DEDICATION

Losing a son is the hardest thing I have ever gone through.
Knowing he is now in the Father's eternal embrace
is a source of great comfort.
Steven, this book is dedicated to you.

CONTENTS

ACKNOWLEGEMENTS

The birth of a book involves major labor pains and plenty of support from others. This one is no exception.

I am grateful to Lori and Mo Kraus for their warm hospitality while this project was in its initial stages. Kari Jones spent many hours reading, critiquing, and discussing with me the content of this work. Her input was invaluable.

Several dear friends went over the manuscript and made helpful recommendations–Sarah Clarke, Carlos Vargas, Martin Lisle, Dennis Scott, and Clayton Dougan. Nelda Lockamy very graciously assisted with the proofreading. Kathie Scriven gave valuable help with the editing. Alan Yoshioka expertly smoothed out the text. Glenn Clark contributed financially to make the project a reality. I am greatly indebted to all of you for helping this book to be born. I am especially thankful to my beloved wife, Wendy, for her constant support, encouragement, and prayerfulness.

Most of all, I am grateful to the Lord Jesus Christ for the privilege of sharing with others the results of years of reflecting on, preaching, and delighting in His magnificent parable of Luke 15. It has left an enduring impression on me, rendering me deeply awed at the wonderful God revealed in this story.

FOREWORD

Regardless of whether you are a new Christian, a mature Christian, or not a Christian at all, this book is a "must read." It has given me to a whole new appreciation of just how "amazing" God's grace is. I have had the privilege of preaching the gospel for many years, but this book has opened my eyes to the reason the message can truthfully be called "good news," and why the apostle Paul says the gospel is *"the power of God that brings salvation to everyone who believes"* (Romans 1:16). I have long been convinced that the gospel is the only message of hope for humanity, but the impact of this book on my life has taken my joy in knowing Jesus as Savior and Lord to a whole new level.

You may be discouraged and wondering if God really loves you. Perhaps your joy as a believer in Jesus has diminished. This excellent book will remind you that God loves you far more than you ever imagined. It will prompt you to be free and extravagant in your worship and to experience an *"inexpressible and glorious joy"* (I Peter 1:8). It will dispel once and for all the notion that we have to do something to be brought into favor with Almighty God. You will be left in no doubt that eternal life is indeed the free gift of God.

Truly, this book is the most refreshing exposition of the parable of the Prodigal Son I have ever read. The author, a very dear friend, demonstrates that his writing is the result of many years of study and meditation on the teaching of the Lord Jesus in this parable. The author shows he has a profound grasp of what the gospel really is, of how much the heart of God longs for us to be reconciled to Himself, and of the serious consequences of rejecting God's amazing grace. The book is full of apt illustrations, often from deep personal experience, and the reader is given a glimpse into Jurgen's lively sense of humor.

I have no doubt that the anointing of the Holy Spirit is on this book. It will be the means of bringing great encouragement to God's people everywhere, and of bringing many who don't yet know Him to experience the joy of being welcomed into the forgiving arms of the loving and gracious heavenly Father.

Clayton Dougan,
Evangelist,
Evangelism International,
www.eiministries.org

THE PARABLE

The Gospel According to Luke 15:1-32

(Based on *The Message* Bible)

B y this time a lot of men and women of doubtful reputation were hanging around Jesus, listening intently. The Pharisees and religion scholars were not pleased, not at all pleased. They growled, "He takes in sinners and eats meals with them, treating them like old friends." Their grumbling triggered this story.

"Suppose one of you had a hundred sheep and lost one. Wouldn't you leave the ninety-nine in the wilderness and go after the lost one until you found it? When found, you can be sure you would put it across your shoulders, rejoicing, and when you got home call in your friends and neighbors, saying, 'Celebrate with me! I've found my lost sheep!' Count on it—there's more joy in heaven over one sinner's rescued life than over ninety-nine good people in no need of rescue.

"Or imagine a woman who has ten coins and loses one. Won't she light a lamp and scour the house, looking in every nook and cranny until she finds it? And when she finds it you can be sure she'll call her friends and neighbors: 'Celebrate with me! I found my lost coin!' Count on it—that's the kind of party God's angels throw every time one lost soul turns to God."

Then he said, "There was once a man who had two sons. The younger said to his father, 'Father, I want right now what's coming to me.'

"So the father divided the property between them. It wasn't long before the younger son packed his bags and left for a distant country. There, undisciplined and dissipated, he wasted everything he had. After he had gone through all his money, there was a bad famine all through that country and he began to hurt. He signed on with a citizen there who assigned him to his fields to slop the pigs. He was so hungry he would have eaten the corncobs in the pig slop, but no one would give him any.

"That brought him to his senses. He said, 'All those farmhands working for my father sit down to three meals a day, and here I am starving to death. I'm going back to my father. I'll say to him, "Father, I have sinned against God, I've sinned before you; I don't deserve to be called your son. Take me as a hired hand."' He got right up and went home to his father.

"When he was still a long way off, his father saw him. His heart pounding, he ran out, embraced him, and kissed him. The son started his speech: 'Father, I've sinned against God, I've sinned before you; I don't deserve to be called your son ever again.'

"But the father wasn't listening. He was calling to the servants, 'Quick. Bring a clean set of clothes and dress him. Put the family ring on his finger and sandals on his feet. Then get a grain-fed heifer and roast it. We're going to feast! We're going to have a wonderful time! My son is here—given up for dead and now alive! Given up for lost and now found!' And they began to have a wonderful time.

"All this time his older son was out in the field. When the day's work was done he came in. As he approached the house, he heard the music and dancing. Calling over one of the houseboys, he asked what was going on. He told him, 'Your brother came home. Your father has ordered a feast—barbecued beef!—because he has him home safe and sound.'

"The older brother stalked off in an angry sulk and refused to join in. His father came out and tried to talk to him, but he wouldn't listen. The son said, 'Look how many years I've stayed here serving you, never giving you one moment of grief, but have you ever thrown a party for me and my friends? Then this son of yours who has thrown away your money on whores shows up and you go all out with a feast!'

His father said, 'Son, you don't understand. You're with me all the time, and everything that is mine is yours—but this is a wonderful time, and we had to celebrate. This brother of yours was dead, and he's alive! He was lost, and he's found!'"[1]

You can't really change the heart without telling a story.
—MARTHA C. NUSSBAUM

*Jesus told parables. When he wanted to say something
really profound about God, he went into parable.*
—JOHN DOMINIC CROSSAN

*Jesus did not give the parables to teach us how to live.
He gave them, I believe, to correct our notions about
who God is and who God loves.*
—PHILIP YANCEY

INTRODUCTION

If given the chance to spend an evening over a cup of coffee with an intimate friend of your most celebrated hero, would you be interested?

Who wouldn't be? Most people would seize the opportunity faster than an Olympic sprinter bolting from the starting line. It's not every day you can pick up nitty-gritty details about a famous person you admire. We all have our heroes, and we love to find out more about them.

How would you like to sit down and do exactly that—with an intimate friend of *God?* Actually, He's not just God's friend—He's God's Son.

Even better.

His name is Jesus Christ.

He made astounding claims, but few compare with this: *"No one knows the Son except the Father, and no one knows the Father except the Son and those to whom the Son chooses to reveal Him"* (Mt. 11:27).

When Jesus asserts He "knows" the Father, He uses a word that denotes thorough, accurate, intimate knowledge. He claims to know God at the deepest level. And when He refers to "revealing" Him, He employs a term from which we get the word "apocalypse." It means: to uncover, disclose, or reveal what has been hidden or covered up. Jesus Christ maintains He can pull back the curtain and give us the inside story on God.

An audacious and tantalizing claim!

Near the end of His earthly life, Jesus said to His heavenly Father: *"I have revealed you to those whom you gave me out of the world ... For I gave them the words you gave me"* (Jn. 17:6,8).

Christ's mandate in this world involved spelling out in detail who His Father is. Jesus came to shed light on the true nature of God. Through His deeds and words He brought into the open what we could never have figured out on our own.

Would it interest you to hear what He has to say on this topic?

The Centerpiece of Luke's Gospel

Some who heard Christ speak exclaimed, *"No-one ever spoke the way this man does"* (Jn. 7:46). His words were described by another as *"words of eternal life"* (Jn. 6:68). Among His many life-giving words, it is difficult to find anything that surpasses the *Parable of the Prodigal Son* in Luke Chapter 15. The beauty, poignancy, and charm of this exquisite story have endeared it to millions. Many consider it to be the *magnum opus* of Christ's parables.

This parabolic gem is the *heart* of Luke's whole book. In the middle section of his Gospel, Luke placed his "travel narrative" (9:51–19:44), wrapped around a cluster of parables in chapters 14–16, at the center of which is found the Prodigal parable. Its literary placement at the nucleus of Luke's Gospel highlights the centrality of this story and its message. The previous chapters are appetizers and here we come to the "main course," suggested one commentator.

And it is much more—it is a recap of the central message of the whole Bible. It distills the essence of the gospel, the supreme story the world's great stories are struggling to tell—the epic drama that makes sense of what is taking place on our broken and beautiful planet. It is a "counterdrama" which exposes the falsehood of the other metanarratives about God, people, and the world. Jesus has "retold the story of the whole human race, and promised nothing less than hope for the world," writes Bible expositor Timothy Keller.[1]

However, the popular title, "The Prodigal Son," is misleading. The main character in the drama is the father—a father who is wonderful beyond words. *Rivet* your attention on him. Follow closely what he says and does. You will be looking at a stunning picture of God, drawn by His Son.

Three Lost and Found Stories

Luke 15 contains three parables delivered in rapid-fire succession. In each case something is lost and then found: a sheep, a coin, and a son. All three stories have a similar finale: they explode into a celebration—especially the last parable of the lost son.

The first two narratives are launched with a hypothetical question: *"Which one of you would not ... ?"* If your sheep or coin went missing, would you not look for it? The point is clear: if people go to great trouble to find a lost sheep or coin, should we not expect God to be concerned about lost *people?*

The first two parables are extremely brief. They afford only a tiny sip of divine mercy, a mere thimbleful that awakens our thirst. We need to drink deeper, and Jesus has one more parable for us: a profound full-blown story—a chalice brimming with rich undiluted grace.

Forgoing His standard opening, Jesus plunges straight into a longer narrative: *"A certain man had two sons ..."*

This is not simply a retelling for good measure. This last parable provides us with a *zoom lens.* Jesus is saying, in effect, "It's important you get this. I am going to give you a glimpse of my Father such as you've never seen. It will blow you away. Pay close attention."

The first two parables are short and sketchy. The third is much more elaborate. "It is more like a complete allegory than any other of our Lord's parables," states one scholar.[2] Some insist a parable is told to drive home one central idea. Other theologians, like Kenneth Bailey, rightly find the "one point per parable" approach far too restrictive and identify "theological clusters" of meaning that join to elicit a single response.[3]

If ever a parable of Christ possessed rich "theological clusters," it is the prodigal story. In this parable there is a marked change of pace as Jesus slows down to incorporate detail, emotion, and drama into the narrative. There is dialogue. There is character development. Now we have more than a simple line drawing—we have a full-blown portrait!

Christ's objective is unmistakable—He longs for people to discover what His Father is *really* like. He proceeds to give us a stunning vision of God that overturns our mistaken ideas about the Almighty. The Teacher from Nazareth seeks to lead us out of the confines of our restricted God-views into a wider place, a place that is fabulously large. If we are to know God as He truly is, this story is non-optional reading.

Bringing God into Focus

Prior to Christ, the Eternal God was perceived in a limited and indistinct manner, as if viewed through a badly focused telescope. Job acknowledged: *"And these are but the outer fringe of his works; how faint the whisper we hear of him!"* (Job 26:14). Moses admitted, *"Lord God, I am your servant. I know that you have shown me only a small part of the wonderful and powerful things you will do"* (Deut. 3:24 ERV). The psalmist confessed, *"Clouds and thick darkness surround him"* (Psa. 97:2). There was a lot of guesswork going on.

The foremost "let's get acquainted" moment in the Old Testament took place at Mount Sinai, where God appeared in clouds of smoke, fire, and thunder. The Israelites trembled and prudently viewed God from a safe distance. They had much to learn about the One Jesus called Father. The apostle John goes as far to say, *"No one has seen God at any time"* (Jn. 1:18 NKJV). People had a hazy picture of the Lord of glory.

What the teller of the parable does is to adjust the lens. The fuzzy image sharpens into a distinct, full-color, close-up, high-definition picture. Jesus brings God into focus.

And what He shows us is absolutely staggering! No one had *dared* to think of God in such terms.

British theologian N. T. Wright explains:

> Jesus didn't tell parables to provide friendly little illustrations of abstract theology. He told parables because what He was doing was so different, so explosive, and so dangerous, that the only way He could talk about it was to use stories.[4]

It was risky to challenge the deeply entrenched beliefs of first-century Judaism. Many of Jesus' countrymen were fanatically devoted to their religious tradition—particularly the scribes and Pharisees. To raise a contrary voice to the prevailing views held by these religious zealots was perilous business. They were not fond of new ideas. Jesus put His life on the line by using parables to torpedo their theology.

A Truth-Packed Parable

One biblical scholar claimed that this story "has made a greater impression on human consciousness than any parable Jesus ever uttered."[5]

It is a compact, uncluttered narrative that is amazingly profound. The storyline is compelling. Not a single word veers off target, not one is superfluous. Each phrase is packed with meaning like the bending branches of an overladen fruit tree.

No one but the Master could have given us this story; only He could have told us so much in so few words. Kenneth E. Bailey said of this narrative, "nearly everyone has a sense of awe at its inexhaustible contents."[6]

One author called the story of the Prodigal Son "the most divinely tender and most humanly touching story ever told on our earth."[7] Another comments: "Its vivid strokes have caught human history."[8]

An eighteenth-century writer extolled the value of this parable, saying: "What would not Christ have deserved of humanity if He had done nothing else than delivered this parable ... ?"[9]

It was destined to be our Lord's most famous story.

No other parable has touched so many hearts. Bishop J. C. Ryle stated there is probably no chapter of the Bible that has done greater good to the souls of men.

A "Meaningful" Parable

A Sunday School teacher once explained to her students that a parable in Scripture is an earthly story with a heavenly meaning. Later on, when quizzed on the lesson, a child responded, "A parable is a earthly story with a *heavy* meaning."

That's not bad!

Many of them have *heavy* meanings. And none more so than the third parable of Luke 15. This story gets down to bedrock; it addresses the heaviest theological question of all: What is God like? "The gravest question before the Church is always God Himself," asserted a man of great wisdom.[10] Thirteenth-century scholar Thomas Aquinas wrote, "The end of ends for an intelligent creature is to see God as He essentially is." The prodigal story is designed to help us do that.

Admittedly, Almighty God is far too expansive, too luxuriant, too all-encompassing to be explained by one short story. A million parables would not suffice. However, Christ's narrative unerringly takes us to the *central* issue; it plunges us into God's heart. It tells us how He feels about us and acts toward us. It brings to light the unspeakable goodness of His innermost nature.

Filtering out the Brightness

Frankly, the God of glory intimidates us. His bigness overwhelms us. Everything about Him is awesome—His power, holiness, exaltedness, majesty, and perfection. He lives in inaccessible light and He is too dazzling for us to look at. It would be like looking at the sun. We can't handle it. Scripture states no one can see God's face and live (Ex. 33:20).

However, solar viewing becomes possible when people use special eclipse glasses. These have strong filters that cut out harmful ultraviolet and infrared light and allow human eyes to behold the sun.

Is there any similar device that would enable us to look at God without getting blinded?

This is where Jesus comes in.

His story in Luke 15 is like a filter that lets us gaze at God without being bedazzled by His overpowering greatness. It affords us a close-up look at His inner nature yet spares us being overpowered by His majesty.

And what we see takes our breath away.

In this parable God dares to expose His very heart. He places it before us like a motor taken apart and laid out in pieces on a workbench.

Read the story with reverence and wonder. We tread on holy ground.

Handle with Care

A word of caution: Jesus' parable is loaded with spiritual dynamite that could seriously alter your concept of God. It may force you to discard your cherished definitions of Deity. It may rearrange your theology. It may make your heart skip a beat. It may well lead you to experience the extravagant embrace of the Father and bring you to a freedom and joy you have not known before.

I couldn't help but write this book. Jesus' story has hijacked my heart and taken me into a new world. It has left me stunned, elated, astonished, entranced, shocked, laughing, comforted, intoxicated. It has given me a fresh vision of God's heart that takes up so much room inside of me that I couldn't hold it in. It has spilled out on the pages you are reading. This book is my attempt to process the most astounding reality in the universe—the love of God. I am grateful you have joined me in this adventure.

English poet W. H. Auden stated, "the way to read a fairy tale is to throw yourself in."

Similarly, the purpose of Jesus' parable is not simply to inform but to *involve*, not just to engage our intellects but also to captivate our hearts. It invites us to become participants in the narrative. It draws us into its reality that we too may find ourselves overwhelmed by a love that is larger, deeper, and wider than anything we have known. It calls us to taste a joy and peace not of this world. It summons us to step into the kingdom of heaven—the large story where God reigns and goodness runs wild.

This paradigm-changing parable could well be titled: *"You thought you knew what God was like? Think again!"* or *"Crazy Story; Unbelievable God."* It gives us a heart-stopping glimpse of the one Jesus addressed as *Abba*.

And keep in mind: this is not *another* flawed attempt to explain the Lord of the universe. It is not one more "respected opinion," nor the consensus of the latest symposium. Neither is it hearsay or conjecture. This is God according to Jesus. This is the Authorized Version of God—as told by His Beloved Son.

When it comes to this topic, He is the only one who *really* knows what He's talking about.

The historic Christian doctrine of the divinity of Christ
does not simply mean that Jesus is like God.
It is far more radical than that.
It means that God is like Jesus.

—D. Elton Trueblood

Jesus is what God looks like in sandals.

—John Dominic Crossan

God needs definition.
Jesus is that definition.
God is like Jesus.

—Brian Zahnd

CHAPTER ONE

The God who looks like Jesus

"So He spoke this parable to them, saying ..."

LUKE 15:3 NKJV

Jesus was never nominated "Rabbi of the Year."

Had the award been given by popular acclaim, He would have won it hands down. Never had a teacher of the Law attracted such crowds.

But He was blacklisted.

For starters, He didn't have the right credentials. But that wasn't the *real* problem.

The Jerusalem elite boycotted Jesus because He refused to stay within the established boundaries of piety. He was too unscripted. His outrageous compassion overtaxed the restraints of Judaism. He trampled on too many of its homemade taboos.

"Obedience keeps the rules," one writer said. "Love knows when to break them."[1] That's what got Jesus into trouble.

It annoyed a lot of people.

Particularly *religious* people.

Once a troupe of moral watchdogs got on His case for the disreputable company He kept. His critics belonged to two important religious groups in Israel: the Pharisees and the teachers of the law. We will be forever indebted to these unidentified faultfinders. Their criticism elicited from Jesus His most unforgettable parable.

Charles Dickens rated it the greatest short story ever written. For many, myself included, it ranks as their all-time favorite parable. After two thousand years, it continues to be a fountain of refreshing living water for thirsty hearts.

Scandalous Piety

"Tax collectors and other notorious sinners often came to listen to Jesus teach" (Lk. 15:1 NLT).

Jesus consorted with irreligious people no self-respecting rabbi would be seen with. He was, as one writer put it, a "receiver of wrecks."[2] Not exactly conventional Jewish piety.

"This made the Pharisees and teachers of religious law complain that He was associating with such sinful people—even eating with them!" (Lk. 15:2 NLT).

His "misconduct" was twofold:

- He received "sinners"
- He ate meals with them

The word translated "receive" is a strong term. It has the sense of welcoming warmly, accepting with open arms. To offer friendship to the riffraff was bad enough, but to dine with them was *scandalous*. And this was not an isolated incident. The tense of the verbs indicates Jesus engaged in this annoying behavior on a regular basis.

There was a magnetic quality about the Carpenter from Nazareth. People flocked to Him in the thousands. They tore roofs off houses (Mk. 2:4) and trampled one another (Lk. 12:1) to get near to Him. Lawbreakers and outcasts were especially attracted to

Him. Something about Jesus resonated with their deepest longings. He radiated hope.

It is fascinating that the only perfect person who ever lived was so attractive to the notoriously imperfect. Author Philip Yancey commented: "Somehow Jesus had mastered the ability of loving people whose behavior He disapproved. That's a lesson the church has not been so good at learning."[3]

In particular, Christ was sought out by those on the fringe of society—the disabled, the homeless, the poor, the marginalized, the untouchables, the downtrodden, the misfits. The controversial Rabbi demolished the notion that some lives matter more than others. The religious elite saw the sinfulness of the outsiders; Jesus saw their *sacredness*. He healed them, befriended them, taught them—and dared to eat with them.

Outrageous behavior for a Jewish rabbi!

Meals with a Message

Meal-sharing in the first century had meaning far beyond the consumption of food. It reflected clearly defined social boundaries. It indicated who was part of one's circle and who was not. To share a table with someone was a sign of reconciliation, trust, and brotherhood.

The term "companion" comes from a root word which means: "bread fellow"—one with whom we share bread. Historically there has been a close connection between friendship and meal sharing.

Pious Jews were scrupulous about whom they dined with and whom they didn't—and the irreligious outsiders were definitely *not* on the list. It was unthinkable the Rabbi from Nazareth would brazenly disregard these "sacred" rules and share meals with scalawags, prostitutes, scoundrels, slumlords, and lawbreakers.

This was more than just a matter of proper social etiquette. It was a theological issue. In first-century Judaism, the division between the "righteous" and the "sinners" was not just a line in the sand—it was more like a Berlin Wall.

When Jesus freely dined with people on both sides of the divide, He was shaking the foundations of Jewish religious and moral beliefs. He was challenging their very understanding of God. In effect, He was throwing open the doors of the kingdom of heaven to everyone. He was demonstrating that every person is valuable and loved by God.

One writer remarks, "The most comforting aspect of Jesus, is He surrounded Himself with screw ups. I really believe He'd have liked me, too."[4]

Not surprisingly, the "friend of sinners" came under heavy fire from the religious establishment. They accused him of frequenting the wrong places and befriending the wrong people. Instead of shunning outcasts, He sought them out. The Jews contended He was knocking down the fence between the pious and the sinners, between the clean and the unclean. He was moving ancient landmarks—and it had to stop.

The Subversive Story

These events are what provoked Jesus' famous parable. He turned to His critics and said, "Let me tell you a story …"

The flinty-eyed religionists readied themselves to listen. They had no idea what they were in for. Their understanding of God was about to be stretched beyond recognition. If they thought the Rabbi from Galilee was shocking—now they were going to hear about His Father! They were about to learn what one writer called "the preposterousness of God." Putting truth into story form, Christ overturned their theological apple cart.

Biblical scholar Eugene Peterson throws light on the provocative stories Jesus was in the habit of telling:

> Jesus' favorite speech form, the parable, was subversive ... As
> people heard Jesus tell these stories, they saw at once that they
> weren't about God, so there was nothing in them threatening
> their own sovereignty. They relaxed their defenses. They
> walked away perplexed, wondering what they meant, the
> stories lodged in their imagination. And then, like a time
> bomb, they would explode in their unprotected hearts ... He
> was talking about God; they had been invaded![5]

Luke 15 is a classic example of Jesus' subversive storytelling. He smuggles truth into people's minds under the cover of a narrative. While engaging the audience's imagination, Christ launches an attack on their ideas about the nature of Deity.

Essentially the Rabbi from Nazareth was saying, "Ultimately this is not about appropriate social behavior—the underlying issue here is theological. It is evident you do not know God. Allow me to tell you what He is like."

What follows is His renowned *Parable of the Prodigal Son*—a window into the character of the One Jesus called *Abba*. It is no mere bedtime story. It is a blaze of truth and passion. It is a lightning flash illuminating the primary theological issue: Who is God? It is groundbreaking truth about the Lord of heaven and earth.

Christ declared, *"For I tell you that many prophets and kings wanted to see what you see but did not see it, and to hear what you hear but did not hear it"* (Lk. 10:24).

Our Concept of God Is Crucial

Our mental picture of God is an essential part of our "operating system." One philosopher contended that more consequences for our life flow from this one issue than any other. Our emotional health, relationships, attitudes, and values are all impacted by our God-concept. We all live at the mercy of our ideas about our Maker.

"What we believe about God is the most important truth we believe," stated one writer, "and it's the one truth that does the most to shape us."[6] Our life is an expression of our view of God.

- Is God a power broker who demands obedience?
- Is He an impersonal force that can be tapped into?
- Is He a stern judge eagerly awaiting the day of reckoning?
- Is He a fussy moralist obsessed with rules?
- Is He a cosmic watchmaker who lets things run their course?

The way we perceive God defines how we engage life. "Nothing counts more in the way we live than what we believe about God," points out Eugene Peterson. "A failure to get it right in our minds becomes a failure to get it right in our lives."[7] False notions about Him sabotage our hearts and disfigure our lives. Bad theology produces bad living.

> *What is the Father like? This is the most important question of our existence.*
>
> —MICHAEL PHILLIPS

Another writer asserts, "At the root of all that is wrong with humans is a false and ugly mental image of God."[8] Spiritual wholeness cannot exist apart from a correct view of God.

This is why we must pay close attention to Jesus of Nazareth. His life was a true reflection of the heart and nature of God (Jn. 12:45; 14:9,10; Heb. 1:3). He spoke as one who has "seen" God (Jn. 6:46; 8:38), and "knows" God (Mt. 11:27; Jn. 10:15).

No one else does.

According to Scripture, every other member of Adam's family suffers from spiritual blindness. We are in the dark about God, and fundamentally—*that's* what is wrong with the human race.

How It All Started

This "brain damage" came about in the Garden of Eden through the fatal event known as "The Fall." Satan approached Eve with a question: *"Do I understand God told you not to eat from any tree in the garden?"* (Gn. 3:1 MSG). The Deceiver called into question the goodness of the Creator and cast doubt upon His trustworthiness.

Eve fell for the Lie about God. A false and ugly picture of God was planted in her mind. It was the Lie that led to the Fall, and the Fall sealed the Lie in human hearts. At the root of our fallenness is a *warped* picture of our Creator.

When God came seeking Adam and Eve, they fled with fear and hid among the trees of the garden. God was perceived as an enemy; they now believed He was *against* them.

They were dead wrong.

God is opposed to sin. It is a cancer He hates with a passion, and will ultimately eradicate. It brings horrific consequences—but in no way does it alter His love for people.

Sin did not change the Creator—but it changed our first ancestors. It messed up their minds and rendered them incapable of seeing things as they are. It trapped them in a fallacious vision of their Maker. They could no longer perceive the truth about God's heart. "For man has closed himself up, till he sees all things thro' narrow chinks of his cavern," wrote English poet William Blake.[9]

Author A. W. Tozer stated:

> Satan's first attack upon the human race was his sly effort
> to destroy Eve's confidence in the kindness of God.
> Unfortunately for her and for us, he succeeded too well.
> From that day, men have had a false conception of God,
> and it is exactly this that has cut out from under them the
> ground of righteousness and driven them to reckless and
> destructive living.[10]

Spiritual Malware

To use computer terminology, our operating system has been invaded by the Great Hacker, Satan. He has infiltrated and corrupted it. A malicious virus is now running in the background. Ever since our exit from Eden, our "computers" have ceased to run properly. And to make matters worse, the inbox of our mind gets filled with junk mail every day.

One theologian expressed it like this:

> Sin is about losing our right minds, such that we are no longer able to see the goodness and love of the Father, and thus no longer free to live life in His unearthly assurance and blessing. We are left to live our lives in and out of fear and anxiety and dread.[11]

This flawed understanding of God affected not only our first parents—but the entire human race. Scripture describes the condition of people's minds with terms such as "darkened," "blinded," "confused."

This inner distortion skews the way we view God. We see Him through the lens of our fallenness. Our darkened reasoning projects its inner confusion upon the Most High and fabricates a god in the likeness of our brokenness and guilt. Our minds are filled with false notions about God. No malady is more widespread—or more damaging. A. W. Tozer points out, "Nothing twists and deforms the soul more than a low or unworthy conception of God."[12] "There is no one single fact more responsible for our waywardness than this," contends another writer.[13]

Clearing Theological Fog

"Our whole business in this life is to restore to health the eyes of the heart, whereby God may be seen," asserted Saint Augustine. And few portions of Scripture are better suited to help us than Luke 15. It is much more than a heart-warming story. It is a direct assault on wrongheaded thinking about God.

The teller of this parable had come to lead people away from the lie and back to the goodness and wonder of the real story. He was like "a man who smashes the window in a stuffy room and allows us all to breathe."[14]

There is an oft-told story of a young boy who was busily drawing with his crayons. When his mother asked what he was doing, her son replied: "I'm drawing a picture of God." Seeking to straighten out his faulty theology, the mother pointed out, "You can't draw a picture of God. No one knows what He looks like." Unperturbed, the little fellow shot back, "They will when I get finished!"

What we have in Luke 15 is God's Son painting a full-blown picture of His Father. And what an awesome portrait it is! The Scriptures affirm that God is good, but the description Jesus gives us takes goodness to levels we never dreamed of.

Only Christ could have given us this daring disclosure of Deity.

Words Are Too Weak

Nobel Prize–winning author André Gide, in his novel *La Symphonie Pastorale*, writes about a Swiss pastor who adopts a young blind girl named Gertrude. The pastor takes on the demanding task of explaining to the sightless girl the beauty of alpine meadows, the vivid colors of the flowers, and the magnificence of the snow-capped mountains. He struggles helplessly against the inadequacy of language to convey the splendor and wonder of the Swiss Alps. Words are too clumsy to carry such a message, but words are the only tools he has, and he perseveres in his frustrating endeavor.

Gertrude eventually is able to get an operation to repair her eyesight and, afterwards returns to the pastor's home. At last she is able to see and experience the sights she had only heard about before. "My eyes opened on a world more beautiful than I had ever dreamt it could be," she exclaims. "Yes, truly I had never imagined that the daylight was so bright, the air was so brilliant, and the sky was so vast." The reality far exceeds the verbal description.

The Alps cannot be reduced to words—much less the God of glory. Yet for many centuries, people's understanding of the Supreme Being was largely limited to words. Sages, prophets, and teachers gave us verbal messages from and about God. Great words, wonderful words—but nonetheless, *words*. And words are wholly inadequate to explain the Lord of the universe. Language is not equal to the task. It is unable to bear the weight of what needs to be said.

We needed more than to *hear* about God—we needed to *see* God. And that's why Jesus came. *"The Word became flesh and made His dwelling among us. We have seen His glory"* (Jn. 1:14). The glory of God became visible to human eyes. The Bible declares, *"No one has ever seen God; the only God, who is at the Father's side, he has made him known"* (Jn. 1:18 ESV). God unveiled Himself in Jesus of Nazareth.

The apostle Paul explained it this way:

> God said, "Let light shine in the darkness." And He has let light shine in our hearts too. He gave us light that shows how bright and wonderful God is. We see this light when we look at the face of Christ. (II Cor. 4:6)

"In Jesus Christ you see God face to face," stated Bible teacher T. Austin-Sparks.

God Seen Clearly

Christ came to reveal God. He came to take away our spiritual blindness. Through His life, actions, and words we finally get a clear picture of the High King of heaven—and He turns out to be more wonderful than we ever imagined!

"Jesus reveals a God entirely different to the monstrous bore we routinely imagine God to be," comments British theologian Mike Reeves.[15]

Is there anything *more* beautiful than Jesus "wading waist-deep into the muck of life, weeping with the broken, rescuing the lost, and healing the sick"?[16] Others looked upon the wayward with disdain; Jesus looked with eyes of compassion. Others saw empty pockets; Jesus saw empty hearts, and He infused them with faith, hope, and love. People flocked to hear His life-giving words and to receive His health-giving touch. He spread heaven wherever He went.

> *Christianity "puts a face on God." Jesus is God's face.*
>
> —E. Stanley Jones

The world has *never* seen anything like it.

"You who suffer, come to Him, for He cures," writes Victor Hugo. "You who tremble, come to Him, for He smiles."[17]

It is little wonder Russian novelist Fyodor Dostoyevsky exclaimed: "I believe there is no one lovelier, deeper, more sympathetic and more perfect than Jesus ... there is no one else like Him."[18]

And here's the amazing thing: Jesus of Nazareth shows us *more* than the beauty of a human life—He shows us the beauty of *God*. Jesus was God made visible, knowable.

Jesus made the astounding assertion that all His words and deeds had their source in God (Jn. 5:19; 8:28; 14:10). When one of His followers requested that Christ show him God the Father, Jesus replied, *"Whoever has seen me has seen the Father"* (Jn. 14:9). In other words, Jesus was saying, "I am your picture of God."

Never before had the Divine Lord been so perfectly mirrored in a human life. Jesus of Nazareth is the clearest view of God the world has ever seen.[19]

God looks like Jesus.

It has been rightly affirmed that every false theology in history has been a failure to take this fact seriously.

So look closely. Jesus is a Messiah who brings a "you-have-heard-it-said-but-I-say-unto-you" message *not* just about ethics—but also about God. The Divine Son is not simply a messenger—He *is* the message. When Jesus loves, heals, forgives, blesses, suffers, bleeds, and dies for us, *this* is the way God acts. This is who God is.

There was a second-century heretic named Marcion who said, in effect, I like the God of Jesus. He's a God of love and mercy. But I don't like the God of the Old Testament. He's a God of anger and violence. Marcion rejected the God of the Old Testament in favor of the "benevolent" God of the New Testament. The early church denounced that mistaken notion, and said, no, we're not going down that road. That was an important decision. To reject Old Testament Scripture is an ancient heresy called Marcionism. However, to say Jesus is a *superior* revelation of God—is Christianity. Jesus Christ is the definitive word about God (Lk. 10:22; Jn. 1:18; Col. 1:15; Heb. 1:1-3).

When God Gave Us an Image

In the Ten Commandments people were forbidden to make an image of God. The Lord was saying, "You don't know what I'm like. Don't presume you do. No images allowed."

Then one day God proclaimed in effect, "Now I'm going to show you what I'm really like." And His Beloved Son came into this world in human form. The Bible calls Him the *"Word,"* the *"image,"* and the *"exact imprint"* of God (Jn. 1:1; Col. 1:15; Heb. 1:3). The Apostle

Paul declares that the glory of God is seen *"in the face of Jesus Christ"* (II Cor. 4:6). Finally we have a true likeness of God—Jesus.

One author wrote: "Jesus was God letting people see the beauty of His face and listen to the music of His voice, and feel the irresistibly gentle drawing power of His presence."[20]

When we look at Jesus of Nazareth our hearts leap as we say to ourselves: "Is God *really* like that?" It seems too good to be true! But this is what the gospel affirms.

Missionary statesman E. Stanley Jones contended: "If the best of men should try to think out what kind of God they would like to see in the universe, they could not imagine anything better than that He should be like Jesus."

At the feet of such a God we gladly bow, forever captivated.

The most important truth we can learn about God, and the most *wonderful,* is this—God is *exactly* like Jesus. He is the definition of God. He is the explanation of God (Jn. 1:18). He is the revelation of God (Mt. 11:27). One scholar stated: "Jesus is God's résumé to the world."[21]

Listen again to the apostle Paul: *"The god who rules this world has blinded the minds of unbelievers. They cannot see the light, which is the good news about our glorious Christ, who shows what God is like"* (II Cor. 4:4 CEV).

The writer to the Hebrews attests that the Son of God is the *"flawless expression of the nature of God"* (Heb. 1:3 PHILLIPS).

Other versions give this translation:

- *"The exact likeness of His being ..."* (ISV).
- *"He is a perfect copy of God's nature ..."* (ERV).
- *"This Son perfectly mirrors God ..."* (MSG).

It has been well said that "God is Christlike, and in Him is no un-Christlikeness at all."

No longer do we need to wonder how God feels or thinks about us. The Son of God came, not just to redeem humans, but also to *reveal* the heart of the Father. He dispels the darkness of our confused thoughts about the Most High.

Please scrap your images of God as a distant faceless bureaucrat, an almighty abstraction, a celestial scorekeeper, a self-serving despot, or cosmic killjoy. Revamp your idea of God.

God is like *Jesus.*

For many years I believed in the deity of Christ without realizing its radical implications—*God is like Christ.* The Lord of glory is just as wonderful as Jesus. The discovery swept me off my feet. It put a new song in my mouth and joy in my heart. If God is as beautiful as the Man from Nazareth—then He's got my heart, my life, and everything else!

The Greatest Prize

Author Anthony de Mello tells the story of a monk who in his travels found a precious stone and kept it. One day he met a traveler, and when the monk opened his bag to share his provisions with him, the man saw the jewel and asked the monk to give it to him. The friar did so readily. The traveler departed, overjoyed with the unexpected gift that was enough to give him wealth and security for the rest of his life. However, a few days later, he came back in search of the monk, found him, gave him the gem, and entreated him, "Now give me something much more precious than this stone, valuable as it is. Give me that which enabled you to give it to me."

Those who came to Christ went away with many precious gifts such as healing, wisdom, forgiveness, and freedom from spiritual bondage. But those who returned with the request: "Give me that which enabled you to give it to me," became partakers of a greater treasure still. It was given to them to *know God*—the greatest prize of all.

It was for this reason Christ came.

As we delve further into His parable, may the devastating beauty of the God revealed in Jesus of Nazareth lay waste the lies we have believed about Him.

For *that* is the purpose of this subversive story.

PRAYER

*O God, Your exalted holiness is blinding and frightful. It makes
us stand far off. However, when we look at Jesus of Nazareth,
the express image of God, we see Your heart—and it makes our
hearts beat faster. We never realized You were that wonderful.
Thank you, Father, for Your delightful Son. We praise You
for His unbounded goodness, His tender compassion, His
overflowing love, His moral perfection. We thank You for His life
poured out for us at Calvary. How wonderful it is to know that
when we see Him, we see the Father. You have made Yourself
known, and we are speechless before the wonder of it. Amen.*

*Through Jesus we may look into God's Fatherly heart
and sense how boundlessly He loves us.
That would warm our hearts.*

—MARTIN LUTHER

*Jesus revealed an enormous amount of information about
His heavenly Father through a single word: Abba.*

—JAMES BRYAN SMITH

*Do you believe that God is your Father, or do you still
find that news too good to be true?*

—BRENNAN MANNING

CHAPTER TWO

The God who is father

"And He said, A certain man had two sons ..."

LUKE 15:11

When Jesus crafted His parable, He did not select a king, a warrior, or a merchant to portray God. He chose a *father*, a man with two sons.

This was not incidental.

The Teacher from Galilee is drawing our attention to the defining characteristic of God—His fatherhood. He is creator, king, judge, and sustainer of the universe. But above all He is Father. This is not merely one of His many roles. This is the foundational truth about God. It is not simply a metaphor. It is who God really is.

The First Word about God

Often "sovereignty" is the jumping off point in our reflection upon God and what He's up to. Sovereignty is a vital truth,[1] but it is not our starting point. It describes His relationship with creation, but there is a more fundamental, pre-creation truth about the Almighty.

Long before He was ever called the Supreme Lord of the universe, He was called "Father" by His Son, the second Person of the

Trinity. The first word about God has to do, not with rulership, but with *family*. It has to do with a shared life of love, joy, and wonder.

What we find at the center of the universe is a Father pouring His favor upon His Son in the overflowing fellowship of the Holy Spirit. We find a Son delighting in the One He calls Abba.

This is the *ultimate* fact about God: He is a Father.

One theologian writes:

> What makes God, God? It is the relationship of total and mutual self-giving by which the Father gives everything to the Son, the Son offers back all that He has to glorify the Father, with the love of each being established and sealed by the Holy Spirit, who proceeds from both. The doctrine of the Trinity tells us that relationship—personality—is at the heart of the universe.[2]

The Eternal Father

Fatherhood did not begin when Adam and Eve had children. It goes right back to the distant reaches of eternity and into the essence of God Himself. The Eternal One is not a divine bachelor living in heavenly solitude—He is a Father who rejoices in His Son in a relationship of mutual openness, other-focused love, and everlasting delight.

"For it is only when you grasp what it means for God to be a Trinity that you really sense the beauty, the overflowing kindness, the heart-grabbing loveliness of God," writes theologian Mike Reeves.[3]

We get a snapshot of this fellowship when, at Jesus' baptism, the Father exclaims from heaven, *"You are my beloved Son, in whom my soul delights!"* This deep, rich togetherness is glimpsed in Christ's words *"The One who sent me stays with me … He sees how much joy I take in pleasing Him"* (Jn. 8:29 MSG).

Something wonderful is happening here!

This is not a cold, stiff father-son formality. This is a free-flowing sharing together of delight, passion, and goodness. It gives richness to the concept of "fatherhood" that exceeds all human experience.

The Tri-Unity of God

From the early days of the Christian community, its members found themselves forced by the Christ-event to rethink their view of God. How did monotheism fit with the Divine Lord having a Son? And who is this Holy Spirit? There was more going on inside of God than they had previously realized.

Their understanding of God was *stretched.*

There is only one God, to be sure. However, the *one-ness* of God came to be seen, not only in His uniqueness (Dt. 6:4), but also in His *united-ness* (Jn. 10:30,38). Within the oneness of the Deity, there is a plurality of persons. God exists in relationship, in the intimate interrelatedness of Father, Son, and Holy Spirit. The term used to describe this Three-in-One Divinity is "Trinity."

And if God is love from all eternity, then before Creation He could *not* have been alone. Love cannot exist in solitude. Love takes place within a relationship. It requires more than one person. It presupposes a plurality.

"It is not well for God to be alone," commented British author G. K. Chesterton. It is His *threefold-ness* that makes love possible in God. God is love—because God is a Trinity. And this is what makes Trinity such good news.

The Christian idea of God as Three-in-One should not be viewed as a mathematical puzzle, a philosophical conundrum, or some kind of bizarre riddle. Rather, it is the marvelous truth that the essence of God is found in *relationships:* Father, Son, and Holy Spirit live in a community of such love, intimacy, and openness that the Three ultimately are One. It is a fellowship of joy and wonder and creativity and glory.

This is what goes on at the heart of reality—and it is the most beautiful relationship in the universe!

The center and nucleus of the universe is not a machine or a monastery—it is a dance, a ballet, a whirlwind of delight between Father, Son, and Holy Spirit. Early Greek theologians used the word *perichoresis* (related to our word "choreography") to describe it. The matrix of everything is a Triune togetherness whose beauty, exuberance, and marvel no human words or metaphors can possibly describe. This Divine Community lives in an unending, joy-filled interchange of love.

Tyrant or Trinity?

The late Christopher Hitchens, author of the book *God Is Not Great: How Religion Poisons Everything,* was not simply an atheist; he was an anti-theist. He believed the existence of God was a bad idea.

Hitchens said in an interview:

> I think it would be rather awful if it was true, if there was a permanent, total, round-the-clock divine supervision and invigilation of everything you did. You'd never have a waking or sleeping moment when you weren't being watched or controlled and supervised by some celestial entity from the moment of your conception to the moment of your death. It would be like living in North Korea.

Mr. Hitchens presents a good case! However, it is most helpful to note how he describes the deity in whom he does *not* believe: an all controlling Divine Despot who is keeping tabs on everyone—the Heavenly Policeman.

To be honest, I find myself in hearty agreement with Hitchens on this point because, quite frankly, I don't believe in that god either. Who would want to be a worshipper of such a god?

Such a deity, in fact, does *not* exist.

The God revealed in Christ shows Himself to be *not* a self-centered dictator but an other-centered fountain of goodness. He is not a tyrant, but a Triune community of love.

And that makes *all* the difference.

Why Trinity Is Important

Travel back in your mind for a moment to the beginning of time, before Creation, and imagine a God who is *not* a Trinity: a solitary, all-powerful, self-sufficient Supreme Being. He relates to no one, answers to no one, speaks to no one. He is independent and alone, living in secluded splendor.

His thoughts do not go beyond Himself, because He is *all* there is. He knows nothing of relationships, dialogue, intimacy, love, friendship, serving, or giving. He has no need to practice consideration, patience, respect, generosity, self-sacrifice, compassion, or kindness. He takes no one else into account, because no one else is there. His existence revolves entirely around Himself.

If such a God were to create a universe, would He make a world of people where it's all about family, community, and relationships? Would He come up with the idea of something called marriage, where two lives merge and live together as one? Would He establish love as the supreme virtue?

It is *highly* improbable.

Would He give us the capacity for humor and enjoyment and laughter?

Not likely.

Would it ever occur to Him to become human and to share His glory with us?

It would *never* cross His mind.

If the Solitary Deity had created us it would be to obtain service and worship. It would be all about His supremacy and our subservience; He would be king and we would be servants. It is not people and relationships that would interest Him but *compliance*. This God would *demand* that we bow and obey—you get with the program or you're in *big* trouble.

That's the kind of universe we would expect from the all-powerful Unaccompanied Boss.

You end up with a heavenly Hitler.

Trinity Changes Everything

But … what if this God were actually a Trinity: a community of love and goodness and creativity and joy? What if this Divine Being were made up of a Father and a Son who love each other with eternal passion in the abounding fellowship of the Spirit? His creative activity would be entirely different, would it not?

We would envisage such a God to make a world where people experience the joys of marriage and family and friendship, and where love is valued as supreme. A realm where there is joy and goodness and beauty and wonder. A planet of sunsets, strawberries, butterflies, waterfalls, roses, and hummingbirds.

Such a God would create people in His image in order to lavish upon them His love and goodness. And it would not be surprising that, if things went awry, He would respond in mercy and compassion, and, if necessary, act sacrificially to rescue His creation.

It is also conceivable that this Divine Community of love would go a step further and invite humans to be part of His family as sons and daughters.

A totally different scenario develops when we have a Father-Son-and-Spirit God, instead of a Celestial Caesar. The Trinity is more than just another item in the creed. It is *bedrock truth* about God that radically transforms the whole story.

The Solitary Deity ends up looking a whole lot like a Middle Eastern deity who rewards suicide bombers and terrorists with heaven.

The Triune God ends up looking like Jesus giving His life for His enemies on a cross.

Slight difference.

This is the God Jesus made known to us—the stunningly beautiful God of overflowing love and joy, who is Father, Son, and Spirit.

A Trinitarian Gospel

The gospel is a Trinitarian affair. It leads us into the love of the Father, through the grace of Jesus Christ, by the fellowship of the Holy Spirit. It calls us to participate in the life and joy of the Triune God. It's not simply a ticket to heaven. It teaches us to live now as beloved daughters and sons of the heavenly Father.

Theologian James I. Packer wrote:

> For everything that Christ taught, everything that makes the New Testament new, and better than the Old, everything that is distinctly Christian as opposed to merely Jewish, is summed up in the knowledge of the Fatherhood of God. "Father" is the Christian name for God.[4]

The first phrase in Jesus' teaching about prayer is *"Our Father."* Our understanding of God needs to start here—and what a glorious truth it is! Martin Luther said if he could truly comprehend the first two words of the Lord's Prayer, he would never be the same again. The stunning fact that God has become our Father is ultimate cause for wonder and joy.

It is significant that the apostle Paul launches each of his letters in the New Testament with a reference to *"the God and Father of our Lord Jesus Christ."* Paul is underscoring a vital fact: if we are to think correctly about God, we must think of Him as Father. The ultimate truth about God is not some abstract quality or "omni" attribute, but the unspeakably wonderful fact of His *fatherhood.*

Adoption into Abba's Family

The goal of the gospel is not merely salvation but *adoption.* It is about our inclusion in the Father's loving embrace. *"God decided in advance to adopt us into His own family by bringing us to Himself through Jesus Christ. This is what He wanted to do, and it gave Him great pleasure"* (Eph. 1:5 NLT). Faith in Christ introduces us into an intimate, trusting relationship with God, whom we are not to address as "Your Honor," but "Abba." We are no longer orphans, but sons and daughters of the Most High.

"God became a man," states C. S. Lewis, "to turn creatures into sons."

Nineteenth-century spiritual sage George MacDonald wrote, "This is and has been the Father's work from the beginning—to bring us into the home of his heart ... This is our destiny."[5]

Could there be better news than *that?*

What Does "Abba" Mean?

There has been much discussion in recent years whether or not *Abba* is truly a childhood term meaning "daddy." Some suggest the word simply meant "father" and denoted a profound personal relationship and respect for a superior. They argue that, although *Abba* has been adopted into modern Hebrew as "daddy," in Jesus' native language of Aramaic, it was essentially equivalent to "father."

On the other hand, it is interesting to note that, although Paul wrote his epistles in Greek, he used the Aramaic term *Abba* twice (Rom. 8:15; Gal. 4:6) and intentionally did *not* translate it into Greek. This is significant. It lends support to the idea that the word Jesus chose to address His Father *did* express a special level of intimacy and openness. The Greek New Testament retains the original Aramaic word—highlighting God's purpose that new generations of disciples would also come to know Him in an *Abba*-like way.

We should take note that the confidence to approach God in childlike openness is not built on a single word. Christ taught we must enter the kingdom with the simplicity of little children (Lk. 18:17). Furthermore, the wide-open "come unto me" accessibility of Jesus (Mt. 11:28; Jn. 7:37) demonstrates the unrestrained freedom with which we can come to God with all our sins and all our need.

Additionally, we are exhorted to approach God "boldly" (Eph. 3:12; Heb. 4:16). It is not with cautious timidity but with unreserved, fearless confidence that a believer can draw near to his heavenly Father. The apostle John adds *"perfect love casts out fear"* (I Jn. 4:18). Reverence is appropriate, but God's children need not cower before Him. We can run into His arms, assured of His unfailing love.

Timothy Keller comments: "The only person who dares wake up a king at 3:00 AM for a glass of water is a child. We have that kind of access."[6]

Intimacy and Reverence

A word of caution is fitting: "One of the scourges of our age, is that all our deities are house-broken and eminently companionable. Far from demanding anything, they only ask how they can more meaningfully enhance the lives of those they serve."[7]

We do well to shun the popular theology of the Marshmallow Deity: the God who is soft and indulgent. With us but not above us.

Immanence without transcendence. Comforting but never convicting. No demands. No rules. It's all cool.

The God of delightful tenderness is also the God of awesome otherness. The joyful freedom of running into our heavenly Father's arms does not preclude prostrating ourselves before Him in worshipful surrender. Most people in Scripture who encountered God needed to be told *not* to fear. Paradoxically, He is the fearsome Lord whose love casts out fear. He inspires both rejoicing *and* reverence. A true knowledge of God combines these two components.[8]

Biblical scholar Eugene Peterson shares this insight:

> The two elements come together in worship … The acts of reverence and intimacy need each other. The reverence needs the infusion of intimacy lest it become a cool and detached aesthetic. The intimacy needs to be suffused in reverence lest it become a gushy emotion.[9]

Hardwired for Heaven

Philip Yancey stated that *all* we ever really wanted was to be desired by the Maker of all things. In the depths of our hearts there is a yearning for something more than food, money, pleasure, or success. There is a desire that consistently comes up short, even in the best human relationships. It is longing to be loved, to know unconditional acceptance.

This inner ache is a longing for home. It exists because we were created to live within the Father's embrace. We were made to experience security, belonging, appreciation, and affection in a relationship with our Maker. It is what we were wired for, and our hearts know it all too well.

This is where the parable of the prodigal strikes a chord with us.

It tells us of a man who lost a son. It's about a father with an inconsolable ache on the inside, who looks down the road a thousand times a day longing for the boy to return. This gentleman weeps and waits and yearns for a son who has not the faintest notion of how much he is loved.

Christ is describing how God feels about lost people. This is heart-stirring truth about the heavenly Father!

"If we take all the goodness, wisdom and compassion of the best mothers and fathers who have ever lived," comments author Brennan Manning, "they would only be a faint shadow of the love and mercy in the heart of the redeeming God."[10]

Fatherhood reaches its ultimate and richest expression in the One Jesus called Abba.

> *God formed us for himself, and has given the human such a vastness of thirst for happiness as He alone can answer.*
>
> —JOHN NEWTON

A Longing to Belong

The story is told of a student who returned to his college after going home for a family funeral. Very soon his grades plummeted. His counselor thought the grandfather's death had affected the boy, and time would bring healing, but his grades only worsened. Finally the boy confessed the real problem. While at home, he had leafed through his grandmother's old Bible, and there he discovered in the family record that he was an adopted son. "I don't know to whom I belong," he confessed to his counselor. "I don't know where I came from!"

This deep sense of alienation lurks within the innermost chambers of each human heart. We have all felt orphaned, lonely, and spiritually dis-located.

One cannot help being struck by the decadence and despair showcased in modern films and novels. A deep sense of emptiness and loneliness pervades contemporary society as one recipe after another fails to deliver the goods sought after. People are searching for something that cannot be found.

Are we not hearing a cry that says: "Is there anybody who truly cares about me? Is there anyone who can hold me and give me a sense of belonging?"

There is.

Our True Home

Our deep yearning to feel secure—to be cherished, to drink deeply of lasting joy—is not there by accident.

It is what we were *made* for. We were created to belong to a heavenly Father.

Sin turned us into orphans.

But somebody came for us. God's Eternal Son took on our humanity, died, and rose again to draw us back into the tender ferocity of a love that is vaster, richer, and deeper than *anything* we can imagine. It is only in the Father's strong embrace that our guilt goes, our fears fade, and our heart finds its true home.

Christ brings us into a richness that touches the deepest desire of our hearts. This is the theme of His parable and the most wonderful truth in the universe: *God wants to be our father.*[11]

George MacDonald put it so well: "The one eternal, original, infinite blessing of the human soul is when in stillness the Father comes and says, 'My child, I am here.'"[12]

PRAYER

Heavenly Father, how can we praise You enough for the unexplainable mercy and incomparable honor of being your children—chosen, adopted and loved through your Eternal Son, Jesus Christ. That You should now say to us "This is my beloved son/daughter in whom I am well pleased" is knowledge too wonderful for us, it is high, we cannot attain it. May the witness of Your Spirit to our spirit regarding our adoption drown out all other dissenting voices. Grant us to know more of the goodness, passion and love of Your Father heart. Pour out Your grace upon us that we may live an Abba-conscious life that increasingly reflects the family likeness of the wonderful God to whom we belong. In the name of Jesus Christ, our Lord, amen.

It is the grand design of Satan to lessen
our opinion of God's goodness.
—THOMAS MANTON

God is better than we thought.
Much better than we feared.
Better even than we dared to believe.
—JOHN ELDREDGE

I implore you in God's name,
not to think of Him as hard to please,
but rather as generous beyond
all that you can ask or think.
—ABBE HENRI DE TOURVILLE

CHAPTER THREE

The God of extreme goodness

"So the father divided his wealth between his two sons."

LUKE 15:12 ERV

The prodigal's father is clearly a prosperous and honorable man. He owns a large estate and has servants. He is well known and highly respected in the community.

And he is remarkably *magnanimous.* The first thing we see the father doing in the parable is *giving.* He generously bestows an inheritance upon an ungrateful son.

None of his neighbors, however, would describe his action as generous. It is instead downright foolish.

His younger boy has requested to speak with his father. After some preliminary small talk, he gets to the point. "Dad, I know this estate is going to be mine someday, but I may be too burned out by then to make the most of it. So, if you don't mind, I want it now—while I still have some pizzazz left."

All eyebrows in Jesus' audience shot up.

To request an inheritance ahead of time was almost unheard of. It amounted to wishing the old man would hurry up and die. The son's impertinence was *way* out of bounds.

Jesus' listeners fully expected the father to hit the roof.

Here the story takes a shocking twist.

Giving Riches to a Rascal

The man doesn't dispatch the spoiled brat to boot camp until he gets his attitude straightened out. In fact, he doesn't even seem to take offense. Without further discussion, the lord of the estate gives in to this outrageous request.

Each one of his two sons is given his share of the property. Apparently the younger boy obtains his portion in hard cash and his brother inherits the farm. According to Jewish custom, one part of the inheritance went to the youngest and two parts to the elder.

The freeloader waltzes out with one-third of the father's hard-earned wealth!

It was at this point everyone in His audience turned to each other with a puzzled look and gasped, "Whhhaaattt?"

"In just two sentences, Jesus has set in motion a startling drama that grips every Jewish heart in his audience," one scholar points out.[1]

Such rash open-handedness with the ungrateful rascal is preposterous! Has the father not thought about what the moocher might do with all that money? A most irresponsible handling of family affairs!

The whole episode is a huge embarrassment to the father. His reputation would plummet. He most certainly would disqualify himself for leadership in the community. The villagers would mock.

"*A foolish son brings grief to his father*," states the book of Proverbs. Some sons are skillful at doing that. And this money-hungry fellow certainly is one of them.

The Art of Blowing an Inheritance

"Not many days later, the younger son gathered all he had and took a journey into a far country" (Lk. 15:13 ESV).

It comes as no surprise that Mr. Moneybags soon packs up, swaggers out the door, and hits the road. Distant places are beckoning. Unlike the sheep and the coin in the first two parables, he doesn't get lost—he *goes.*

Not only does he leave town, he leaves the *country.* This is evidenced by the fact he finally ends up on a pig farm. Such farms were not to be found in Israel; pork was not a part of the Jewish diet. This fellow is getting as *far* from home as possible.

Why does the boy not find an apartment close to home so he can visit his dad on a regular basis? Why does he have to go to "a far country"?

We all know the answer, don't we?

Out there *nobody* knows him! No one will be keeping tabs on him or informing dad of his activities. There will be nothing to prevent him doing as he pleases. He has the money, he has the craving, he has the freedom—and he's going to live it to the max!

So Junior does exactly that.

"And there he squandered his property in reckless living" (Lk. 15:13 ESV).

This is the part of the story where the prodigal son earns his name. "Prodigal" does not mean "wayward," but "wasteful." It comes from Latin roots that mean "forth" *(pro)* and "to drive" *(agere).* It describes a person who drives forth his money—who spends with reckless abandon, who squanders until nothing is left.

The boy starts living life to the hilt. He knows his dad wouldn't approve—but the old man is no longer around! He plunges headlong into a lifestyle he always dreamed about. He really whoops it up. And, of course, the whole wild escapade is paid for with the funds he got from his father.

In the Beginning

Not unlike this story, the Bible starts out with a stunning display of God's lavish goodness. God created a marvelous world of beauty, harmony, and indescribable perfection for the human family. Seven times God contemplated His handiwork of hummingbirds, roses, waterfalls, concord grapes, butterflies, penguins, and sunsets, and exclaimed, "It was good." Everything our first parents could possibly desire was lavished upon them. Their home was appropriately named Eden: a place of pleasure.

Adam and Eve were ushered into a world far more astonishing than any fairy tale. They did nothing to deserve it. John Piper points out, "You can't deserve to be created. You can't deserve, as a non-being, to be put into a lavish garden where all your needs are met by a loving Father."[2] The first two humans stood wide-eyed in the middle of an explosion of extravagance, beauty, and goodness.

With uninhibited delight they drank deeply of the Creator's intoxicating pleasures.

And they learned one great lesson: *God is good.*

Expansive Goodness

The God who is Father, Son, and Holy Spirit had no need to create a universe; He enjoyed unrestrained happiness and fulfillment. When the Triune God decided to create, it was not to satisfy some personal need but to share His abundance. Creation is the overflow of uncontainable benevolence. Seventeenth-century theologian Richard Sibbes said it well: "God delights to communicate and spread His goodness."[3]

God's goodness is an outgoing, limitless, overflow of generosity. There is an expansiveness about it; it is unstoppable, it is inexhaustible. The Creator delights to give, He seeks to give, He lives to give. That's what God is all about!

C. S. Lewis gives us this delightful description: "In God there is no hunger that needs to be filled, only plenteousness that desires to give."[4]

Goodness is the truth about God revealed on Mt. Sinai when Moses made his daring request: *"Please, show me Your glory"* (Ex. 33:18). How would the Lord answer? By displaying His power? His holiness? His majesty? The Divine response is significant: "And the LORD said, I will cause all my *goodness* to pass in front of you" (Ex. 33:19). This is God's glory—His superlative goodness! He delights in giving and bestowing His favor.

The classical Greek author Athenaeus rightly affirmed, "Goodness does not consist in greatness but greatness in goodness."

This joyous fact about God is underscored from the very first pages of the Bible. A cursory reading of the creation account leads us to believe our Maker purposes to provide every good thing in abundance for those who trust in Him. "Genesis 1 is a song of praise for God's generosity," comments Old Testament scholar Walter Brueggemann.[5]

> *Infinite sharing is the law of God's inner life.*
>
> —THOMAS MERTON

Essentially the Creator is saying to us, "I have given you the whole world to enjoy. Explore it, develop it, care for it, and delight in it. But you must trust me in this: All my desires for you are unfailingly good, and I am withholding the fruit of the forbidden tree for good reason. Do not eat of it or you will die."

The Great Deception

Surrounded by untarnished beauty, abundance, and perfection, Adam and Eve had overwhelming reasons to believe in the goodness of God.

But the great Deceiver came into the scene—and that confidence was shaken. The bill of goods the Enemy sold them was this: "Don't expect God to satisfy all your desires. As a matter of fact, there are things He *doesn't* want you to enjoy. Don't be fooled—He is not as good as you think."

"God is not good"—is the greatest *lie* in the universe.

Our first parents swallowed it, turned away from their Maker—and stepped off the precipice.

The resulting wreckage defies description.

In a world "ruined by the Fall," the question that continues to face us is: Is God's goodness believable?

This is the great controversy of the biblical narrative and of human history. The Evil One does all he can to make people believe that the promises of sin are more satisfying than the promises of God. He orchestrates tragedy and chaos to give credibility to his lies about God. He uses falsehood and confusion to blind people's minds to the inexhaustible riches of our Maker's benevolence.

The central issue on planet Earth is this: *Is God good enough to be trusted?* This is the Great Debate. And ultimately each person is forced to take sides.

Where Is God?

The struggle to believe God is truly good is one I have had to confront personally—in a most painful way.

Our five children grew up in Bolivia, where my wife and I have served as missionaries for over 35 years. Steven, the second youngest, was a ray of sunshine in our home—a remarkably talented, bright, creative boy.

However, in his late teens, Steven developed a bipolar condition, and his life slowly began to unravel. My wife and I watched in despair as our beloved son succumbed to depression, sleeplessness, and suicidal tendencies. Attempts to help him were unsuccessful, and in the early hours of June 14, 2010, the unthinkable happened. Steven ended his life.

We were stunned. Could this actually be happening to us? It felt like a truck had run over our hearts. Pain and confusion barged into our lives and took up permanent residence. That was the worst day of my life.

"God, we were praying for our son—why didn't you answer?"

Within a matter of hours we were on a flight from Bolivia to Canada to attend the funeral service of our 18-year-old son.

Does this sort of thing happen to *missionaries?*

Yes, it does.

Are they not exempt from tragedies like this?

No, they aren't.

The truth of the matter is: *nobody is.*

In a world engulfed by suffering, what makes us think faith will stop bad things from coming our way? In response to the idea that belief in God equals happiness, the German martyr Dietrich Bonhoeffer retorted, "The cross of Christ destroyed the equation." The only perfect person who ever lived died a cruel death. We live on a planet where awful things can happen to *anyone.*

Looking for Answers

A tsunami of pain washed over us. Our son was gone. The bitter ache of loss seeped down into the depths of our souls. Deeper than words could say. How much pain can a soul absorb?

My faith went into crisis. "God, where were you when Steven died? Was that the *best* you could come up with?"

How do you continue to believe in a God who permits this sort of thing to happen to you? How do you follow the way of trust in the face of raw heart-rending pain? Why does a loving God allow an 18-year-old son to fall victim to suicide? How do you square *that* with the goodness of God?

My faith staggered.

As I grappled with this troublesome issue, I noticed in the biblical record that I was not the first to ask this question. "God ... why?" was the thorny question debated all through the book of Job. The psalmists repeatedly cried out in despair when their world fell apart. *"Why, O LORD, do you stand far off? Why do you hide yourself in times of trouble?"* (Psa. 10:1; see too Psa. 42:9; 44:23; 74:1,11; etc.).

The "Why?" question has been hurled at God many times. It was heard at the dawn of history when Adam and Eve wept before the grave of their murdered son. And it has reverberated down through the centuries.

An Unexpected Answer

I finally turned to the gospels. Surely Jesus Christ, God incarnate, would throw some light on this distressing issue.

Jesus of Nazareth lived a life of unsurpassed goodness. He healed broken lives. He showed compassion to people in pain. He put an end to suffering wherever He went. This Messiah was marvelous.

Just when everything looked so hopeful, though, things took a turn for the worse. Jesus was apprehended, sentenced, and cruelly executed on a Roman cross. His life ended in the most horrible and painful way. The best man who ever lived was subjected to the worst torture ever devised.

The problem of suffering just got *more* complicated. Here is a Messiah who doesn't theorize about pain, He *tastes* it. He doesn't explain suffering—He *experiences* it!

And then ... a Bible verse I had read many times caught my attention. Before dying, Jesus uttered a loud cry: *"My God, my God, WHY have you forsaken me?"* (Mt. 27:46).

Just a minute. That's *our* question!

He takes the question we have been throwing at God, and now, in a cry of anguish—He asks it too! Now we have the man who was God, crying out: *"God ... WHY!"*

How do we explain *that?*

The Suffering God

Is it possible God was responding to our question in an unexpected way? We were looking for answers, but, in the words of one writer, "instead of hearing an answer we catch sight of God Himself scraped and torn. Through our tears we see the tears of God."[6]

Could the Cross be God's answer?

Not a series of philosophical arguments. Not an explanation— but a *crucifixion*.

The crucifixion of God.

Nothing in the history of mankind is more astounding than God pierced and bleeding on a cross. God—a victim of evil. Who could ever imagine the Almighty would be subjected to suffering in its worst possible form? Why would a God with unlimited power allow such a thing?

Light began to break into my darkness. I began to see the Cross in a new way. I realized God does not view our suffering from afar in His distant heaven but says, "I will suffer with you." One writer put it this way: "The Cross is God taking on flesh and blood and saying, 'Me too.'"

This crucified God says in effect: "I understand, I feel your pain. I am not indifferent to your suffering. I share it, and I purpose to put an end to it." Theologian Jürgen Moltmann wrote: "God weeps with us so that we may one day laugh with him."[7]

My question was: "Where is God in all of this suffering?" And now I caught sight of Him—omnipotence agonizing and bleeding on a cross, a victim of cruel, deadly violence. "Instead of explaining our suffering God shares it," writes one philosopher.[8]

My question slipped out the back door and walked away. There are moments when it shows up again, but I now know where to find the answer.

Trusting in the Dark

There are many things about the ways of God my minuscule mind does not comprehend. I am unable to unravel the mystery and the why of suffering. I don't understand why the life of our son ended tragically at age 18. Neither do I understand why some of my friends have lost their child, their spouse, or their health.

But in the midst of a world that throbs with suffering stands the cross of a suffering God. It speaks with greater force and eloquence than words ever could. The profundity of its message, of its "terrifying beauty," is light years beyond any verbal explanation.

The Cross tells us that God does not stand on the *outside* of human suffering. He Himself suffers—with us and for us. The Cross is the revelation of God's compassion.

"But God demonstrates His own love for us in this: While we were still sinners, Christ died for us" (Rom. 5:8).

We may not understand God's ways, but we can now see His heart.

What we have is not an explanation for everything, but a Sovereign Lord who understands and cares. English theologian John Stott confessed: "I could never myself believe in God if it were not for the Cross.... In the real world of pain, how could one worship a God who was immune to it?"[9]

Dietrich Bonhoeffer was right: Only a suffering God can help.

His Face Is Towards Us

A father and his young daughter drove home from the cemetery where the body of a wife and mother had been laid into a cold, dark grave.

Their home had never felt so empty.

That night the little girl wanted to be with her daddy. As they lay in the dark silence a little voice was heard, "Daddy, are you there?"

"Yes, I'm here."

"Daddy, it's dark. It's so, so dark. Daddy, is your face toward me?"

The father turned and said, "Yes, my face is toward you."

He embraced the little one until she finally slept.

After a while he slipped from the bed and fell to his knees. "God," he said. "It's dark. It's so, so dark. I have never seen it so dark. Is your face toward me?"

And God said, "Yes, it is."

How do we know God's face is toward us?

We have one answer— THE CROSS.

Whatever suffering you face, look to the Cross and ask yourself if you can trust this suffering God.

—GLEN SCRIVENER

We cannot comprehend or explain everything God does, but after Calvary we know beyond a shadow of doubt He is trustworthy. His concern for us is undeniable. The Cross stands as final, irrefutable proof of the love of God. We can trust, not because God has explained Himself, but because He has shown us His *heart*.

Dispelling Doubt

Losing a son has left a permanent hole in my heart. There are moments when I am overcome with grief. Sometimes I feel a stab of pain when I drive past the place where we had our last meal, or I shop in the store where he once worked.

But I no longer wrestle with God over this loss. It's *not* that He gave me an explanation. He gave me a revelation of His heart. He pointed me to the Cross.

And that was enough.

It was there my doubts about God's goodness were crucified and buried. I don't have all the whys figured out. I don't understand the ways of God. But a God who gave His life for me on a cross ... is a God I can trust.

After being diagnosed with cancer, Timothy Keller wrote about the relevance of the Cross:

> Do you see what this means? We don't know the reason God allows evil and suffering to continue, or why it is so random, but now at least we know what the reason isn't, what it can't be. It can't be He doesn't love us. It can't be that He doesn't care. He is so committed to our ultimate happiness that He was willing to plunge into the greatest depths of suffering Himself.[10]

Philosopher Peter Kreeft pointed out: "There is ... one good reason for not believing in God: evil. And God himself has answered this objection not in words but in deeds and in tears. Jesus is the tears of God."[11]

Overturning the Lie

Someone said bluntly: "God is good, and the devil is bad. Let's not get it confused."

Extreme outgoing goodness lies at the center of who God is. It is expansive and relentless. This beneficence is reflected in the generosity of the prodigal's father. It was demonstrated in Creation. God is wonderfully and inexhaustibly good.

One Christian leader pointed out, "God's original purpose for human life is that it should be lived in faith, faith in the goodness of God."[12]

But God's goodness was denied by Satan in the Garden of Eden. We were lied to. We were told God cannot be trusted, and the Lie took root in human hearts. People's minds have become terribly confused.

Earth no longer looks like Eden because we swallowed the Lie. This is what turns paradises into pigpens. It is why our lives veer in wrong directions. It is why things have taken a turn for the worse on our planet.

Scottish writer Oswald Chambers made this perceptive statement: "The root of all evil is the suspicion that our Father is not good."

This is the central issue at stake in our planet. Is God's goodness believable? Is His love real? Can He be trusted? This is the bottom line.

This is one reason why Jesus came. He came to make, and even *to be*, the final statement about God's goodness.

What Christ has to say on the subject takes our breath away. The wild extravagance of God's goodness surpasses anything we ever imagined. It has the intensity of a hurricane and the softness of a rose petal. It inspires happy dancing and holy wonder.

Our sin could not deter God from pursuing us. As a matter of fact, it brought about an even *more* lavish display of His unheard-of generosity—as we are about to discover in Jesus' story.

PRAYER

Good Lord, You are the beauty behind all beauty, the music behind all music, the virtue behind all virtue, the truth behind all truth, the love behind all love. Open my eyes to your abounding goodness. Thank you for Your Son Jesus, the supreme testimony to Your extravagant goodness. Thank you for the Cross, the ultimate expression of its overflowing, overcoming reality. As I taste and see that God is good, may my heart beat with gratitude and wonder. When I forget the source of every good gift, renew a thankful spirit within me. When I turn from what is good, bring me back, and lead me in the way everlasting. Amen.

The reason there is so much pain in the world
is because God is not controlling.
He gives people their own will,
to help or, sadly, to harm.
—DONALD MILLER

God has such a deep reverence for our freedom
that He'd rather let us freely go to Hell
than be compelled to go to heaven.
—DESMOND TUTU

I do not think the forest would be
so bright, nor love so sweet, if there
were no danger in the lakes.
—C. S. LEWIS

CHAPTER FOUR

The God who grants dangerous freedom

"Not long after that, the younger son got together all he had, set off for a distant country ..."

LUKE 15:13

With scarcely a farewell, the boy shoulders his backpack, strides out the door, and starts down the driveway. Before turning onto the road, he manages a feeble wave—and then he's gone.

Through tear-filled eyes, his father watches him leave.

He would give anything to know how to talk to the boy. But those words cannot be found, and the last opportunity to say something has just walked out the door.

Any attempt to deter his son is pointless. The young man's heart has left long ago, and his feet are simply trying to catch up. The father stands transfixed by pain, and watches him depart.

The whole affair likely fuels a lot of talk in the village. Why does the man let the kid get his hands on the inheritance? Why does he let him walk off with the money? Anybody can see his life is about to spin out of control. Surely the father could manage his affairs in a better way.

We can only surmise about the events that have led up to this painful moment. Has tension been growing between father and son? Has communication broken down? We are not given details.

However, the phrase *"not long after that"* speaks volumes. Here is a young man eager to break free from parental control. He chafes under his father's rules and wants out. Living under the same roof with his older brother is also no piece of cake. Junior wastes no time in making his departure.

A Parent in Pain

"All stories begin with a lump in the throat," writes author Frederick Buechner. This one certainly does. With his insides in turmoil, the father chokes back the tears as a large piece of his heart walks away into the distance.

It is a heart-rending scene that has been repeated a million times over all over the planet.

The man could have chased after him to say, "Son, wait! Why don't we talk this over?"

He *doesn't* do it.

The man loves the boy as much as any father could. His heart throbs with pain. His tears flow, but his feet do *not* move.

Why not?

This leads us to another perturbing question …

Why did the Creator act likewise in the Garden of Eden? Why did He simply look on as His beautiful world wandered away from Him into poverty, hunger, war, violence, injustice, corruption, and a thousand other evils? Why did God allow this prodigal planet to spin out of control?

Surely the Creator could do a better job of managing His affairs. Could He not be more proactive? He has plenty of power at His disposal to restrain evil. Why not use it?

It's the age-old question: If the Lord of creation is good, why does He allow so much that is bad? Why do horrible things happen in His world?

There are no *easy* answers.

However, Luke 15 provides some helpful clues. Let's look at this thorny issue through the lens of this chapter.

Three Parables: One Message

Luke states Jesus told them "this parable." Singular. What follows are *three* stories. Plural. Evidently the three are meant to be part of a whole.

The first two are routine search-and-rescue stories. When a sheep strays from the flock, the shepherd scours the countryside until he finds it. When a coin goes missing, the woman turns the house upside-down until she recovers it.

However, in the third parable there's a new twist. When the son leaves home and gets "lost," the father *stays* home. Unlike the shepherd and the woman, he makes no attempt to go and search for him.

How do we explain this?

Is a sheep worth more than a son? No, it isn't.

Is a coin of greater value than a boy? Of course not.

Why then, when the sheep is lost, the shepherd combs the hills for it, when the coin disappears, the woman ransacks the house for it—but when the boy goes missing, the father makes no attempt to find him? A search is made for the sheep and the coin. Why not for the son?

Here's one basic reason: *There is a vast difference between sheep, coins, and sons.*[1]

The sheep will not be found unless the shepherd goes out and searches for it. The coin will not be recovered unless the woman looks for it. The son, however, unlike sheep and coins, can come home *whenever* he so desires. And, if forced to return against his will, would likely take off at the first opportunity.

This is a fundamental rule in parenting: we *can't* handle sons as we do sheep and coins.

The father of our story understands this very well. And no one understands it better than God.

A Prodigal Planet

When the Creator designed the universe, on one tiny piece of dust called planet Earth, He placed some creatures called "humans." These headstrong individuals decided they did not want to live under the Father's roof, and they struck out on their own. Their *modus operandi* was "This is my life and I am going to live it my way." Before long they were squandering their inheritance and making an overall *mess* of things.

We ended up with a world full of mortals who pay little or no attention to their Maker. Some believe He doesn't exist.

Why do they get away with that?

Why doesn't God put His foot down? (figuratively speaking.)

The rest of the cosmos dutifully operates according to the Creator's game plan. The rain falls, the sun shines, the wind blows, the grass grows, and fish swim. Everything works marvelously like clockwork.

But in one corner of this symphony of beauty and goodness there is an insurrection going on. We have *Homo sapiens* who have turned their backs on God and live their lives without Him.

This was the original "prodigal" story.

Rather predictably, the "distant country" project crashed and burned. Planet Earth is *not* exactly doing well, if you've noticed.

Check your local newspaper for details. Someone should declare this world a disaster zone; all manner of tragic things happen. We have suicide bombers, human trafficking, environmental destruction, oppressive regimes, corrupt judiciaries, nasty neighbors, rebellious kids, and a thousand other problems.

The planet suffers, animals suffer, people suffer ... and—not unlike the father in our story—it appears God *also* suffers.

Love, Freedom, and Suffering

Why are humans allowed this dangerous freedom? Shouldn't the Sovereign Lord be running a tighter ship? Why doesn't He step in and set things right? Isn't that part of His job description?

Well, what do we suggest the Almighty do? Cut off the oxygen supply until everyone smartens up? Give the planet a good shake and put the fear of God into people? Flex His omnipotence and force people to get their acts together? A bit of arm-twisting might be effective.

He could easily do that, but that raises a problem. God would then be treating us *not* as humans, but as animals or objects. Something vital would be lost. The difference between sheep and coins and sons would be obliterated.

That, apparently, is something our Maker *refuses* to do.

God has no interest in having a world made up of sheep and coins. It's *people,* not puppets and robots, He wants—sons and daughters with whom He can have a genuine relationship of love. He wants us to know Him, to walk with Him, to revel and dance in His goodness.

Granting Godlike Freedom

By crafting us in His image, the Creator endowed us with the capacity to create, to reason, to imagine, to laugh, and to wonder. A heavenly hush must have come over the angels as they saw Him fashion such remarkable godlike creatures.

And then He granted us the greatest treasure of all. He gave us the capacity to experience the incomparable wonder and beauty of that which lies at the essence of God.

He enabled us to *love*.

And that involved the dignity of freedom.

> *Without choice there is no love. So God made us in his image. God already had pets. He wanted people.*
>
> —BRUXY CAVEY

It was not given to animals. They simply do what they were created to do. They are governed by instincts.

Not so for humans.

People have been equipped with an internal on-off switch at the center of their being, a freedom that is absolutely unique in the whole scheme of creation. It is something sheep and coins do not possess.

The switch is called *choice*. We can say yes or no to God.

Spiritual writer Henri Nouwen put it this way: "I am loved so much that I am left free to leave home."[2]

A Daring Venture

Is it not dangerous to dish out this kind of freedom? What if humans abused it? What if they chose evil instead of good? Violence and oppression could run rampant. A tsunami of misery and suffering could engulf the world. Why run such a risk?

The answer comes down to this: if love is going to be the main point of this drama, if this is what God is most interested in, then each person must be granted the freedom to choose. Love cannot be forced, manipulated or programmed. It can only exist where there is plenty of elbow room to choose for or against it.

Love relinquishes control. It does not insist on its own way (I Cor. 13:5).

Freedom to Choose

There were many trees in the garden, and Adam was told not to eat of *one* of them (Gn. 2:16,17). "The command which presumes the freedom to obey or disobey is the first command given in our Scriptures. It defines us as creatures of freedom," points out Eugene Peterson.[3]

In order to have a world where genuine love happens, people must have the liberty to make choices. "Love must live in the freedom not to love," observes Frederick Buechner.[4] Freedom of choice opens the door to any worthwhile experience of love, goodness, and joy—and it also opens the door to evil. Love cannot exist apart from that freedom.

God could use His power to *make* us obey Him. But there is *one* thing He could never obtain by force.

He could not make us *love* Him.

And that happens to be what He is *most* interested in.

In his book *God and Human Suffering,* Douglas John Hall points out: "God's problem is not that God *is not able* to do certain things. God's problem is that God loves. Love complicates the life of God as it complicates every life."[5]

Danish philosopher Søren Kierkegaard exclaims, "Wonderful love, even his omnipotence is under the power of love!"[6]

So why would a loving God create a world where evil can happen? Is He not concerned with our happiness?

Much more than we can *imagine.*

People, Puppets, and Pawns

God's concern for our ultimate happiness led Him to create us with the capacity to love and to be loved. He gave us the freedom to make choices. In so doing, He placed within our reach the highest joy this universe knows.

Lewis points out that God gave us free will "because a world of mere automata could never love and therefore never know infinite happiness."[7]

If the Creator were a self-serving autocrat, He could have designed a universe where everything ran strictly according to His plan, where every creature unerringly did as commanded. The Lord would be indisputably *in charge.*

In such a world, the "wrath of God" would not exist because nothing displeasing to Him would ever be allowed to happen. No one would have the freedom to disobey. The Almighty would control everything, and *only* His will would be carried out.

God could *easily* have set things up like that.

When people are merely puppets and pawns, there are no unpleasant surprises: no boundaries are violated and no rules are broken. Such creatures will never disappoint or upset you. On the other hand, neither will they do anything noble, praiseworthy, or heartwarming. Things just happen as scripted in a bland, monotone, dreary fashion.

In such a world, love does not exist. Joy is absent. It's not a place to which you would want to move!

"Chase away the demons and they will take the angels with them," noted the Canadian singer-songwriter Joni Mitchell.

God had a much better idea.

He desired more than flawless order and robot-like compliance. He wanted *relationship*. He wanted joy and wonder and goodness and romance and adventure.

"He is a king who wants not subservience but love," points out Philip Yancey.[8]

The Lord therefore decided to empower humans with a godlike freedom of choice. He conferred upon them the capability of genuine love and the dignity of making praiseworthy decisions. One writer put it this way, "By giving them freedom to disobey, God made it possible for them to love. By giving them the power to act foolishly, He made it possible for them to be wise."[9]

In the process, this God of love did something no power-hungry despot would ever do—He granted them the ability to break His heart.

Now we have a *real* story!

One author points out, "Always remember, it's simply not an adventure worth telling if there aren't any dragons."[10]

And no one is sure *what* is going to happen next. British writer Dorothy L. Sayers rightly declared: "The Christian faith is the most exciting drama that ever staggered the imagination of man."[11]

The Perils of Freedom

Once a university student came home and announced, "I'm not sure if I can keep on believing in God." His father responded, "Son, that is your freedom—your *dangerous* freedom."

A perilous liberty, indeed.

What is this frightful autonomy that allows us to choose God or Satan, good or evil, light or darkness, heaven or hell? How is it we are permitted to believe in or blaspheme the One who gives us our next breath?

Why are we granted the enjoyment of strawberries and sunsets and sex while we simultaneously turn our backs on the Maker of it all? How is it we can freely spurn the love of God, trample it underfoot, and even *crucify* it?

What grave choices have been placed in our hands! And how recklessly we manage this dangerous freedom!

In their book, *The Sacred Romance,* Brent Curtis and John Eldredge write:

> The wildness of giving us freedom is even more staggering when we remember that God has already paid dearly for giving freedom to the angels. But because of his grand heart he goes ahead and takes the risk, an enormous, colossal risk. The reason he didn't make puppets is because he wanted lovers. Remember, he's inviting us up into a romance. Freedom is part of the explanation for the problem of evil. God is the author of some storms directly; but he is the author of the possibility of all storms in giving us freedom. And *we* opened Pandora's box.[12]

Who's the Real Culprit?

Are human choices not behind the bulk of suffering on our planet? It is people who carry out acts of bullying, rape, extortion, terrorism, infidelity, abuse of power, gossip, slander, and theft. "What region of the earth is not full of our calamities?" asked Virgil, the Roman poet. Are "natural disasters" not due, to a large extent, to the curse that came upon the world through human sin (Gn. 3:17)? Can most of the world's misery not be traced back to our selfish, cruel, and prideful choices?[13] You and I are the reason why the world is as it is.

It has been pointed out that while belief in God after the Holocaust may be difficult for some, belief in man after the Holocaust is *impossible.* It leaves little doubt regarding the capacity of humans for evil.

After the tragic death of Princess Diana in 1997, author Philip Yancey was contacted by a television producer and asked why God could have allowed such a terrible accident. "Could it have had something to do with a drunk driver going ninety miles an hour in a narrow tunnel?" replied Yancey. "How, exactly, was God involved?"[14]

Furthermore, it should be noted that humans do not act alone in perpetrating wicked deeds. Scripture testifies to the existence of a malevolent spirit behind the evil in human history. Those who do not submit to God's rule are acted upon by evil forces (Jas. 4:7; Eph. 2:2). As singer Bob Dylan put it, "you're gonna have to serve somebody." We live in "enemy occupied territory" that is under the control of one described by Jesus as *a murderer from the beginning* (Jn. 8:44). Bad things happen because people submit themselves to this dark power.

The Bible states that the tragic events that befell Job were carried out by Satan (Job 1). The apostle Peter described people suffering physical ailments as *"oppressed by the devil"* (Acts 10:38). When tragedy, natural disasters, and disease strike, we are not seeing the face of God but the face of His adversary. Although these events are often termed "acts of God," perhaps it would be more accurate to say: *"An enemy has done this"* (Mt 13:28).[15] We are living in a battle zone.

Theology on a Bus

On one occasion, when taking a long bus trip in southern Bolivia, I struck up a conversation with another passenger. As we traveled through the night, the topic turned to spiritual matters. Overhearing our discussion, another traveler blurted out: "If God is good and just, why does He allow so much suffering and injustice in the world?"

What a question to have thrown at you at 3 o'clock in the morning! I prayed, "God, I'm going to need some help with this one."

Turning to the man, I said something like this: "The suffering and injustice you are talking about was *not* part of the world when God made it. He created a wonderful and perfect paradise. But that changed when our first parents followed Satan's lead and ate of the forbidden tree. As a result, a flood of evil came into this world. That wasn't God's doing, it was ours. We opened the door through our rebellion. *We* are to blame."

The man listened attentively.

"However," I continued, "God saw our plight and sent His Son, Jesus, into this world. The Son of God gave His life to rescue us from evil and from the suffering it brings."

"The horrible death by crucifixion He underwent tells us clearly that God is not indifferent to our pain. He voluntarily suffered, died, and rose again to get rid of sin and suffering forever."

"Tragically many people do not want Christ in their lives. They reject His offer of forgiveness and salvation. And then they complain that God allows so much evil and suffering in the world! As I see it, God is not the one responsible. We are."

That seemed to satisfy the questioner in the aisle. He responded, *"Muchas gracias,"* and returned to his seat. Breathing a sigh of relief, I said, "Thank you, Lord."

The Peril of Rejecting God

The human race thought life in the "distant country" was going to be a great fling. We were *wrong*. The feast turned out to be a famine. Before long we ran into things like guilt, shame, poverty, loneliness, and hunger.

Untold suffering resulted. Life in God's world without God does not fare well.

And the story doesn't end there.

The freedom to reject God goes beyond this life into the next. No one is forced to go to heaven. If someone is determined to live without God, there is a place available for him. It is called Hell. What could be *fairer?* God thinks of everything.

Frederick Buechner speaks with clarity on the subject:

> People are free in this world to live for themselves alone if they want to and let the rest go hang, and they are free to live out the dismal consequences as long as they can stand it. The doctrine of Hell proclaims that they retain this same freedom in whatever world comes next. Thus the possibility of making damned fools of ourselves would appear to be limitless.[16]

Scripture states that the Sovereign Lord takes no pleasure in the death of the wicked (See Ezek. 33:11). It causes Him to weep, as Christ wept over the city of Jerusalem when its leaders turned against Him (Mt. 24:37,38). His desire is that none should perish (I Tim. 2:4). He commands us to repent because He longs to see us delivered from the destruction sin brings.

Tragically, many pay no heed.

Hell Is a Choice

People do not end up in Hell simply because God damned them to go there. It is a choice people make. Eternal death is not punishment for sin; it is the inevitable *consequence* of sin, as a crash landing is the consequence of jumping off a building. To choose sin is to choose death.

Hell is what we finally wind up with when we choose hatred over love, evil over goodness, greed over generosity, resentment over forgiveness, darkness over light. Ultimately, Hell is the choice of those who reject God's love and forgiveness offered to us in the gospel. If we refuse to follow Christ and end up in Hell, this is not the vengeance of God, but the *end result* of sin. It is, as one scholar put it, "the supreme self-torture of a freely chosen enmity against love."[17]

J. I. Packer said bluntly,

> Nobody stands under the wrath of God save those who have chosen to do so. The essence of God's action in wrath is to *give men what they chose*, in all its implications; nothing more, and equally nothing less.[18]

There are many who choose *not* to welcome God into their lives. What makes this a damnable choice is this: God is the fountain of life—the *only* source of life. Without God we perish. To say no to God is to say no to life; it is to choose death. Outside of Him—there is *nothing* but death. "Once a man is separated from God, what can he do but wither and die?" asks Lewis.[19]

> *Hell is the place where you say, "No, I don't want your love."*
>
> —ERWIN MCMANUS

Hell is the insanity of saying no to the light, love, and goodness of God. Lewis has been quoted as saying that Hell is that moment when God says to the rebellious sinner, "All right then, have it your way." George MacDonald stated, "The one principle of hell is—'I am my own.'" If a person insists he doesn't want God, that dreadful option is open.

"Hell is just a courtesy for those who insist they want no part of forgiveness," writes Robert Capon.[20]

Henri Nouwen comments that "just as the father of the prodigal son let his son make his own decision God gives us the freedom to move away from God's love even at the risk of destroying ourselves. Hell is not God's choice. It is ours."[21]

Listen to G. K. Chesterton: "Hell is God's great compliment to the reality of human freedom and the dignity of human personality." God takes our decisions very seriously—a most sobering fact!

Operation Redemption

The Lord of creation did not just stand idly by as we blindly stumbled to perdition. This is where the story takes another strange twist.

Enter Jesus of Nazareth.

He was the incarnation of the love of God. At untold cost to Himself, He came to recover that which was lost. He came to heal and forgive. He came to put an end to this nightmare of evil and suffering.

Then human hands committed the *greatest* evil of all—the sobering murder of God's guiltless Son, Jesus Christ, on a Roman cross. The crucifixion followed hours of ruthless flogging and humiliation. In the midst of all this horror, Jesus cried out, *"My God, my God, why have you forsaken me?"*

Where was *God* when Jesus was subjected to this living hell?

Scripture gives us this astounding answer: *"God was in Christ reconciling the world unto Himself"* (II Cor. 5:19).

Isaiah, the prophet, declared: *"But He was pierced for our transgressions, He was crushed for our iniquities; the punishment that brought us peace was upon Him, and by His wounds we are healed"* (Isa. 53:5).

The Cross was where God carried the weight of the world's evil on His own shoulders. It was "God's strange unlooked-for victory over the evil of our world," writes N. T. Wright.[22]

When Abraham Lincoln's body was brought from Washington to Illinois, it passed through the city of Albany and was carried down a main street. A black woman stood upon the curb and lifted her little son as far as she could above the crowd. She was heard to say, "Take a long look, honey. He died for you."

One writer added, "if I could, I would lift up your spirit to see Calvary. Take a long look, He died for you."[23]

The Final Celebration

Evil will come to an end on the prodigal planet. When the resurrected Messiah ultimately brings His redemptive mission to full completion, *all* of creation will be reconciled back to God (Col. 1:20). All that is broken will be made whole. That which was lost will be found. Life will reign in the final celebration of goodness and joy.

The Father calls everyone home to the eternal banquet of the kingdom. He is *"not willing that any should perish"* (II Pet. 3:9). The invitation is extended to all.

But we have the dangerous freedom to say no.

The Amazing Drama

Why do bad things happen in God's world? We don't have the whole answer. But it has something to do with being a part of a story where there is God and Satan, pleasure and risk, freedom and foolishness, ecstasy and pain, adventure and mystery, beauty and danger. It is what can take place when the main point of the drama is *love.*

One author pointed out, "If you want to look at the stars, you will find that darkness is necessary."[24]

Listen to Lewis:

> Some people think they can imagine a creature which was free but had no possibility of going wrong; I cannot. The happiness which God designs for His creatures is the happiness of being freely, voluntarily united to Him and to each other … And for that they must be free. Of course God knew what would

happen if they used their freedom the wrong way: apparently
He thought it worth the risk.[25]

We were not created to be a sheep or a coin. We were given
dignity and freedom. We were made in the likeness of the King of
the universe to be loved by Him, and to love Him in return. In all
of Creation there is no greater privilege.

And there *never* will be.

There is something we need to say to God, every morning of
every day ...

Thank you.

PRAYER

Thank you, O God of goodness and grace, that You did not create us to be sheep or coins but to know You and be loved by You. Thank you for calling to us when we were hiding from You. Thank you that, when we were soiled with sin, the strong pull of Your mercy drew us to Yourself. Batter and bend our stubborn will and make it fully Yours. Overwhelm, override, over-awe us with your beauty, grace and love. Grow us slowly, persistently, and deeply, Lord, to be people whose hearts are set on You alone. Amen.

Somehow I had fallen for the deception
of judging the natural world as unspiritual
and God as antipleasure. But God invented matter,
after all, including all the sensors in the body
through which I feel pleasure.

—PHILIP YANCEY

Pleasure is designed to raise our sense of
God's goodness, deepen our gratitude to him,
and strengthen our hope of richer pleasures to come.

—J. I. PACKER

Angels can fly because they take themselves lightly.
Never forget that the devil fell by force of gravity.
He who has the faith has the fun.

—G. K. CHESTERTON

CHAPTER FIVE

The God who made pleasure possible

"… and there squandered his wealth in wild living."

LUKE 15:13

The lights, the music, and the sensual delights of the far country look so tantalizing, so irresistible. Heaven is beckoning; life is about to begin.

That well-worn path has all the appearances of a direct highway to glory. What fabulous heights of pleasure lie ahead!

Or so it *seems.*

Upon arrival the prodigal throws himself into the predictable activity of "squandering" his father's hard-earned wealth. The word literally means "to scatter." It can refer to winnowing—tossing grain up in the air and letting the wind blow away the unwanted parts. It works well with wheat—not so well with money. But that's what the boy does with his inheritance.

We are not given specific details on the wild living (or "riotous living" as the King James version describes it), but our imagination has no difficulty filling in the blanks. It appears our high-flying friend sins up a storm.

Later on in this parable his elder brother states the prodigal has devoured his father's property with prostitutes. It is likely true.

The Allure of Pleasure

The enticements of pleasure easily beguile us. Is it not a thirst for pleasure that prompts the younger son to snatch his inheritance ahead of time? Is pleasure not the magnet that draws him all the way to the far country? And once there, is it not pleasure that devours his inheritance and devastates his dignity, leaving him destitute and distraught?

What is this force that pulls so *strongly* on human hearts?

The promise of pleasure has little trouble in hijacking our attention. Dangerous and disloyal longings arise that brazenly disregard the convictions we hold, or the faith we proclaim. Alluring desires tug at our soul.

Sometimes we give in. Other times we turn away with a sigh, wondering what to do with these crazy urges.

Often we shove the chaotic desires away and dutifully follow our daily routine, but they return and camp by the back door. We sign on for more religious activity and disciplines, but the unruly impulses persist.

How did these deep yearnings weasel into our hearts? Why do they refuse to go away? Does God want us simply to suppress them and focus on being good and responsible? Are we just supposed to settle down and be Mr. Nice Guy? What about the wild restlessness inside, the longing for adventure and excitement? Were our hearts designed only to be tamed and squelched?

Who Invented Pleasure?

For centuries philosophers have debated "the problem of evil," but an equally valid but rarely discussed question is "the problem of pleasure." Where did *that* originate? Why is sex fun? Why do we find beauty, food, music, and humor enjoyable? How do we account for these delights?

English writer G. K. Chesterton felt Christianity gives the only plausible explanation. He saw pleasure as scattered remnants washed ashore from a shipwreck. We are the survivors of the sinking of a golden ship that went down before the beginning of the world. Here and there, relics of a glorious past are to be found— tokens of a time when pleasure flourished in lavish abundance. They are leftovers from Paradise.

These vestiges of beauty, joy, and sheer goodness on our scarred planet resonate deeply with our hearts. They are reminders that we were meant to live in a better world that once was. They are traces of the "enormous bliss" (as John Milton put it) of a garden named Eden.

These delights stir longings to find more. Like a trail of bread-crumbs, they direct us to the Lavisher of these good gifts. They point us to the Author and Finisher of joy, who conferred upon us these pledges of His goodness and love.

Christian philosopher Dallas Willard described God this way:

> Undoubtedly He is the most joyous person in the universe. The abundance of His love and generosity is inseparable from His infinite joy. All of the good and beautiful things from which we occasionally drink tiny droplets of soul-exhilarating joy, God continually experiences in all their breadth and depth and riches.[1]

Happiness and Holiness

Certain theological notions equate holiness with somberness and raise a general suspicion of happiness. According to this view, spirituality should be tight-lipped and grim-faced. Godliness should look like gloom.

Here is an amusing example:

> A young Scottish preacher lived seven miles up the river from the church where he served. One Sunday the snowdrifts made road travel impossible, and he skated down the river to the church service. Called before the bar of his presbytery for breaking the Sabbath, his defense was that skating was the only way he could get there. "Young man," said the Moderator, "there is just one question. Did ye or did ye not enjoy the skatin'?"[2]

Faithful followers of the grinch God!

In their zeal to curb sin, rather than welcoming legitimate enjoyments as God's good gifts, some have *outlawed* them. This false spirituality does not honor the Bestower of these blessings, and it has more affinity with Pharisees than biblical revelation. It follows the lead of the Deceiver and not God. Christianity does not call for the negation of earthly bliss but its celebration and sanctification.

"Laughter," suggests author Anne Lamott, "really is carbonated holiness."

"Evil's greatest triumph," asserts Philip Yancey, "may be its success in portraying religion as an enemy of pleasure when, in fact, religion accounts for its source: every good and enjoyable thing is the invention of a Creator who lavished gifts on the world."[3]

The Spoilsport God

This "wet blanket" perception of God was the distorted view sadly held by many throughout Christian history.

Danish philosopher Soren Kierkegaard remarked: "Christ turned water into wine, but the church has succeeded in doing something even more difficult: it has turned wine into water."

Tormented by his guilty past, Augustine of Hippo promoted the idea that sexual pleasure was to be avoided. He infamously declared sex to be sinful even within marriage. A repressive view of sexuality came into vogue that regarded sex as incompatible with holiness.

The Protestant Reformation encouraged a more positive attitude toward sex. The reformers insisted marriage was the institution established by God for the expression of human sexuality. The honorability of the sexual relationship in marriage gained acceptance—a development applauded by many to be sure!

> *I myself, who have spent a good part of my life in sorrow and gloom, now seek and find pleasure wherever I can.*
>
> —MARTIN LUTHER

Scripture disapproves of sexual immorality, but within the context of marriage celebrates sex as a delightful gift of God. The first chapter of the Bible affirms sex was created by God (Gn. 1:27), commanded by God (Gn. 1:28), and approved by God (Gn. 1:31). The Old Testament book, *Song of Songs,* unabashedly exalts the beauty and wonder of *eros* in marriage.

What kind of a God would include such an erotic book in His Bible? He obviously doesn't subscribe to a repressive view of marital sex. He dares to encourage its enjoyment.

Rivers and Swamps

The marriage bed, however, not unlike a riverbed, needs borders and limits. Fierce wildness needs containment. As narrow canyons turn rivers into raging torrents, so the rock walls of commitment and responsibility allow love's passion to run deep and strong. There it can remain focused and channeled. Its holy excitement can freely flow and cascade in all its intended force and exuberance.

The removal of the walls does not endlessly expand the richness of sexual delight. On the contrary, the river spreads across the countryside and turns into a swamp. It is diminished. The sacredness of sex is sabotaged. It is cheapened and reduced to shallow, self-centered indulgence. It stagnates.

Borders are vital.

Not much white-water rafting goes on in marshlands.

Staying afloat in these waters is no simple matter. The basic skill of laying down your life for another person is essential—it involves life-long learning. Navigating around the jagged rocks of selfishness, pride, and lust is no easy task. Capsizing is common.

Complications exist for both married and singles. We live in a fallen world and we are broken people. We desperately need God and His grace. We often need forgiveness. But God's roadmap for sexual expression helps us to find order in a disordered world, to choose rivers over swamps.

Pleasure Was God's Idea

Far from opposing pleasure, God is the inventor of it. *All* of it. Satan is powerless to create, and can only bend and twist the good that God has created. It is not pleasure itself, but its misuse we must guard against. The capacity to enjoy pleasure is a magnificent legacy from our Creator.

God's first word to humans was not a prohibition but a call to enjoyment: *"You are free to eat from any tree in the garden"* (Gn.

2:16). God created physical pleasures and affirmed them to be very good (Gn. 1:31). Roses, cherries, beaches, music, wine, laughter, sex, and sunsets were *His* idea. He does not frown on pleasure; He is *"the living God, who gives us richly all things to enjoy"* (I Tim. 6:17 NKJV).

This was liberating truth for Martin Luther, who stated: "I who have hitherto spent my life in mourning and sadness, now seek and accept joy wherever I can find it."

The Perils of Pleasure

However, as the prodigal discovers, life's delights are not only enjoyable but perilous. They can intoxicate and enslave. They can overpower and impoverish. They can subtly attach themselves to our lives like leeches and suck us dry. They are able to transform themselves into idols that demand worship. They even morph into taskmasters.

Pleasures were never meant to be gods or tyrants. They are not entitlements. They are *gifts*—and that presupposes a Giver. They don't just *happen* to be here. They come to us courtesy of Someone. Crafted with love. Designed for joy. Bestowed by a Generous Benefactor.

We must never *forget* that.

The gift of pleasure was never meant for selfish indulgence, or to be relished in isolation, or without restraint.

It was intended to be enjoyed, shared, and most importantly—to be received with *gratitude*. Don't miss that last part. It was given to draw our hearts to the Giver.

Down the Slippery Slope

When the Giver is ignored, a downward spiral begins. In Romans 1:18-32 the apostle Paul describes the undoing of societies as they turn from God. They follow a predictable pattern: idolatry, immorality, sexual perversion, and social chaos. They skid into a moral pigsty.

It's a direct downhill route that runs from the Father's house to the famine in the far country.

Notice how this journey gets underway: *"For although they knew God, they did not glorify Him as God, nor were thankful"* (Rom. 1:21 NKJV).

It starts with *thanklessness.*

This is the tipping point. "Basically and radically all sin is simply ingratitude," noted Swiss theologian Karl Barth.[4] "Ingratitude is the essence of vileness," adds philosopher Immanuel Kant.

More than a hundred times the Bible summons us to live, eat, pray, and abound in thanksgiving. *"So then, just as you received Christ Jesus as Lord, continue to live in Him, rooted and built up in Him, strengthened in the faith as you were taught, and overflowing with thankfulness"* (Col. 2:6,7). Gratitude is central to the life God made us for.

G. K. Chesterton came to faith through an experience of over-whelming gratefulness for the sheer gratuity of being. He pointed out, "When it comes to life the critical thing is whether you take things for granted or take them with gratitude."[5]

He penned these words:

> You say grace before meals. All right. But I say grace before
> the concert and the opera, and grace before the play and
> pantomime, and grace before I open a book, and grace before
> sketching, painting, swimming, fencing, boxing, walking,
> playing, dancing and grace before I dip the pen in the ink.[6]

Chesterton saw clearly that each moment and each breath in God's world is an undeserved gift. To be surrounded by unexplained mercy and unsolicited favor is an astonishing *miracle*. Every day is an opportunity to awake to new wonder and praise as we taste and see the goodness of God.

Enjoyment honors the Creator's purpose and is, in fact, a participation in the divine joy.

Theologian Jürgen Moltmann makes this observation:

> When I love God I love the beauty of bodies, the rhythm of movements, the shining of eyes, the embraces, the feelings, the scents, the sounds of all this protean creation. When I love you, my God, I want to embrace it all, for I love you with all my senses in the creations of your love. In all the things that encounter me, you are waiting for me.[7]

"Religion was not designed to make your pleasures less," rightly affirmed nineteenth-century preacher Charles Spurgeon.[8]

Two centuries ago, a deeply spiritual man offered this wise counsel: "There are but two lessons for the Christian to learn: the one is to enjoy God in everything; the other is to enjoy everything in God."[9]

The Forgotten Father

The prodigal son has given little or no thought to the *source* of his good fortune. He is so busy grabbing all the gusto that the benefactor fades entirely from his mind.

Everything he enjoys in the distant country has been, in fact, financed by his father. The designer clothes, the gourmet meals, the five-star hotels, the extravagant parties, the tall cold ones he enjoys sipping ... it is *all* paid for with dad's money. It is the generosity of the man he has walked away from that makes all this enjoyment possible.

He owes a huge debt of gratitude to his father. Is "thank you" ever said?

Or does he ever consult him on the wise management of his wealth?

Apparently not.

If only he let the man who has given him the money show him how to use it, the story could be so different. The inheritance could catapult him to a lifetime of financial stability.

Instead, it becomes his *downfall*.

With his father out of the picture, the son stuffs himself on a smorgasbord of self-centered indulgence. It does not turn out well. The father's wealth, without the father's wisdom, is not a good mix. Ingratitude is the son's undoing.

Dangerous Heights

For over 20 years my family and I lived and worked in one of the highest cities in the world. Potosí, located in the Andes Mountains, is at an altitude of 13,400 feet. Rather close to heaven.

Many of our visiting friends, unaccustomed to the altitude, suffered from the shortage of oxygen. Vomiting, headaches, and other discomforts often made their stay less than enjoyable. Our doors were wide open to visitors, but many thought twice (and breathed deeply!) before braving the challenges of the high altitude.

Six months after birth, our youngest was diagnosed with a pulmonary disorder and her heart became enlarged. The doctor suggested Elisa could remain in the high altitude as long as she stayed free of colds or coughs. Our daughter did fine for a few months, and then winter came, and she caught a cold. Very quickly her condition deteriorated.

We immediately made plans to travel to a lower altitude. We loaded up the car, and with everyone on board, drove down the road that winds its way through the mountains to the nearby city of Sucre.

As we made the descent, we could see changes in Elisa. Color returned to her cheeks, she regained vitality, her condition improved noticeably. The lower elevation worked wonders.

She was finally able to *breathe* again!

It would be over a year before we could return to our home in Potosí. During that time our daughter grew stronger, and was finally able to adapt to the rarefied air of the highlands.

> *When something good becomes a god, the pleasure it brings dies in the process.*
>
> —KYLE IDLEMAN

Those who would scale the lofty peaks of pleasure run similar risks. The unchecked craving for greater highs is dangerous business; it has brought many down to the depths of despair. Pleasure has power to delight and to destroy.

Philip Yancey comments that

> in a world estranged from God, even good things must be handled with care, like explosives … Eating becomes gluttony, love becomes lust, and along the way we lose sight of the One who gave us pleasure. The ancients turned good things into idols; we moderns call them addictions.[10]

The wild pursuit of sensory delight has taken its toll on many a life. The prodigal is one of them. He has become a different person. Gone is his radiant vitality, the sparkle in his eyes, the lightness in his step, and his self-respect.

His body is captive to out-of-control passions. Thrills are getting harder to find. His friends turn out to be freeloaders. Everything unravels.

The Perilous Pursuit

Endless pleasure has a way of going horribly flat. Aimless boredom sets in. We are left with tedious emptiness.

Chesterton's dictum seems all too true: "Meaninglessness does not come from being weary of pain but from being weary of pleasure."

Indian-born apologist Ravi Zacharias contends:

> Pleasure without God, without the sacred boundaries, will actually leave you emptier than before. And this is biblical truth, this is experiential truth. The loneliest people in the world are amongst the wealthiest and most famous who found no boundaries within which to live. That is a fact I've seen again and again.[11]

Likewise, C. S. Lewis comments:

> No natural feelings are high or low, holy or unholy, in themselves. They are all holy when God's hand is on the rein. They all go bad when they set up on their own and make themselves into false gods.[12]

The delights of earthly bliss need to remain strongly connected to God. When severed from the Giver, and unguided by His light, they become toxic. We cannot do without God in our lives or in our pleasures. We were made "to live, move and have our being" in Him. To live elsewhere leaves our spirits gasping for oxygen.

These words from Lewis are worth embedding in our minds: "God cannot give us a happiness and peace apart from Himself, because it is not there. There is no such thing."[13]

The Pleasures of God

After visiting an old friend, I was winding my way home on a country road on Vancouver Island. As I drove along a route thickly bordered by trees, I drank in the verdant glory of the west coast of Canada. The fir trees pointing heavenward reminded me of the source of all this artistry.

I drove past a narrow lane that snagged my attention. I stopped and walked back for a better look. It was a long driveway enveloped by a canopy of maple trees. Its magical beauty was enhanced by a rich splatter of color from the autumn leaves. It looked like a tunnel to wonderland. It was stunning.

I stood entranced, overcome by a sensation of enormous joy. Something broke in upon me that was deep, beautiful, and exquisite. It made me shiver with delight.

I drove on, intoxicated, singing, shouting, and praising God. Other motorists must have smiled, wondering what drug I had gotten high on.

No one would have guessed it was *beauty*.

Fullness of Joy

In the center of our being there is an irrepressible longing for joy. There are moments when we catch glimpses and hear echoes of it. But it is always too fleeting and too faint. Our hearts hunger for more.

This God-implanted desire will not be truly satisfied until we are face to face with the Giver of all goodness. Our inner thirst beckons us to turn our feet and hearts homeward, to the One in whose presence there is fullness of joy and pleasures forevermore (Psa. 16:11).

"What would it be to taste at the fountain-head that stream of which even these lower reaches prove so intoxicating?" ponders Lewis.[14]

Timothy Keller remarks:

> The most rapturous delights you have ever had—in the beauty of a landscape, or in the pleasure of food, or in the fulfillment of a loving embrace—are like dewdrops compared to the bottomless ocean of joy that it will be to see God face-to-face (1 John 3:1–3). That is what we are in for, nothing less.[15]

Forget about clouds and harps and boredom. Get ready for a hurricane of holy gladness.

PRAYER

*Creator God, You are the Giver of every good gift, the Source
of all earthly bliss. Thank you for inventing enjoyment and
for bestowing on us the capacity to experience it. Teach us to
receive Your good gifts with joy and thanksgiving. Forgive us for
pursuing pleasure in ways that dishonor Your purposes. Numb
our ears to the persistent calls of the idols of lust, consumerism,
vanity, and power. Life's simple pleasures are indeed good, but our
hearts long for something more. "From the best bliss that earth
imparts, we turn unfilled to Thee again," confessed one writer.
Our hearts were made for You and only You can satisfy them
fully. Open our eyes to the wonder of Your beauty, goodness, and
love, and teach us to drink deeply and daily from the Fountain
that never will run dry, which is Christ Jesus our Lord. Amen.*

Human history is the long terrible story
of man trying to find something other than God
which will make him happy.

—C. S. LEWIS

Many go fishing all their lives
without knowing that it is not fish
they are after.

—HENRY DAVID THOREAU

The poverty in the West is a different
kind of poverty—it is not only a poverty
of loneliness but also of spirituality.
There's a hunger for love,
as there is a hunger for God.

—MOTHER TERESA

CHAPTER SIX

The God we cannot live without

"After he had spent everything, there was a severe famine in that whole country, and he began to be in need."

LUKE 15:14

L ife in the fast lane of the far country is fabulous.
At least for a while.
Before long, however, it is not uncommon for speedsters to arrive at a crazy twist in the road, and soon they find themselves on a downward track. It starts getting darker. The joy ride turns into a jolt ride, with potholes, bumps, and ruts.

That's what happens to our prodigal friend.

Just when the spendthrift's bank account runs dry, "a severe famine" shows up.

Where does that come from?

Famines have a habit of making their appearance when you least want them. They happen all over the globe, but they are particularly prone to show up when you have "wasted your substance with riotous living." They don't always arrive immediately, but they usually turn up sooner or later.

From Partying to Pigs

In desperation the young fellow manages to land a job on a farm. *"Then he went and joined himself to a citizen of that country, and he sent him into his fields to feed swine"* (Lk. 15:15 NKJV).

Actually, it isn't a job. The phrase "joined himself" comes from a word which literally means "to glue." It appears the boy forces himself upon a hapless rancher who gets "stuck" with the prodigal. The man can't get rid of the pesky fellow and finally sends him out to herd the hogs. The prodigal becomes a parasite on a pig farm!

One needs to be Jewish to appreciate fully this part of the story.

Pig-lovers are few in number, but Winston Churchill apparently was one of them. He once said jestingly, "I like pigs. Dogs look up to us. Cats look down on us. Pigs treat us as equals."

One would be hard pressed to find such words on the lips of a first-century Jew. Their repugnance towards pigs was *extreme*.

According to the Mosaic Law, pigs were "unclean" animals, unfit for human consumption. Pig avoidance was an essential part of Hebrew piety—touching or even mentioning them by name was out of bounds! Pigs epitomized all that was detestable and unholy, and were thought to be the abode of demons. History records instances of Jews who preferred to be *killed* rather than eat pork.

No son of Israel would be caught dead herding hogs. An ancient Jewish axiom warned, "Cursed is he who feeds swine." It was the *ultimate* disgrace.

However, in Jesus' parable, the son of a respectable Jewish gentlemen has become a tender of pigs! He has joined the society of the swine. A more degrading scenario cannot be imagined.

A Jew's Worst Nightmare

And if that weren't bad enough, the pig keeper is so famished that the slop in the hog trough starts to look appealing. *"And he was longing to be fed with the pods that the pigs ate …"* (Lk. 15:16 ESV). The phrase is strongly worded, indicating an intense desire. Not only is he living with the swine, but he feels tempted to *eat* with them. That's what you call hitting rock bottom!

It is generally agreed that the swine were feeding on carob pods that grow on a small shrub, common in the Mediterranean region. The plant was valued mostly as a source of feed for livestock.

But now the prodigal yearns to feed on the porkers' pods. For a good Hebrew boy, properly raised in a kosher kitchen, this culinary choice is unthinkable!

Jesus' audience winced when He got to this part. For a Jew, this was as *bad* as it gets! The prodigal is cutting himself off from any possibility of being received back in a Torah-abiding Jewish community. He has thoroughly contaminated himself and is now an unclean outsider. He has burned his bridges and there is no going home.

Everything has gone terribly wrong. He has made a grab for riches and ends up broke. He has sought freedom and finishes up enslaved. He has chased after pleasure and lands in a pigsty. He has given himself to feasting and winds up starving. He has looked for life and is now on the verge of death.

The Story of Mankind

The prodigal's plight is a dramatic portrayal of humanity's ill-fated story. A gloomy chapter for planet Earth began the day Adam and Eve abandoned paradise for the "far country." They stepped out from under the blessing of God, smack into the curse of sin. Darkness settled upon our world. Chaos invaded the cosmos.

Lucifer laughed.

Our first parents wept.

Creation groaned, as the tectonic plates of its moral foundations shifted in a precarious way.

As the progenitor of the human race lay down to sleep that night, gazing at the evening sky, never could he imagine what lay ahead for the multiple billions of his descendants.

It would have *terrified* him.

The tsunami of sorrow. Indescribable tragedy and trouble.

Auschwitz, atom bombs, apartheid, 9/11.

Sorrow would come, as Shakespeare put it, not as "single spies, but in battalions."[1]

A Fatal Moment

Sir Isaac Newton, the brilliant scientist, worked long hours studying the nature of the physical universe, often laboring by candlelight. By his side sat his beloved dog.

On one occasion, Newton rose to leave the room. The dog jumped up to follow him, bumped against the desk, and knocked over a candle. The scientist's papers caught fire and in moments his hard labors were reduced to ashes.

When Newton saw what remained of his research, heartbroken he threw himself into a chair and wept bitterly. Turning to his dog, he stroked his head and said, "You will never, never know what you have done."

On that fateful day in Eden, when our first parents turned to follow the Great Deceiver, God could well have said, "You will never, never know what you have done."

An avalanche of evil in one choice.

An ocean of sorrow in one bite.

A hell of suffering in one act.

A descent into darkness in one step.

Scottish philosopher Thomas Carlyle observed: "Sin is, has been, and ever shall be the parent of misery."

The Root of the Problem

What is this insidious, destructive poison? This mysterious root of all our evils? This forbidden fruit? This toxic attraction, so loved by humans, so hated by God? What is this unmentionable, uncomfortable, politically incorrect term called *sin?*

"If you have not learned about sin you cannot understand yourself, your fellow-men, the world you live in or the Christian faith," states J. I. Packer.[2]

The term "sin" in Scripture first shows up in Genesis 4. God warns Cain with these words: *"Sin lies at the door. And its desire is for you, but you should rule over it"* (Gn. 4:7). Sin is not simply a blunder. It is a dark force that seeks to control us. It dogs our steps and grabs us by the throat to do its bidding. It seeks with deadly intent to destroy us. It has infiltrated and set up camp in our heart.

Karl Barth points out:

> Sin is not confined to the evil things we do. It is the evil within
> us, the evil which we are. Shall we call it our pride or our
> laziness, or shall we call it the deceit of our life? Let us call it
> for once the great defiance which turns us again and again
> into the enemies of God and of our fellowmen, even of our
> own selves.[3]

Giving in to sin involves transgression (I Jn. 3:4), and its payoff is death (Rom. 6:23). We should not underestimate our plight. If the truth were known, we have likely broken every one of the Ten Commandments thousands of times. We have scorned the laws of heaven and have heaped judgment upon ourselves (Rom. 2:5). Only *fools* fail to tremble.

However, sin is not merely a legal dilemma, an impersonal infraction, or a failure to abide by God's rulebook. There are deeper issues involved. Sin is first and foremost the violation of a *relationship*. As Scot McKnight points out in his book *Embracing Grace*, sin is essentially a *relational* issue. It is a disrupted connection with God and others. It is the damaging of trust, the betrayal of love, the severing of a relationship. It is flight from God.

In His prodigal parable, Christ portrays sin by using a family metaphor. He tells of a father whose adult son curses him and shamelessly runs off with the family's inheritance.

> *Sin means to lose contact with God, and to be guided by Him no longer.*
>
> —PAUL TOURNIER

That is what we have all done. We have snubbed the Father of Glory, the Giver of every good gift. Not only have we broken His law, we have broken His heart. We have dishonored Him and have brought ruin to ourselves and to His creation.

Sin is a relational matter. It is a disconnection. It is rebellion, it is treachery, it is alienation, and ultimately it is *suicide*.

The Deadliness of Sin

What makes sin particularly devastating is that it afflicts us with a profound blindness. It makes us incapable of knowing the Father. It brings darkness to our hearts and shuts down our perception of His love and goodness.

When we do not see the Father's face, when we do not live in the freedom, security, and confidence of His lavish embrace, life unravels. We succumb to fear, anxiety and frustration. We live in a world of hopelessness, self-centeredness, brokenness, and disappointment. By derailing our capacity to know the Father's joy, sin robs us of any true basis for assurance or hope.

Anselm, the eleventh century Christian scholar, cautioned, "You have not yet considered the exceeding gravity of sin."

Sin's Bitter Fruit

Sin is its own punishment.[4]

Listen to God's words through His prophet Jeremiah: *"Your wickedness will bring its own punishment. Your turning from me will shame you. You will see what an evil, bitter thing it is to abandon the Lord your God and not to fear Him"* (Jer. 2:19 NLT).

"We are not punished for our sins, but by them," points out philosopher Elbert Hubbard.

E. Stanley Jones explains: "You cannot 'get away with it,' for it registers itself in inner deterioration, in the inner hell of not being able to respect yourself, in compelling you to live underground in blind labyrinths."[5]

Sin devours us on the inside. It leaves us orphaned, estranged, and empty. It corrodes our spirit.

Ravi Zacharias comments that sin, "which we so tragically minimize, breaks the grandeur for which we were created. It brings indignity to our essence and pain to our existence."[6]

"When … a man turns away from God," states French thinker Simone Weil, "he simply gives himself up to the law of gravity."[7] He may think himself capable of making good and noble choices, but he has stepped off a cliff, and the downward pull of sin is inescapable. He has turned his back on life and has chosen death.

Sin is grievous to God, not just because it offends His holiness, or challenges His authority, but because it *destroys* the people He created and loves. It sabotages their peace, joy, and freedom. It seduces their hearts. It draws them away from the Fountain of life and goodness. It creates hell.

Not Just a Destination

Hell is more than a place. It involves an inner condition, a *state* of hellishness fabricated by a multitude of sinful choices. "It's not a question of God 'sending' us to Hell," says C. S. Lewis. "In each of us there is something growing up which will of itself be Hell unless it is nipped in the bud."[8]

Lewis explains:

> People often think of Christian morality as a kind of bargain in which God says, 'If you keep a lot of rules, I'll reward you, and if you don't I'll do the other thing.' I do not think that is the best way of looking at it. I would much rather say that every time you make a choice you are turning the central part of you, the part of you that chooses, into something a little different from what it was before. And taking your life as a whole, with all your innumerable choices, all your life long you are slowly turning this central thing into a heavenly creature or into a hellish creature: either into a creature that is in harmony with God, and with other creatures, and with itself, or else into one that is in a state of war and hatred with God, and with its fellow creatures, and with itself. To be the one kind of creature is heaven: that is, it is joy, and peace, and knowledge, and power. To be the other means madness, horror, idiocy, rage, impotence, and eternal loneliness. Each of us at each moment is progressing to the one state or the other.[9]

Hell is an inner bent toward evil whose end is utter destruction. It is an influence, an illness of the heart, a power that grips every human life. And we are powerless to free ourselves from its clutches.

We desperately need redemption. We need Jesus—the One who came to eradicate hellishness, and bring heaven back into the heart. He reconnects us with God, life, and love. His grace is the divine cure for the brokenness of those who dwell in the far country.

Love and Anger

The "wrath of God," frequently mentioned in Scripture, has nothing to do with God having "a short fuse" or "losing His cool." The Almighty does not have an anger problem. Nor does He lack self-control. Biblical writers celebrate the riches of God's goodness, forbearance, and long-suffering (Rom. 2:4), and affirm that He is "slow to anger."

The issue is not an anger problem—it is a *love problem*.

Anger is an integral part of love. When a son or daughter becomes the target of sexual or physical abuse—who could possibly *not* be angered? Anger energizes us to leap to the defense of a loved one in danger. Anger is not incompatible with love; it is a *direct* consequence of it.

"Anger is the fluid that love bleeds when it gets cut," observed Lewis.[10]

"Love implies anger," asserts one writer. "The man who is angered by nothing cares about nothing."[11] The greater our love for someone, the greater our capacity for anger at what is destroying their life.

Early Christian apologist Tertullian pointed out that God "can only be completely good if he is the enemy of the bad, so as to put his love of good into action by hatred of the bad."[12]

"It would hardly be kindness if he didn't punish sin, not to use every means to put the evil thing far from us," affirmed George MacDonald.[13]

Love takes forceful action against evil. It will do all in its power to free a loved one from a harmful situation. Like a she-bear robbed of her cubs, love is fiercely protective, prepared to take strong measures. It's what true love *does*.

Some situations *demand* anger. And one of those situations is … planet Earth. A lot of wretched stuff happens here. If God loved this planet and its people enough, He would get angry. *Very* angry. And thankfully—He does!

It's called "the wrath of God."

The Good News about Wrath

It is no mistake to say that the love of God and the wrath of God amount to the same thing, described from different points of view. Both constitute an emphatic "No!" to that which endangers His creation. God's evil-eradicating, death-destroying wrath is indispensable to the well-being of the universe. It is not a counterpoint to His love but a vital expression of it.

Croatian theologian Miroslav Volf comments:

> Though I used to complain about the indecency of the idea of God's wrath, I came to think that I would have to rebel against a God who wasn't wrathful at the sight of the world's evil. God isn't wrathful in spite of being love. God is wrathful because God is love.[14]

> *To be truly good one has to be outraged by evil and implacably hostile to injustice.*
>
> —REBECCA M. PIPPERT

The wrath of God is His firm opposition to all that is crooked, broken, oppressive, unjust, and evil. He loves people too much to allow them to be destroyed by sin. His deep hatred of sin is a reflection of the greatness of His love. He will go to any length, pay any price, and make any sacrifice to free people from this toxic poison of the soul.

This is the unmistakable message of the Cross. The horrific death of Christ at Calvary reveals the intensity of God's purpose to annihilate sin and rescue sinners. The biblical record says that Jesus is *"the Lamb of God, who takes away the sin of the world"* (Jn. 1:29).

In his article "Prayer: Rebellion against the Status Quo," David Wells contends that we have sadly lost our anger, but fortunately God has not lost His. "The wrath of God is His opposition to what is wrong … [it] seeks the triumph of truth and the banishment of Evil."[15] It is God declaring: "No, not in my universe!"

It would be appalling if the Divine Lord flew into a rage without warning. But it would be equally appalling if He *never* got angry. The evil of this world is damnable, sickening, horrendous. Someone needs to put a stop to it.

Someone *will*.

The wrath of God turns out to be *very* good news. This love-inspired hostility to all things hateful and harmful gives hope to a world afflicted by the curse of sin. "It is not evil that will have the last word, but good; not sorrow, but joy; not hate, but love."[16]

This is a cause indeed for celebration.

Spiritual Blindness

The deepest treachery of sin is that it makes us deaf and blind to the reality of God's existence. It makes us incapable of knowing the Father and living in the freedom of His boundless love.

Sin sabotages our delight in God and hinders us from seeing that He is not only good but stunningly, overwhelmingly, and indescribably good. His goodness spills out beyond itself like an artesian well gone wild. It is free-flowing, self-giving, self-sacrificial love. It is openhandedness, generosity, lavishness. Tragically human hearts have been *blinded* to this fact through sin.

Unbelief is now in our genes; it is our default setting.

Our blindness to His love cripples us inside. It sends us into a moral tailspin. We can't live *unloved*.

Peter Kreeft points out: "When we believe God is something other than a lover, it is inevitable that we sin."[17]

Over seven centuries ago, Thomas Aquinas wrote: "No man can live without joy. That is why one deprived of spiritual joy goes over to carnal [sinful] pleasures."[18]

We were wired for joy, and if we do not live in the enjoyment of the Father's love, lust will fill the vacuum. It is psychologically inevitable.

We resort to gorging on the carob pods of the "distant country" in a vain effort to sublimate our spiritual hunger. "All sins are attempts to fill voids," stated Simone Weil.[19]

Aquinas identified four common substitutes for God: wealth, pleasure, power, and honor. We attempt to fill the void within through some combination of these fantasies.

There's only one problem. The substitutes are preposterously *unsatisfying*. These "carobs" are devoid of succulence. Jimi Hendrix, one of our modern-day poets, before dying of a drug overdose, said it like this: "There ain't no livin' left nowhere."

Our hearts have a need for something else ... for *Someone* else.

Christ's three parables in Luke 15 highlight the idea of "belonging"—the lost sheep belongs in the fold; the lost coin belongs in the housewife's purse; the son belongs in his father's house. Our true and rightful place is in the house of the Father. We will never feel fully at home anywhere else.

Coming to sense our spiritual bankruptcy prods us to commence our homeward journey. *"Blessed are the poor in spirit: for theirs is the kingdom of heaven,"* declared Jesus.

It is to such a decisive moment the prodigal comes ... and this is the turning point of the story.

Reality Check

"But when he came to himself ..." (Lk. 15:17).

"Night brings out stars as sorrow shows us truths," wrote one poet.[20]

The pig-keeper comes to his senses. His mind clears. He has been living in a dream world—deluded and befuddled. And suddenly the fog lifts.

"He came to himself"—Jesus' phrase is fascinating. Is the plight of prodigal people a type of mental imbalance? Is sin an irrational act? A kind of insanity?

The worst kind.

What could be more wrong-headed than to turn away from a Love so true, so wild, so rich, so free? And what could be more crucial than to awaken to our profound need for God and to the reality of His love for us?

Awakening to the Wonder

A French spiritual guide penned these words: "Be persuaded, timid soul, that He has loved you too much to cease loving you."[21]

Could it possibly be true?

Our hearts struggle to believe it.

God understood our need. And He gave us unmistakable proof of His heart to dispel our doubts, to put the matter beyond dispute, and to end the discussion.

His love was written, not in the clouds, not in stone, not in a letter.

It needed to be said in a more forceful, explicit and indisputable way ... and it *was*.

It was written on a bloodstained *cross*.

Here is unassailable proof of the Father's welcoming, forgiving, loving heart. And it sends a vital message to each person on the planet ...

Come home.

PRAYER

*Lord God, in our wrongheadedness we dared not surrender
to You for fear of what that might mean. In our blindness we
wandered and stumbled and found only disappointment, failure,
and brokenness. Our freedom proved to be false, our pleasures
turned to dust, our sins ensnared us. Can it be that in striving
to avoid You, we turned away from life and goodness and joy?
Strong Redeemer, come and deliver us, for we have lost our way.
Shine Your light into our darkness. Without You we cannot live.
Draw us, cleanse us, mend us, and conquer us. The stirring in
our hearts to be at peace with You, the desire to know You—is
it not born from the miracle of Your desire for us? Replace our
emptiness with the joy of your salvation. Gentle our hearts with
Your loving presence, through Jesus Christ our Lord, amen.*

Man is the creature with a mystery
in his heart that is bigger than himself.
—HANS URS VON BALTHASAR

Homesickness is native to all humans because
we're all children of Adam—the first prodigal son.
The Bible is the story of his long way back.
—JONATHAN MARTIN

The Kingdom of God is where we belong.
It is home, and whether we realize it or not,
I think we are all of us homesick for it.
—FREDERICK BUECHNER

CHAPTER SEVEN

The God who is our true home

*"How many of my father's hired servants
have more than enough bread,
but I perish here with hunger!"*

LUKE 15:17 ESV

The young man in the pigpen sits lonely and forlorn, his back to the cold stone wall. He has come to the end of the line. The only companions left are these abominable swine. They are well fed; he is famished. Never before has he felt so hungry, homeless, and hopeless.

As he marinates in his misery, his thoughts suddenly veer homeward. Wistful memories of his father's house flash into his mind.

"There is no greater sorrow than to recall happiness in times of misery," suggested Italian poet Dante Alighieri.[1]

The delightful aroma of home-cooked meals, the sheer abundance, the laughter, the comfort, and the security.

Precious, painful memories.

123

Why did he ever leave? Why did he make all those wrong turns? As he mulls it over, homesickness settles upon him like an early morning mist. All at once, it dawns on him that he has searched in vain for something that can only be found at home. And he *longs* to be back there.

The Strange Nostalgia

There is a homing instinct firmly lodged in each human heart. We are, as one philosopher put it, "haunted by transcendence."[2] It is a strange nostalgia for which this "far country" called earth has no remedy. This world is not large enough, long enough, nor deep enough to satisfy our inner thirst. Something inside of us longs for more. This earth never truly feels like home.

Life's fleeting pleasures are insufficient. They are "the scent of a flower we have not found, the echo of a tune we have not heard, news from a country we have never yet visited," as Lewis put it.[3] We yearn for something this world cannot provide.

We are all haunted by an unexplainable desire, a thirst for something we cannot name but intensely miss. Paul referred to it when he wrote, *"we are hoping for something we do not have yet …"* (Rom. 8:25 ERV). Another biblical writer spoke of those who *"were longing for a better country—a heavenly one"* (Heb. 11:16).

A Longing for Home

One of the occupational hazards of missionaries is that their sense of having a homeland gets blurred.

I have spent the better part of my life serving in a country where I am seen as a *gringo*. I have a good grasp of the language. I enjoy the people and the food, and function well in the culture. Through a long and tedious process I have even obtained Bolivian citizenship.

However, … I'm still a *gringo*.

No matter how well one adapts to local ways, one is *always* seen as a foreigner.

When I go "home" to Canada, it's great to see family and friends. I delight in the natural beauty of the West Coast, I love walking on forest trails, and I enjoy eating smoked salmon.

However, it doesn't take me long to realize that those with whom I converse live in a world far removed from mine. I am not tuned into the day-to-day realities they face, and their interest in hearing about Bolivia soon wears off. Very quickly we run out of things to talk about.

I am in my "own" country, but once again I feel like a stranger. I am left with the sensation I don't completely belong to either Bolivia or Canada. I end up wondering *where* my homeland really is.

Missionaries are not the only ones.

Homesickness is native to *everybody*.

The word frequently used is "alienation." The popular U2 song expressed it like this: *"I still haven't found what I'm looking for."*

The Elusive Desire

Sixteen centuries ago, Augustine confessed: "There reigns in the broken human heart a feeling of discord, a lack of congruence between what is and what ought to be."

One scholar described our plight with these words:

> There is within us a fundamental dis-ease, an unquenchable fire that renders us incapable, in this life, of ever coming to full peace. This desire lies at the center of our lives, in the marrow of our bones, and in the deep recesses of the soul ... At the heart of all great literature, poetry, art, philosophy, psychology, and religion lies the naming and analyzing of this desire.[4]

The parable Jesus told revolves around this pervasive desire.

And it is the saga of our planet. The lost-ness of the prodigal son reflects the profound lost-ness of the human family. We are all descendants of Adam—the first prodigal son. We are lost people living in a lost world. John Milton, the author of *Paradise Lost,* coined a word that expresses our plight well—"unparadiz'd."[5]

C. S. Lewis depicts our dilemma in this way:

> Our lifelong nostalgia, our longing to be reunited with something in the universe from which we now feel cut off, to be on the inside of some door which we have always seen from the outside, is no mere neurotic fancy, but the truest index of our real situation.[6]

There is an ache in our hearts that won't go away, an inconsolable longing we can never quite satisfy. One author describes this haunting desire for something more as "the constant gnawing sense of having had, and lost, some infinite thing."[7]

Hearts That Are Restless

Where does this cosmic homesickness come from? "We cannot be homesick if we have no home," points out one writer.[8]

Homesickness stems from memories treasured in the mind. It is sorrow over something once known, enjoyed, or possessed.

Is the human race haunted by such a memory?

The biblical record indicates everything began, not with original sin but with original *blessing.* Things got underway in a paradise, the primeval cradle of humanity. There human beings were hand-made by God and infused with divine life in a moment of ecstatic intimacy. The first man burst into being in an ambience the Bible describes as "fullness of joy."

With the light of eternal glory shining upon him, Adam opened his eyes and gazed into the Face of Infinite Love. Was it there the human heart was captivated forever by the wonder-full mystery of love? Was a desire awakened at that moment that could never be erased—or satisfied by anything else?

Very likely.

"We live haunted by the remains of a paradise half-seen in dreams, half-heard in birdsong, half-felt in the aftermath of love's making," pondered one poet.[9]

God's presence was our original habitat, and no other place can *truly* feel like home. We carry within us "a dream of blessedness" that once was, and may someday be again.

> *We all long for Eden and we are constantly glimpsing it, our whole nature is still soaked with the sense of exile.*
>
> —J. R. R. TOLKIEN

Hardwired for Love

Our deep emotional thirst for security, affection, affirmation, and meaning was meant to be quenched out of the fullness of God's goodness and love. "The soul's deepest thirst is for God Himself, who has made us so that we can never be satisfied without Him," wrote biblical scholar F. F. Bruce.[10] "We were made," states Lewis, "not primarily that we may love God (though we were made for that too), but that God may love us."[11] Our spirits were designed to live on divine grace, as a car is made to run on gasoline.

We were never meant to live anywhere but paradise. The need to receive *life* from God is written in our DNA. Our humanity was configured to receive and respond to His love. Our heart has God's fingerprints all over it! We were made to dwell within the sacred circle of infinite joy of the Triune God. That is our native habitat!

Augustine expressed it this way: "God is the country of the soul."

When our soul attempts to live in another "country"—outside of God's love—we find within us an uneasy nostalgia that won't go away. The literal meaning of "nostalgia" in Greek is "a painful yearning to return home."[12] It is an inner ache, a longing for our *true* home.

"If you are really a product of a material universe," asks Lewis, "how is it that you don't feel at home there?"[13]

Humans made by God and *for* God should not be surprised that life that doesn't work *without* Him. The puzzle simply doesn't come together.

The Tug of Heaven

A man stood and watched as a young boy flew his kite in an open field. Because of poor visibility, the high-flying kite was clear out of sight. "How do you know it's still there?" the onlooker inquired. The young fellow's answer was decisive: "I can feel the tug."

Who has not felt the inner "tug" of heaven? Who has not sensed in their heart a longing to drink deeply of goodness, joy, beauty, and love? Who has not tasted pleasure and thought, "There must be *more* of this somewhere else!"

"Our deepest instinct is heaven," writes Canadian author Mark Buchanan. "Heaven is the ache in our bones, the splinter in our heart."[14] It was described by another writer as "God's footprint in the sands of the soul."[15] Scripture refers to it like this: *"He has also set eternity in the human heart"* (Eccl. 3:11).

This restlessness is an internal alarm clock that disturbs us and prompts us to arise and return to the Father. It is a strange inner pull, a homing instinct mysteriously written into the fiber of our being, a call that arises from the depths of our spirit bidding us to come home.

Theologian Karl Barth called it our "incurable God-sickness."

Tilted Heavenward

Author Frederick Buechner relates a story that, in his words, "is almost too awful to tell." A boy of twelve or thirteen, depressed and in a burst of uncontrolled anger, got hold of a gun and fired it at his father, who died soon afterward. When asked why he had done it, the boy replied it was because he hated his father, who demanded too much, and was harsh with him. Some time later, after he had been placed in a detention center, a guard, walking down the corridor late one night, heard sounds from the young fellow's room. He stopped to listen and heard the boy sobbing in the dark, "I want my father; I want my father."[16]

Is this not a parable of our lives?

The God we tried to get away from—and even crucified—whose laws we have trampled on, whose voice we have silenced, proves extremely difficult to avoid. Perhaps impossible. The need for God is engraved upon our hearts. We can systematically eliminate Him from every corner of our lives—only to discover we can't live without Him.

We are *hopelessly* heaven-bent.

Why does the prodigal son not dismiss all thought of his father from his mind, and look for a way out of his predicament in the far country? Surely there is work to be found somewhere. Somebody is bound to give him a hand. What causes him to turn his heart and feet homeward?

Is it not that longing, found in each of our hearts, that cries, "I want my father!"?

Memories of Home

The foremost memory of home that comes to the prodigal's mind is the abundance found there. *"How many hired servants of my father's have abundance of bread"* (Lk. 15:17 DARBY). At his father's table there is food in extravagant supply. It makes his mouth water.

The Bible frequently uses the word "abundance" with reference to God. We read repeatedly of the abundance of ...

- His goodness
- His faithfulness
- His mercy
- His steadfast love
- His compassion
- His forgiveness
- His grace.

How wonderful that God has such items in never-ending supply! The psalmist David takes poetic flight as he describes God's house: *"They are abundantly satisfied with the fullness of Your house, and You give them drink from the river of Your pleasures"* (Psa. 36:8 NKJV). It sounds like a marvelous place to live!

> *His infinite liberality will always exceed all our wishes and our thoughts.*
>
> —JOHN CALVIN

The apostle Paul put it this way, *"Eye has not seen, nor ear heard, nor have entered into the heart of man the things which God has prepared for those who love Him"* (I Cor. 2:9).

The gospel calls all of us to an extravagant banquet in the Father's house. By sitting down to meals with lawbreakers and "sinners," Jesus demonstrated the "wideness" of the invitation. He came to tell us of a God who takes great delight in lavishing His favor upon those who come back to His house. And His resources for doing so are limitless. His storehouses of goodness and grace are inexhaustible.

One theologian throws further light on this:

> In truth we might catch up the whole of the Christian faith in this little word *more*. It is the large room we are invited to inhabit; it is the greater confidence and hope that we dare to profess; it is the greater love that we are astonished to receive, more, always more than we deserve. God is the Name of this "more." Always God exceeds.[17]

The apostle Paul repeated five times in his letter to the Romans that the devastating effects of our sin have been met by the "much more" of the gospel. Our wrongdoings are great and many; the Bible affirms God's grace is much greater still. *"But where sin abounded, grace abounded much more"* (Rom. 5:20 NKJV). Kenneth Wuest, a scholar of New Testament Greek, translates this verse as follows: *"Grace existed in superabundance, and then more grace [was] added to this superabundance."*

You get the distinct impression there's plenty of it!

Someone summed it up with this pithy phrase: "God has got more mercy than you've got mess."

Reluctance to Return

Sadly, many people resist returning to the Father's house. They think their past is unforgivable.

It's not.

They think there's no hope for someone like them.

There is.

They can't accept that God could really love them.

He does.

They struggle to believe God is as good as Christ said He was. He is.

Jesus came to correct all our wrong ideas about God. He did more than explain what God is like—he *showed* us what God is like. His nonstop deeds of kindness gave people a small taste of the extravagant banquet of the Father's house—of His unending provisions of mercy and goodness. Jesus' self-sacrificing death on the cross was the final breathtaking evidence of God's heart of love.

But there's a fast-talker named Satan who tries to convince us it's not true. However, the last time we believed him—it landed us in a pigsty.

Not *exactly* paradise.

Jesus invites us to taste and see that God is good, and to discover that His goodness surpasses all we could ever imagine! He came to dispel all doubts about God's love and to summon us to the feast at the Father's house. He came to bring us home.

British journalist Malcolm Muggeridge understood this:

> In the end, coming to faith remains for all a sense of homecoming, of picking up the threads of a lost life, of responding to a bell that had long been ringing, of taking a place at a table that had long been vacant.[18]

Returning to God is a return to our true home—and our heart intuitively knows it.

HOMEWARD BOUND

Try as he might, the prodigal cannot get his father out of his system. The "far country" is not what it was cracked up to be, and winding up in a pigsty is the *ultimate* nightmare. And in this uncongenial setting, memories of home tug at this heart.

Having to face his father is not an attractive idea. "I'm sorry" are the hardest words to say in any language. Deep-rooted shame blocks the road home, and whether he will be received back is uncertain. His final resort is fraught with difficulty.

But at this juncture it appears to be the only option on the table. He instinctively knows that in the far country he will never be at peace. He will never truly feel at home.

The strange inner pull towards his childhood abode grows stronger until it finally overpowers his reluctance.

He decides to go back.

He climbs out of the pigpen and dusts himself off. With tattered rags on his back and a load of shame on his shoulders, he slowly turns his feet homeward.

If he had *any* idea of what awaited him, he would run home— with all haste.

PRAYER

Good Lord, no matter how deeply we drink of life's pleasures, no matter what we put our hopes in, it always comes short. There's a God-sized hunger in our hearts, a divine thirst that this world cannot fill. There is something beyond that beckons us. We heard it in our favorite music, sensed it when we held our first child, saw it in the shimmer of a sunset on the beach. It's a longing for goodness and wholeness and beauty and joy. It's a longing for You. It's a yearning that only a God whose name is Love could satisfy. Help us to cast aside the false fantasies that so easily dazzle us that we may find our true joy in You, the fountain of life. May the homesickness of our hearts stir us to seek you and live in You, as we wait for that day when we drink freely and fully of the ocean of Your love. Amen.

Compassion means seeing your friend
and your enemy in equal need,
and helping both equally … Herein lies
the holy compassion of God
that causes the devil much distress.

—MECHTHILD OF MAGDEBURG

The great basis of Christian assurance is not how much
our hearts are set on God, but how unshakably his heart is set on us.

—TIMOTHY KELLER

The church is full of prodigals discovering,
to their astonishment, that their father
still loves them.

—N. T. WRIGHT

CHAPTER EIGHT

The God with tear-filled eyes

"So he got up and went to his father."

LUKE 15:20

L ife has become unbearable for the prodigal son. His inheritance is spent, his friends have left, his self-respect is gone, and his options have run out.

There remains one hope of survival—*go home.*

So now the prodigal is on the road—scruffy, disheveled, and bedraggled. He smells like a pig. He is robed in rags.[1] Nobody would guess he is the son of a prosperous landowner. *Everything* has gone wrong, and now he is heading back to the place he wishes he had never left.

Doubts and fears flood his heart. What will his father say? Will he receive him back? Will he disown him? Will the community ostracize him? A torrent of uneasy thoughts bombard his mind as he trudges homeward.

It is here that we come to one of the most moving scenes in the Scriptures. Biblical commentator Alexander McLaren asserts: "The climax of the parable, for which all the rest is but as scaffolding, is the father's welcome ...."[2]

There are many exquisite passages in the Bible. Few compare with this one.

Look closely at the stunning picture Christ paints for us.

The Father Was Looking

"But while he was still a long way off, his father saw him ..." (Lk. 15:20).

How is it the father catches sight of him first? Does he know his son is coming home?

No, he doesn't.

Evidently the father's eyes are scanning the horizon when the prodigal appears in the distance. Had he owned binoculars, he would use them every day. His eyes are *always* on the horizon.

The fact that he spots his son "a long way off" speaks volumes about what is going on in the father's heart. The man cannot get the boy off his mind. For hours he is standing on the porch, staring off into the distance—with a huge lump in his throat. Anguish has taken up permanent quarters in his heart since the day his son left. He has wept many tears and died many deaths. The snatches of news that come to him are not good. His heart aches for a wayward son and longs for his return.

One biblical expositor surmises:

> What servant on the farm does not well understand the sudden lack of interest in all the work, the absent look as schemes of improvement are detailed to him, the many signs that reveal that his heart is with his lost son, and that all else is matter of indifference to him?[3]

It is likely the father has heard his elder son complain: "Dad, why do you waste so much time thinking about that good-for-nothing son of yours? Shouldn't we just get on with life?" But how can you get on with life when your son is *lost?*

When Your Heart Walks Away

Someone suggested that having a child is to have your heart leave your chest and walk around outside your body for the rest of your life. When your child rejoices, you rejoice. When the child suffers, you suffer. You can't help it. It's not just another person out there— it's your *heart!*

When a son or daughter becomes ensnared in drugs, alcohol, or crime, who can gauge the pain in the heart of a father or mother? Is it the child or the parent who suffers most? When a young life spins out of control, parents encounter anguish and despair as never before.

Where do such overpowering emotions come from?

A naturalistic worldview struggles to provide an answer for this. If we are a purely accidental conglomeration of chemicals, how do you explain love and grief, passion and despair, beauty and sorrow? They don't originate in test tubes. We could never expect animated pieces of organic matter or the random firings of neurons in our brain to create such phenomena.

There is an answer that makes much more sense.

They come from *Someone* who made us. They are but a dim reflection of His loving heart.

Take another look at the broken-hearted father in our story, scanning the horizon with tear-filled eyes. He is lost in his pain. He is overcome by sorrow. Daily he waits and yearns and weeps for an absent son.

This is not just a Jewish farmer. This is *God.* This is a picture, painted by Jesus Himself, of the heavenly Father, who looks with yearning towards His "long-lost children." Christ is saying—*this* is what my Father is like!

The Emotional Life of God

Does the Lord of the star-fields get emotionally involved with humans? Does the God of unimaginable power get overcome by sorrow? Does He experience inner turmoil? Is this not just anthropomorphic imagery?

There is a common belief the Sovereign Lord lives in lofty heavenly bliss, unperturbed by "the restless world that wars below." This conception sees God emotionally removed from the realm of human pain and sorrow.

A missionary in Asia was asked by a native if God experienced sorrow. The man replied, "No, God is sovereign. He is all-powerful and holy. He is free from sorrow and sadness that we mortals experience."

The native replied, "If that is the case, then we are not interested in Him."

The missionary was *mistaken*.

The God of the Bible is no stranger to emotions. Jewish scholar Abraham Heschel points out in his book *The Prophets* that "the most exalted idea applied to God is not infinite wisdom, infinite power, but infinite concern."[4] In Jesus' parable, God is depicted as a father in the grip of powerful emotions, agonizing over a lost son. This is not incidental detail. Christ is giving us profound insight into the emotional life of His Father. He is allowing us to look into His heart.

And it makes us catch our breath.

A God of "*Splagchnizomai*"

Look closely at the next phrase in the story, *"his father saw him and was filled with compassion for him"* (Lk. 15:20), or as the New English Translation puts it, *"his father saw him, and his heart went out to him."*

When he sights the wayward son in the distance, there is a volcanic eruption of "compassion" in the father's heart. The word *splagchnizomai* (don't even try to pronounce this!) that Jesus uses denotes a powerful emotional response. Perhaps the closest expression in English is: "gut-wrenching." The term is most frequently used of Christ's compassionate response to human need.

Theologian Karl Barth goes into detail:

> The expression *[splagchnizomai]* is a strong one which defies adequate translation. He was not only affected to the heart by the misery which surrounds Him—sympathy in our modern sense is far too feeble a word—but it went right into His heart, into Himself, so that it was now His misery. It was more His than that of those who suffered it.[5]

A God of *splagchnizomai* compassion cannot view the suffering of this world without suffering Himself. When those whom He created and loves are in pain, so is He. Theologian Jürgen Moltmann points out, "If God were incapable of suffering in every respect, then he would also be incapable of love."[6] Holy love is acquainted with grief.

"Jesus gives God a face," writes Philip Yancey, "and that face is streaked with tears."[7]

Love Suffers

References to God's intense emotions are scattered throughout Scripture. A remarkable example is found in the book of Hosea, when God cries out over His wayward people: *"Oh, how can I give you up, Israel? How can I let you go? ... My heart is torn within me, and my compassion overflows"* (Hos. 11:8 NLT).[8]

What a striking portrayal of God! He speaks as an offended lover, agonizing over the infidelity of His people, suffering the pain of a broken relationship. He feels shunned, hurt, and despairing. His emotions seem almost too strong, too passionate.

> *You may call God love, you may call God goodness, but the best name for God is compassion.*
>
> —MEISTER ECKHART

This God of unlimited power finds Himself unable to coerce love. Philip Yancey writes, "And when His own love is spurned, even the Lord of the universe feels in some way helpless, like a parent who has lost what He values most."[9]

When we open ourselves to love, we open ourselves to suffering. "For it is not in the nature of love to deflect pain," observed Canadian author Mike Mason, "but rather to absorb it, and to absorb greater and greater amounts of it."[10] To love is to make ourselves vulnerable, which comes from the Latin word "to wound." It places our well-being in the hands of others, empowering them to impart joy or to inflict pain. Genuine love runs the risk of getting wounded—and even God's love is not exempt!

There is an African tribe with a unique form of greeting. "Are you well?" says one. "If you are well, I am well," replies the other. In other words, "If you are not well, I cannot be well. If you suffer, I will suffer too."

What a great response! Although it is doubtful that all who say the words truly mean them.

There is One who *does*—God Himself. When the human race "fell," the Lord of heaven could *not* be well. He was hopelessly "unwell." The Lord of the universe could not simply look on as His creatures careened towards destruction. He must act on their behalf.

Compassion literally means to feel with, to suffer with. Frederick Buechner writes, "Compassion is the knowledge that there can never really be any peace and joy for me until there is peace and joy for you."[11]

Goodness That Must Act

In the fourth century, Athanasius, in his famous treatise on the incarnation, reasoned: When "the creatures whom He had created … were in fact perishing … on the road to ruin, what then was God, being Good, to do? Was He to let corruption and death have their way with them?" Athanasius concludes this was *unthinkable.* "It was impossible … that God should leave man to be carried off by corruption, because it would be unfitting and unworthy of Himself."[12]

Athanasius' fundamental argument was: God is good—overwhelmingly good. He is therefore committed to the well-being of His creation, and it is obvious He will intervene in some way. He will not let the ship go down. The Creator will take on the role of Redeemer. *Count* on it.

"It would rather be a wonder if, being what he is, he did not," writes one biblical scholar, for "it is the nature of love, universally, to insert itself into the miseries, and take upon its feeling the burdens of others."[13]

If the true nature of the Lord of creation is rooted in love, then it should not amaze us that He dispatched His Son on a rescue mission when this world was sliding toward destruction. It also comes as no surprise Jesus should go about *"doing good and healing all who were oppressed by the devil"* (Acts 10:38 ESV). It becomes almost *predictable* He should finally lay down His life for us *"that He might bring us back to God"* (I Pet. 3:18). This is what a God of unfathomable goodness and *splagchnizomai* is most likely to do!

More Than a Cliché

One might ask, why would God love people like this? Does He do it ...

- Out of moral constraint?
- As a philanthropic duty?
- Out of religious obligation?
- Because it's His job description?
- Out of theological necessity?

No. None of the above.

God loves to love. He lives to love. There is nothing begrudging or reluctant about it. It is His nature to love. It is His joy to love. "God loves us," insists Lewis, "not because we are lovable but because He is love, not because He needs to receive but because He delights to give."[14]

"God is love" is more than a trite phrase. It is the most daring, paradigm-shifting, heart-grabbing affirmation the Bible makes about God. And, to make sure we grasp it, it is stated twice (I Jn. 4:7,16). Ditch the idea of this being a mere cliché. It's an absolute *game changer*.

The Internal Life of God

Love is not simply something God does; it is who God *is*. Love is not just an attribute of God, it is the *essence* of God.[15] God is love because He is a Trinity, and love is what goes on eternally between Father, Son, and Holy Spirit. Jesus referred to this when He said to His Father, *"You loved Me before the foundation of the world"* (Jn. 17:24).

Trinity is not a theological conundrum. It tells us that within God there is connection, bonding, rapport; there is a relational whirlwind of delight and pleasure. The Triune community is all about beauty and joy and goodness and love.

And there is nothing as wonderful in the entire universe!

C. S. Lewis gives us this insight:

> [Christians] believe that the living, dynamic activity of love has been going on in God forever and has created everything else. And that, by the way, is perhaps the most important difference between Christianity and all other religions: that in Christianity God is not an impersonal thing nor a static thing—not even just one person—but a dynamic pulsating activity, a life, a kind of drama, almost, if you will not think me irreverent, a kind of dance.[16]

What is most astounding is that we were created to be *included* within the divine circle of glory![17] From eternity, Infinite Love, with all its fierce passion, has been turned *toward* us. The Cross was where its fiery flood erupted in volcanic intensity and flows unstoppable. The Spirit of Love now draws sinners home, and the Father's heart beats faster when one of them is spotted in the distance.

We had never *dared* to consider such a thing. It is either the greatest absurdity or the most stunning piece of news we ever came across.

The Strange Deity

Peter Kreeft commented:

> Only love could motivate such madness. Christ's outstretched arms on the Cross are God's answer to our childlike question: 'How much do you love me?' 'This much!' How big is that stretch? It is the distance between Heaven and earth that was bridged by the Incarnation, and it was the distance between Heaven and Hell that was bridged by our salvation.[18]

> *God knows no seasons of change. God has a single relentless stance toward us: God loves us.*
>
> —BRENNAN MANNING

An old Chinese man, after hearing for the first time the story of the loving, sacrificing God, exclaimed to his neighbor, "Didn't I tell you there ought to be a God like that?"

New Testament scholar Larry Hurtado indicates that his research on the religious beliefs of the Roman world did not uncover a single reference to suggest the gods "loved" people. The deities were known for their strength, beauty, wisdom, or prowess in war, etc., but *not* for loving those who looked to them for help. Any assistance from the gods was provided, not out of the goodness of their hearts but "for a price." It was usually a *hefty* one.

The gospel message of a God who passionately loves people—to the point of sacrificing His Son for them—had never been heard of before. Roman gods were not characterized by such behavior! This was a very strange deity indeed!

And a most *wonderful* one!

Longing to Be Loved

This outlandish story resonates with the deepest desire and aspiration of human beings. Tolkien says of the gospel, "There is no tale men more wish to be true." We yearn for it to be so because life's greatest joy is to be loved deeply and unconditionally. There is no longing more deeply entrenched in the human heart. One person put it this way: "What you are really chasing, weary wanderer, is a love that's not caked in conditionality."[19] Love is what gives meaning and richness to our existence. Someone stated bluntly, "When you are out of love, you are out of life." The gospel addresses our need to recover "life" at the deepest level.

Christ came to tell us of a Father whose love exceeds anything we have ever heard. Like the prodigal, we too were seen by Him when we were "a long way off." The Bible affirms that *"even before the world was made, God chose us for Himself because of His love"* (Eph. 1:4 NLV). He has been looking our way with eyes of love since *before* time began.

Love That Passes Understanding

When we consider how hard we tried to get away from God, how horribly we messed up in the "far country," the Father's love makes no sense at all. But this is the stunning miracle of the gospel.

Annie Dillard speaks for many of us:

> I am sorry I ran from you. I am still running, running from that knowledge, that eye, that love from which there is no refuge. For you meant only love, and love, and I felt only fear, and pain. So once in Israel love came to us incarnate, stood in the doorway between two worlds, and we were all afraid.[20]

We struggle to comprehend a love of this caliber. We are baffled by a love that will not quit, that pursues us, that seeks to redeem, to restore, and to receive us back as beloved sons and daughters. "God's love is not wearied by our sins and is relentless in its determination that we be cured at whatever cost to us or Him," wrote Lewis.[21]

This is the love God's Son came to tell us about.

Brennan Manning put it well: "In effect Jesus said: Hope your wildest hopes, dream your maddest dreams, imagine your most fantastic fantasies. Where your hopes and your dreams and your imaginations leave off, the love of My heavenly Father only begins."[22]

He can't take His eyes off of you.

Soak in the *immensity* of that.

PRAYER

Loving Father, You have every reason not to love us. You are holy and we are not. However, our fickleness, our phoniness, and our failures did not and cannot extinguish Your love. The holy fire of Your heart of love startles and scares us. It is too strong, too relentless, too intense. You love us in our sin and brokenness, in our fear and loneliness. You love us, not because we are lovely, but in order to make us lovely. You love us, not with drowsy benevolence, but with ardent, healing, uplifting, life-giving, unsettling passion. We long to be loved, but we are afraid of a Love that purposes to make us lovers, that seeks to overthrow our indifference, our selfishness, our hatred. With trepidation we say, burn and heal us, O Flame of God. Make us the fragrance of Your love. Whisper Your love to our hearts and let us whisper Your love to others. Amen.

God will receive a prodigal son with open arms,
even if he comes home just because he's hungry.
—José María Cabodevilla

We don't come to God, "hat in hand";
He comes to us, grace in hand.
God is more eager to forgive us than
we are to be forgiven.
—James Bryan Smith

God is like a highway patrolman
pursuing you down the interstate
with lights flashing and siren blaring
to get you to stop–not to give you a ticket,
but to give you a message so good
it couldn't wait till you get home.
—Author unknown

CHAPTER NINE

The God who comes running

"... his father saw him and was filled with compassion for him; he ran to his son ..."

LUKE 15:20

I f more beautiful words than these have ever been written in a story line," declares one author, "I don't know what they are." 1 Another scholar suggests there is no greater statement about God in the whole Bible.

When Jesus describes how His Father feels about lost people, He paints a picture that takes our breath away. Has a deity ever been depicted in this manner? The pagan gods dispatched thunderbolts to let people know who was in charge. Jesus portrays the Almighty all out of breath, rushing wildly to embrace a rascal who had been living in a pigsty.

Who has *ever* thought of God in these terms?

Look closely at this scene.

The prodigal is on the road home. His hair is matted, full of tangles and snarls. He looks nothing like the hotshot who had strutted along this road in the opposite direction some time before. His money and his dignity are gone. He smells like a pig-keeper. He is returning bare-footed, empty-handed, and full of shame from his ill-fated escapade in the far country.

His main reason for going home is simple: he is starving to death. He can only think of one place where he stands a chance of getting a hot meal, and that's where he is going.[2]

When night falls he finds a place to sleep by the side of the road. Gazing up at the stars, a thousand questions ricochet through his mind. Will his father care to see him again? Will he treat him as his misconduct deserves? Will he shun him completely?

This trek home is the hardest thing he has ever done.

The stone-paved roads of the Roman world made travel easy, but this journey is *not*. He is going home to face the music for his reckless actions. He cringes as possible scenarios flash through his mind. Shame and apprehension make each step torturous.

However, the dread that holds him back is not equal to the hunger that pushes him forward. Home is his only remaining meal ticket, and so day after day he trudges on.

A Candidate for *"Kezazah"*

The prodigal was keenly aware that one of the dreaded possibilities was *kezazah,* the ancient Jewish "cutting off" ceremony. This was a procedure used to banish someone guilty of serious misdeeds. The public ritual involved breaking a large clay pot before the delinquent in the presence of the villagers, symbolizing that the relationship between the offender and the community has been "shattered." He would now officially be an outsider.

The pig-keeper feels particularly qualified for *kezazah.*

The day finally comes when he crests the last rise, and stands still as he views, in the distance, the village he has known from childhood. Wiping his brow, he takes a deep breath and starts down the final stretch, rehearsing his repentance speech.

As we picture this scene in our minds, we might imagine a typical farm as we know it: a farmhouse at the end of a long driveway with barns and fields nearby. The home where the prodigal has grown up would be quite different. Jewish families in the first century did not live isolated from each other on separate farms. They practiced communal living for social and security reasons.

A normal Hebrew household was an extended family often comprised of forty to one hundred people. Each family made up a small village. The farm fields lay beyond the perimeter of the cluster of homes, and workers would head out to their labors in the morning, and return in the evening. In such a community the father in our story would have made his home.

The fellow with pig dung on his feet is now approaching the village.

When Patriarchs Sprint

From what strategic vantage point does the father spot his son while he is "still a long way off?" We don't know.

But evidently he has been looking. He has *always* been looking.

And when suddenly he catches sight of a forlorn but all too familiar figure in the distance, his heart skips a beat.

In one heart-stopping moment everything else in the world fades from his mind—his cup of coffee, arthritis, stiff back, farm business, protocol, public opinion—*all* is forgotten.

In an instant he is off and running, propelled by the pent-up emotions of a long-awaited moment.

The servants look up surprised. They have never seen the landlord move so fast. They watch as he takes the shortest route through the garden, tramples on flowerbeds, breaks through the hedge, and makes off down the road.

After viewing his hasty departure, the workers give each other a knowing look. This could only mean *one* thing. The long-awaited occasion has arrived. The father's prolonged vigil has come to an end.

And he is now racing through the village with coattails flying.

That is when the prodigal catches sight of him.

An elderly man is coming his way with *great haste.*

The young man stops and shields his eyes for a better look. The runner with old legs and flowing robes—is his *father!*

Reentry Procedure

When a Jewish boy disgraced his family, community protocol forbade him to simply stroll breezily into the village and arrive home. A serious offense could not be dismissed lightly.[3]

To meet directly with his father was out of the question. Several days would have to go by while the boy sat in shame outside the village, exposed to public ridicule, until his father agreed to see him. At that point, the transgressor would be expected to bow and kiss his father's feet and submit to the conditions imposed upon him. This could involve public flogging, restitution, or even expulsion from the community—the dreaded *kezazah.*

But that is *not* the way this story goes.

The dishonored patriarch, who by all rights should be angry and unavailable, is now *breaking* all the rules.

He is making a beeline for his son—going flat out in a *very* undignified manner.

With face flushed and full of anticipation, the elderly father charges unceremoniously down Main Avenue, trampling protocol underfoot, unable to endure the slowness of normal walking.

It is all very un-patriarch-like.

The Heart-Stopping Welcome

The prodigal stands riveted. He is nervous, baffled.

Before he can gather his thoughts or even brace himself, he is hit by a hurricane of affection, a barrage of kisses. Tears of joy flow as the old man, with heart bursting, stands in the street embracing his son.

Pig smell and all.

Push the pause button and put a frame around this breathtaking picture. Don't miss what Jesus is saying to us about God.

This is how the Almighty feels about *each* one of us.

Our sins could not extinguish His love; our rebellion could not turn Him away. He insists on running to meet rebels, fools, and failures like us. *"Who is a God like you … ?"* rightly asks a prophet of old (Mic. 7:18). We cannot but stop and look with wonder at this unruly torrent of grace.

This picture is pure, undiluted awesomeness.

> *No created being can ever know how much God sweetly and tenderly loves them.*
>
> —Julian of Norwich

Drink it in. Feed on it. Feast on it.

Let the beauty and wonder and goodness of it filter down into your heart and soul like water on cracked, parched ground.

Let it take your breath away. Let it captivate you. Let it rearrange your theology.

This is our God and there is no one like Him.

Correcting Our God-View

The question arises: Is *this* the God of blazing holy otherness before whom angels and mountains tremble?

Yes, it is.

Is *this* the consuming fire, the High Lord of limitless power and glory?

That's right.

So He is BOTH terrible *and* tender?

Correct.

Right alongside His flaming majestic holiness we need to place this picture of a racing euphoric father—without diminishing either one.

Chesterton wrote in his book *Orthodoxy* of the challenge of "combining furious opposites." He pointed out that Christianity does this "by keeping them both, and keeping them both furious."[4]

Is Jesus God or man? Both. Is the kingdom of heaven present or future? Both. Does God inspire fear or calm fear? Both. Heresies hang on only one half of the equation. We need to affirm the "furious opposites" and leave the paradox intact. In God's kingdom, the lion and the lamb lie down together.

Without any doubt, the mystery of holiness is *great.*

We serve a God who is imposing and inviting, frightful and forgiving, majestic and meek. We celebrate His otherness and His nearness. He is both our Lord and our Friend. We marvel that He is high and holy, yet winsome and approachable. In His presence we tremble with "joy unspeakable" as perfect love casts out fear.

Ravi Zacharias comments on the fascinating combination in Scripture of the terms "Holy" with "Father":

> When God is our Holy Father, sovereignty, holiness,
> omniscience, and immutability do not terrify us; they leave
> us full of awe and gratitude. Sovereignty is only tyrannical if
> it is unbounded by goodness; holiness is only terrifying if it

is untempered by grace; omniscience is only taunting if it is unaccompanied by mercy; and immutability is only torturous if there is no guarantee of goodwill.[5]

Lewis again: "The most striking thing about our Lord is the union of great ferocity with extreme tenderness ... This is the appearance in Human form of the God who made the tiger and the lamb, the avalanche and the rose."[6]

Another writer comments:

> Our world is ... longing to see people whose God is big and holy and frightening and gentle and tender ... as ours; a God whose love frightens us into His strong and powerful arms where He longs to whisper those terrifying words, "I love you."[7]

This God of awesome delightfulness was made visible and knowable in Jesus Christ. The God of Mount Sinai gave us a fuller revelation of Himself at Calvary. Someone greater than Moses, the temple, and the prophets is here (Jn. 1:17; Mt. 12:6; 17:4,5). The final Word about God is Jesus—the center and soul of our understanding of God. Abba's Son brings into view the breathtaking beauty of the Triune God.

The God of the Pharisees

Sadly, many have in their head a lesser God of their own making. An uptight, disgruntled, overbearing, list-checking deity on the lookout for the latest infraction. The God of extreme scrupulosity.

Sinclair Lewis, in his bestseller *Main Street,* speaks for many when he describes God, who, since dictating the Bible, spends His time snooping around trying to catch people disobeying it.

This was the Pharisees' view of God. And it was this twisted way of thinking that provoked the Rabbi from Galilee to launch this torpedo of a parable—aimed to blow up the lies many have believed about the Father of our Lord Jesus Christ.

If God is as Christ described Him—a father who gathers up his robe and weeps for joy as He runs breakneck with arms outstretched to embrace a son who has messed up as badly as any boy could—then that is the *best news* ever broken on planet Earth, bar none.

Let the truth of the previous paragraph soak into your soul. Please read it *again*.

If your view of God does not include the kind of father Jesus described, it needs to be reexamined. It's due for an overhaul.

The Father on Film

If we were to make a movie of this story, the scene of the breathless father dashing through the village would be set in slow motion. We would see him straining to cover the ground as fast as his sandaled feet can carry him. His heart is bursting. His legs are pumping. He has waited too long to delay this encounter a moment longer. The emotion is building, the longed-for meeting is about to happen, and the village comes to a standstill. Neighbors look on in amazement. Heaven is watching.

The prodigal stands speechless as his ecstatic father hurtles willy-nilly towards him. He can't believe what is happening.

He is about to have the most amazing experience of his life …

It is not only a fabulous moment for a movie. It is a fabulous *truth*.

Beyond Fiction

The teller of this parable would have us know that when the Almighty God spots a returning son or daughter in the distance, the entire universe gets put on hold. All royal protocol, all concern for His personal dignity is tossed aside. The Sovereign Lord rushes in joyful abandon, His garments flapping in the wind, to welcome miserable failures who have been hanging out with pigs.

This is *not* the God most of us have in our heads, and our minds stagger to take it in.

Most Jewish fathers in Jesus' audience would have handled the situation quite differently. Likely they would have stood stiffly on the front porch with crossed arms and eyes full of lightning bolts.

They would have demanded an apology—the bow-and-grovel type. They would have spat out their finest how-could-you-ever-do-something-so-stupid speech. And there would have been consequences—*dire* consequences.

Not this father.

Not by a long shot. It is the furthest thing from his mind.

Because it is the furthest thing from God's mind.

God in a Hurry

It is hard for me to reflect on this moment in our Lord's parable without being overcome by emotion because this is not simply the story of some Jewish boy.

This is *my* story.

I simply cannot comprehend that the high King of heaven throws to the wind all propriety and regal behavior and races breathless toward me with arms outstretched because He is overjoyed to have me back after my latest stint with the pigs.

Can you get your mind around *that*?

Can you believe *this* is how God feels about you?

The Son of God *dares* us to believe it.

What Makes God Run?

Years ago in Argentina, a young preacher was explaining in a sermon that God is never in a hurry. He never has to rush to get somewhere on time. Under no circumstances does He lag behind or get ahead of schedule. He is always punctual.

At the conclusion of the message, an older minister congratulated the young man on his preaching, but pointed out a mistake. "We can't say God is *never* in a hurry. There's one place in the Bible where we see God running—and it's in the story of the Prodigal Son. When the boy returns, the father doesn't wait for him at home—he *races* out to meet him. That's a picture of God. When it comes to showing mercy, He is in a hurry, and He runs."

> *While we run from God, God runs toward us.*
>
> —PAUL TAUTGES

The Lord doesn't forgive reluctantly or grudgingly. He *delights* in mercy. He comes running.

"God is more ready to forgive me than I am ready to offend," stated Charles Spurgeon.[8]

One theologian declared: "The most amazing fact in the world, if it is really true, is the redeeming pardon of God."[9]

"You cannot conceive, nor can I, of the appalling strangeness of the mercy of God," declared one writer.[10] One scholar called it God's "inconceivable" mercy.

The Bible affirms repeatedly that the Lord is slow to anger and great in mercy (Psa. 103:8; 145:8; etc.). "There is a stark contrast between the sluggishness of God's anger and the abundant effusiveness of His love," comments John Piper.[11]

When Heaven Makes Haste

What makes God run?

Any chance to show *mercy.*

When the opportunity arises, He's off and running! There's no hesitation or reluctance. He can't wait to do it.

We all know how difficult it is to forgive someone who has hurt us deeply. It doesn't come easy to us.

Not so with God. Few things give Him greater pleasure. Nothing makes Him run faster.

Is this not the *scandal* of the gospel?

It is not hard to believe that the sovereign Lord is holy and just and powerful. We would expect God to be like that. But for Him to get up and bolt down the road every time a home-sick scoundrel shows up on the horizon—that's embarrassingly undignified behavior for the Lord of the universe! Totally *ungodlike.* What ever happened to royal protocol? No earthly monarch would ever demean himself in this way. And for the Most High God to do so—is outrageous.

But that's not all.

It gets *worse.*

The Undignified God

Follow the Son of God as He stumbles up a hill with a cross on His lacerated back. He has been scourged and mocked and spat upon. He is then crucified—pinned to a Roman cross with heavy wrought-iron nails through His wrists and feet. Subjected to the cruelest form of execution ever invented by humans, He is left to agonize, bleed, and die (Lk. 23:20-48).

In the second century, Melito, Bishop of Sardis, penned these words:

He that suspended the earth was Himself suspended.
He that fixed the heavens was fixed [with nails].
He that supported the Earth was supported on a tree.
The Master was exposed to shame,
God put to death![12]

We expect God to be worshipped. Not *tortured.*
We expect God to be reverenced. Not *mocked.*
We expect God to live. Not *die.*

Could anything be more shocking?

One scholar pointed out that "Christianity is the only religion whose God bears the scars of evil." It is, in the words of Chesterton, "the strangest story ever told." Maximum dishonor was heaped on the High King of glory.

How do we explain *that?*

The Crucified God

Is this what God was willing to do to reconcile wayward people back to Himself? Is this how far He was prepared to go to fix the disaster caused by our sin?

Was the Cross, in effect, God running to meet us, saying, "I will not resign myself to having you far from Me. I am prepared to suffer humiliation, pain, and even death in order to have you back. No price is too high, no suffering too great. I will not rest content until you are back in my loving embrace."

"This is real love—not that we loved God, but that He loved us and sent His Son as a sacrifice to take away our sins" (I Jn. 4:10 NLT).

When Jesus, the God-Man died on a hill outside of Jerusalem, the Bible records that the earth shuddered and darkness enveloped the planet.

Well might creation gasp.

The story of the Creator agonizing on a cross is either the greatest absurdity ever invented by a human mind, or the most staggering revelation of the heart of God.

Christian faith dares to believe the latter.

It dares to believe, in the words of one writer, that "God makes Himself known in this moment of hell."[13]

It dares to believe that the One Jesus called Father is a God of unimaginable goodness. He is wonderful beyond description. His mercy is an unstoppable torrent and His love is a consuming fire.

Not What We Expected

We are prone to think God angrily responds to our failures with a *kezazah* ceremony, and that a prolonged time of sitting in shame outside the gate will be required before we can hope for forgiveness. We anticipate a stern reception and stiff consequences. We expect to have to work long and hard "as a hired servant" to get back into His good graces.

The Prodigal Son story *demolishes* this type of thinking. It turns our Pharisee theology on its head. Instead of a frowning, indignant bookkeeper, Jesus tells us of a heavenly Father who dances in sheer joy at the sight of a homecoming prodigal. When a returning rebel appears in the distance, God *runs*.

All the reasons (and there are many!) for God *not* running to meet us were nailed to a cross outside of Jerusalem. They were thoroughly obliterated—*forever*. Justice does not stand in the way of mercy. Justice now *applauds* as mercy hurtles towards us. Love now races *unhindered*.

Abba's Son would have us know that heaven echoes with the sound of running feet. Angels look at each other with a smile. They have seen this before. It happens every time a wayward son or daughter returns home. And the hosts of heaven watch awestruck as once again the King of glory flings everything aside and races wildly down the road to welcome another lost-and-now-found child.

It's *more* than a parable.

It is the most amazing truth we will ever learn.

G. K. Chesterton was a brilliant English journalist whose eccentricities fit the stereotype of the proverbial absent-minded professor. In a moment of bewilderment he sent his wife a telegram: "Am in Market Harborough. Where ought I to be?" Her reply was: "Home."

Home is where we *all* ought to be.

If you still find yourself a long way from the Father's house, this story is an invitation from heaven. If you had any idea what awaits you, you wouldn't wait a minute longer. You would come home. This involves placing your trust in the One who died to forgive you and reconcile you to God. It means committing your life to the Lord Jesus Christ.

And when you do, you will encounter *extreme mercy*.

You will experience the greatest Love in the universe.

Frederick Buechner put it well:

> Repent and believe in the gospel, Jesus says. Turn around and believe that the good news that we are loved is better than we ever dared hope, and that to believe in that good news, to live out of it and toward it, to be in love with that good news, is of all glad things in this world the gladdest thing of all.[14]

PRAYER

God of mercy, we do not read in Your Word that You are rich in wrath, or rich in justice, or rich in power. Scripture affirms You are rich in mercy. Where would we be if that were not the case! We praise You that Your mercy is unfailing, it is tender, it is abounding. It is greater than our accumulated offenses. It is wider than our persistent failures. It trumps our messes and astonishes our hearts. It brings us to our knees and puts a song of praise on our lips. We hope in Your mercy, wonder at its lavishness, and rejoice in the fact that it endures forever. Stir our hearts, O Lord, that we may not only be receivers, but givers of mercy, sharing with others that which we receive from You in such excessive abundance. In Christ's Name, amen.

*It costs God nothing, so far as we know,
to create nice things: but to convert
rebellious wills cost Him crucifixion.*
—C. S. Lewis

*If trust must be earned, hasn't God unequivocally
earned our trust with the bark on the raw wounds,
the thorns pressed into the brow,
your name on the cracked lips?*
—Ann Voskamp

*The Cross is the price God pays
to get to us in spite of our sins.*
—E. Stanley Jones

CHAPTER TEN

The God who takes our shame

"Filled with love and compassion, he ran to his son ..."

LUKE 15:20 NLT

It was one of the greatest cringe moments of my life. My friend Chris and I had just walked home from our high school and had arrived at his house, an old-style home with a large porch. We stood jabbering about something, when a newspaper delivery boy came along. As he started up the path toward the house, newspaper in hand, I blurted out, "Hey, wait a minute. Let me show you how you do that."

I considered myself quite a pro at delivering newspapers. Having done paper routes for years, I had developed considerable expertise in tossing folded newspapers onto porches as I rode past on my bicycle.

I snatched the newspaper and gave it one of those fold jobs I was good at. Here was a fine chance to show this novice how it was done. Then, I leaned back like a baseball pitcher to make the throw. Now this kid was going to see an *expert* do it. Adding the ol' flick of the wrist as I released the paper, I watched the newspaper take flight and arc through the air.

And *then* it happened.

The newspaper did *not* land on the porch. It landed in the *living room*—demolishing a large window in the process!

Ouch!

Did I ever make a fool of myself on that one!

Shame and Dignity

We all have memories that make us wince, moments when we wished the ground would swallow us up. Our personal "hall of shame." Those embarrassing experiences remain indelibly etched in our mind.

There are few things in life we are more eager to avoid than shame and humiliation. We dread the thought. We put a high value on our personal dignity.

However, in the Middle East, the price placed on personal dignity is not just high—it's *astronomical.* Few things are as highly prized as a "good name," and virtually every social interaction has to do with shame and honor. The prodigal parable takes place in this kind of setting. There are huge "shame" issues going on in His story, and if we are to get the full impact of what is taking place in the narrative, it is crucial we pay close attention to this cultural dynamic.[1]

"East is East, and West is West, and never the twain shall meet."[2] Rudyard Kipling got that one right. Easterners are puzzling to Westerners. "The East and West seem condemned to be topsyturveydoms to each other," remarked Chesterton. We have no tools to process bizarre events such as "honor-killings."[3] And the people of the East are equally confused about what goes on in the West.

Unlike the guilt-based culture of the West, Middle-Eastern societies are shame-based. Maintaining honor and avoiding disgrace is a major concern. The big question is not so much whether an action is right or wrong, but if it is honorable or shameful in the eyes of the community. Public disgrace is to be avoided at all costs. Miguel de Cervantes put it this way: "A man dishonored is worse than dead."

It bears noting that words like shame, reproach, and honor show up constantly in the Scriptures. These are prominent concepts in the lives of the people in the biblical narrative. They lived in an honor-shame society.

The Undignified Father

When the Teacher from Nazareth came to the part in His story where the elderly landowner dashes down the road to meet his son, his listeners would have *gasped*. Respectable elders *never* ran. This was a major indiscretion.

Kenneth Bailey, an expert on Middle Eastern culture, explains that "an oriental nobleman in flowing robes never runs anywhere."[4] Aristotle stated, "Great men never run in public."[5] It was considered improper and undignified.

The father in Jesus' story is engaged in very unbefitting conduct. Children and servants ran—*not* patriarchs. The specific Greek term for "running" in this parable is used to describe athletes competing in races. For an elderly man to sprint top speed through the village went against all cultural norms. It was a flagrant social blunder.

When Listeners Get Jolted

Christ had a fascinating habit of inserting shocking or bizarre elements into the parables He told. His parables are *not* nice bedtime stories; they are wake-up calls that startle and prod people to think. The racing patriarch was definitely one of those shockers.

By violating social convention, the prodigal's father is shaming himself publicly. He is recklessly discarding the honor Easterners value so highly.

Furthermore, robes are not suitable attire for running. In order to dash out to meet his son, the father finds necessary to gather up his long garment, and as he does so, he would expose his legs. This too is a disgraceful act. In Eastern culture gentlemen maintain their dignity.

But this patriarch *doesn't*. He storms down the street, bare legs flashing in the sunlight, trampling his honor underfoot. We must not miss this. The father is acting in a way that heaps shame upon himself. More than one person hearing this parable must have turned to his neighbor and said, "Have you ever heard of such a thing?" This is undignified behavior for a patriarch.

Insult and Injury

You will recall the father's dignity has taken a beating right from the *beginning* of this story. Let's backtrack for a moment.

For a son to say, "Dad, I want my inheritance now," is a slap in the face for the father. In the Middle East, elders are respected and honored. To shame them is unthinkable. The boy's obnoxious behavior is way out of line.

One scholar checked out this story with people from all over the Middle East. His conversations always took the same form:

> "Has anyone ever made such a request in your village?"
> "Never!"
> "Could anyone ever make such a request?"
> "Impossible!"
> "If anyone ever did, what would happen?"
> "His father would beat him, of course!"
> "Why?"

"The request means—*he wants his father dead!*"⁶

What measures does the insulted father take to defend his honor?

None at all.

He allows the young brat to expose him to the mockery of the neighbors. The father's reputation in the village takes a beating.

The Disgraced Dad

We should keep in mind that, when the father hands over the inheritance, he doesn't pull it out of the family safe or bank account. His wealth is his property—sheep, goats, camels, crops, houses, and land. In order to comply with his son's request, the father would have to auction off one-third of his possessions.

A good portion of his assets go *down* the drain. Jewish people in ancient times zealously maintained ownership of their land. It was a matter of family honor. Various safeguards were in place in the Law of Moses to ensure that land was not permanently lost.

This forfeiture of property is a major embarrassment for the father. It means more than material loss; it means a loss of *honor*. His reputation in the community takes a plunge.

The son gets the money, his father gets *disgraced*.

And surprisingly ... the father *accepts* the humiliation. The patriarch swallows the bitter pill out of love for his son. He is willing to suffer a loss of dignity with the hope that, at some point, his boy is going to come around.

However, the insolent fellow is only getting started!

Luke records he "set off for a distant country." The word used suggests much more than simply heading out to see the world. It literally means: "He traveled away from his own people." Miroslav Volf points out in his book *Inclusion and Embrace* that the prodigal son's departure from his father's home is his attempt to become a non-son—to terminate his sonship. The boy, in essence, is severing ties with his family, his people, and from everything he has been given.

The father is getting rejected—and dishonored!

The young fellow takes the direct route to Good Times City, and there the escapade gets seriously underway. He foolishly blows the *entire* inheritance.

The reports filtering back to his village are not good. Rumors are flying.

Added *shame* for the patriarch.

Making Dad Look Bad

When the spendthrift's bank account runs dry, he hits the skids and makes an embarrassing landing in a nearby pigsty. Now the father has a son who is a *swine-herder*—not something a Jewish man would boast about!

And finally, when he hits rock bottom, our hapless friend gets up and comes home.

The scoundrel who has dishonored his father in every possible way has a lot to answer for. He should be on knees, licking the dust, eating humble pie, kissing his father's feet, and begging for forgiveness. The epitome of penitence.

But that's *not* what takes place.

The white-haired gentleman sees him coming, hikes up his robe, and runs. Notice what's going on here: the man, who has already been thoroughly disgraced by his son, now runs with uplifted garments—and disgraces himself *further.*

This scenario has *shame* written all over it!

The love of the father for this boy is so enormous he is prepared to look undignified, laughable, and downright ludicrous. *Nothing* deters him. No price is too high. He is willing to suffer humiliation to get his son back.

This gentleman leaves us dumbfounded!

What is Jesus telling us about God?

We need to look closely at this. What comes to light is an aspect of the Father's character that is almost unbelievable.

The Shaming of God

In the Garden of Eden our first parents received from their Creator a wonderful inheritance—a world of beauty, goodness, and abundance. But, following the lead of the Serpent, Adam and Eve opted for enjoying the gifts—*without* the Giver. They turned their backs on God and struck out on their own.

Sounds rather *prodigal-like,* doesn't it?

Humanity rejected and dishonored God in the garden. We turned up our nose at the One who had given us everything.

It was no *minor* insult.

How would this disgraced Deity respond?

He came looking for us, calling out, "Adam, where are you?"

Can you sense the *pain* behind those words? God's most prized treasure in Creation had turned against Him. We don't see firebolts. We see a seeking God with an *aching* heart.

This God *surprises* us. (And He always will.)

The Lord of swirling galaxies and distant star-fields was spurned on this speck of dust called planet Earth. Yet He allows it and *bears* the shame.

Life on our planet was about to take a steep downward plunge into the awful consequences of our *"thou shalt surely die"* choice. Satan's promised Eden wasn't exactly paradise.

However, the Creator had a stupendous promise for us. He essentially said, "This is *not* how things are going to end. I did not create you to perish. I created you to experience my love and joy, and I will do whatever needs to be done to make that happen. A Liberator will come. He will defeat the Serpent and bring you back."[7]

He was referring to Messiah and His death on the Cross.

Long centuries would go by before He came.

Meanwhile, God's good creation was overgrown, not only with thistles and thorns, but with cruelty, violence, tribal wars, oppression, injustice, and chaos. It was ugly, and the sovereign Lord could easily have *washed* His hands of the whole mess.

He didn't.

He persisted in loving fallen humanity, and He set in motion His plan to salvage His creation.

A Good God Who Loves Bad People

A man named Abraham and his descendants were chosen. From this family the Liberator would come. God identified Himself with the Hebrew nation with a view to bringing about redemption to the whole world.

> *In a nutshell, the Bible from Genesis 3 to Revelation 22 tells the story of a God reckless with desire to get his family back.*
>
> —Philip Yancey

This was a barbaric time in history. Tribal deities were constantly at war with each other. Genocide, infanticide, and human sacrifices were commonplace. Savagery reigned. It was a nasty world to live in.

The Old Testament documents massacres, atrocities, and bloody conquests. And it records God's involvement in those barbaric chapters of history.

The question arises: How could a holy God be a part of such ghastly situations? Does He sanction genocide? Does He approve of violence?

Did Christ not teach us rather to bless those who curse us, turn the other cheek, and forgive seventy times seven? And were these not His words: *"Love your enemies that you may be children of your father in heaven"?*

If God does *not* sanction retaliation and violence, if self-sacrificing love and forgiveness are what He is all about, what in the world was He up to in the Old Testament? What do we make of those gruesome stories of destruction? How do we reconcile these two different pictures of the Almighty?

Putting His Reputation at Risk

This is a difficult issue, but consider this possibility: Could it be the Lord was meeting savage ancient peoples where they were, in all their primitive barbarity—in order to move them in a better direction? Was He walking with them in their messy situation with a redemptive purpose in mind? Was He so committed to rescuing them that He was willing to take upon Himself the shame of being identified with their brokenness and fallenness?

Much in the Old Testament clearly does *not* fully reflect God's true character. Rather, it reflects His patience and willingness to bear with His chosen people in order to take them to a better place. The Children of Israel little understood how radically their God differed from other pagan deities; they had a lot to learn. God became a part of their fouled-up story in order to make them a part of His.

Undeniably, there are other issues going on, but this explains a lot of what was taking place in those difficult Old Testament passages.

God's love was so robust that He was willing to look contemptible in order to redeem fallen people. He embarrassed Himself and tarnished His reputation by calling Himself *their* God. He was prepared to be the God of Israel, even though His Name would be dishonored, profaned, and even blasphemed as a result (Isa.

52:5; Ezek. 36:22). He hung around with people who made Him look bad.

It is the scandalous *shaming* of God.

But wait—it gets even *worse.*

Fast forward to Jerusalem, 33 A.D.

The Ultimate Disgrace

Jesus the Messiah was betrayed by one of His followers and arrested. The religious bureaucrats staged a mock trial and sentenced Him to death. The Romans then proceeded to execute Him in the most horrible manner ever devised by human minds. He experienced the supreme dishonor of hanging naked on the spikes of a Roman cross. There, before the gaze of a mocking crowd, He agonized, bled, and died.

There is a crucial difference between death by crucifixion and other methods of execution. The guillotine, for instance, brought about a quick and relatively painless death. This eighteenth-century invention was designed to end life abruptly while inflicting a minimum amount of suffering.

Crucifixion was designed to do the *opposite.*

It aimed at inflicting a *maximum* amount of suffering for a pro- longed period. It was painful and slow. In fact, the word "excruciat- ing" (tremendously painful; causing intense suffering) comes from two Latin words: *ex cruciatus,* or out of the cross. Crucifixion was the defining word for extreme pain.

Roman statesman Cicero called crucifixion "the most cruel and disgusting penalty." Jewish historian Josephus described it as "the most wretched of deaths."

Death on a cross caused extreme physical agony, but there was something *worse*—it subjected the person to extreme shame and humiliation. Crucifixion was designed to expose the victim to maximum public ridicule and contempt, and was strategically carried out near crowded, busy junctions. This method of execution meant ultimate disgrace, and in a society where honor is prized above all—this was the *most* dreaded part.

N. T. Wright explains: "Crucifixion was a powerful symbol throughout the Roman world. It was not just a means of liquidating undesirables; it did so with the maximum degradation and humiliation."[8]

Another scholar writes: "By pinning them up like insects, crucifixion was deliberately intended to display and humiliate its victims. It was always carried out in public ... [and] was deliberately designed to be loathsome, vulgar, revolting and obscene."[9]

The Cross never finds its rightful place in a man's heart until it takes his breath away.

—F. W. BOREHAM

In ancient Rome the repulsive four-letter word *crux* (cross) was not to be uttered in polite company. First-century Jews were horrified by crucifixion and viewed it as a sign of a divine curse.[10] It is no wonder that one biblical writer refers to the *"open shame"* (Heb. 6:6) of crucifixion and speaks of *"the disgrace He bore"* (Heb. 13:13 NLT).

In his account of the Passion, Matthew says very little about the physical sufferings of Jesus (Matt. 27:27-44). He directs our attention elsewhere. For Matthew, the Cross is mostly about man's mockery of God. It is a cross of shame.

Where Was God?

In the book *Bevis: The Story of a Boy,* by eighteenth-century novelist Richard Jefferies, a young boy is fascinated by a picture of Jesus dying on a cross:

The Crucifixion hurt his feelings very much; the cruel nails; the unfeeling spear; he looked at the picture a long time and then turned the page saying, "If God had been there, He would not have let them do it."[11]

If *God* had been there! The supreme irony is this: He *was* there. He was the one hanging on the cross!

Here we stand thunderstruck.

If nothing worse can befall a human being, what can we make of the bloody disgrace of *God* on a cross? Could anything be more bewildering, more astonishing, more atrocious?

For the Lord of the universe to enter His own creation and become human is enough of a mindblower. But for Him to be spat upon, mocked, tortured, and killed by His rebel creatures leaves us speechless. God came and we murdered Him. Who can possibly get his mind around *that?*

Jerusalem, 33 A.D.

Imagine for a moment a traveler who arrives at Jerusalem the day Jesus of Nazareth was executed. As he approaches the city gates, he glances over and sees the Galilean suffering the agony of crucifixion. Then he hears the man on the cross cry out, "My God, my God, why have you forsaken me?"

What conclusion would the stranger draw? Would he think, "Wow, there's the Son of God giving His life to redeem the world?"

Hardly.

The onlooker would surely conclude: "There's another God-forsaken lawbreaker dying for his crimes." Certainly *that's* what it looked like: another villain paying for his wrongdoing.

But the traveler would have been *dead* wrong!

This was no God-forsaken lawbreaker.

No, this was God *unwilling* to forsake the lawbreakers of the world. This was God stooping so far down to lift up fallen people that He *looked* like a lawbreaker. He was *"numbered with the transgressors,"* says the Bible (Mk. 15:28). Three "criminals" were executed that day, but one of them was a holy God shaming Himself in order to free us from *our* guilt and shame.

Nothing more shocking has ever happened in the history of the world.

This was the *shaming* of the King of Glory.

A hymn writer expressed it like this:

Bearing shame and scoffing rude
In my place condemned He stood,
Sealed my pardon with his blood,
Hallelujah, what a Savior![12]

This is what He was willing to do to get us back.

In the language of the prodigal parable, this is the part of the story where the father lifts his robe, exposes his legs, runs, and brings dishonor upon himself. *This is God disgracing Himself as He rushes to meet us in our sin and shame.* Here we see the "ludicrous depths of self-humiliation [to which God] will descend in his wild pursuit of mankind."[13]

That's the gospel. That's the Cross.

And *that's* the Father Jesus wants us to know.

The Truth about God

God is not a ruthless warrior who delights seeing people slaughtered. Scripture states that He takes no pleasure in the death of the wicked. Rather, He is a God who sacrifices *Himself* for the wicked. He is a God who looks like Jesus dying on a cross. He is a Calvary-like God.

The Cross is the *final* statement about God.

It is a mistake to point at those violent Old Testament stories and state, "That's what God is like." We can only say that with confidence when we get to the Gospels. It is the crucified Christ who gives us a clear picture of the heart of God and His self-sacrificing love. It is Jesus who shows us what God is *really* like.

"Do not think, sinner, that God is stony-hearted. Thou hast a heart of stone, God has not. The hardness is in thyself, not in Him," preached Charles Spurgeon.[14]

He's right. The problem lies in *us,* not in God. The real problem is *our* sinfulness and hardness of heart. We are the ones in need of repentance.

In the 1960s a book came out titled: *I'm OK—You're OK.* Who are we trying to kid? A more truthful motto would be: "I'm a mess and so are you!" The words of Buechner are sadly true: "Our best moments have been mostly grotesque parodies. Our best loves have been almost always blurred with selfishness and deceit."[15] Scripture declares that *"the heart is deceitful above all things, and desperately wicked"* (Jer. 17:9). We are a *long* shot from being "okay."

When human beings were given the opportunity to do as they *wished* with the Lord of heaven, the outcome was not pretty. He was rejected, mocked, tortured, and subjected to a horrendous death. Members of our race carried out the crucifixion of God. And the conspirators were not *thugs.* They were the most outstanding citizens in the land. This was *humanity's* response to the beauty of God's presence!

We are guilty of high treason.

"The Cross is the unveiling of man's rebellion against God," states Karl Barth.[16]

Nowhere does the stark reality of man's evil heart come to light as when human hands murdered the Son of God. The death of Christ was not just something done for us—it was done *by* us. The Cross *unmasks* what humans have become. It confronts us with the ugly truth about our deep-seated antagonism toward God. It rips to shreds our pious illusions. "To put it candidly and rather bluntly," said one writer, "we know we are sinners because of what happened on Good Friday."[17]

Scottish theologian James Stewart writes: "And will anyone deny, with Jesus hanging there, that sin is the critical enemy, the most dangerous insatiable thing in the world, and that he personally needs to be forgiven?"[18]

What happened at Calvary should have turned the Almighty against us forever. It *didn't*. He turned our damnable act into an *atonement,* and nail-marked hands now welcome us back into God's infinite embrace.

Coming Home

When the miracle of repentance finally does take place and we come back to Him after our stint in the far country, God doesn't give us the third degree. He doesn't demand, "What did you do with all that wealth I gave you? Did you squander *all* of it?"

Rather, He *covers* our shame with the best robe. Over our rags is "gladly thrown ... a veil of loving oblivion."[19] He gives us a ring and shoes, and celebrates our return with a banquet. Instead of shaming us, He forgives us. Instead of rehearsing the failures, He honors us, and rejoices over our homecoming.

Who ever heard of a God like *that?*

Is it any wonder the gospel turns people into lovers and worshippers of God?

Isaac Watts' hymn says it beautifully:

Were the whole realm of nature mine
That were an offering far too small.
Love so amazing, so divine
Demands my soul, my life, my all.

As guest of honor at the party, the prodigal wears the special robe. No one dares dredge up the past. The "far country" is not brought up. That chapter is *closed*. The only comment about it comes from the father: "This my son was dead, and he is alive. He was lost, and is found. Let's celebrate."

There is *one* place in the universe where we can stand tall again. It is at the foot of the Cross—where God bore our shame.

PRAYER

God of grace and glory, we have been victims and agents of sin. We have brought shame upon ourselves. However, when we were bereft of dignity, freedom, and joy, You came for us, and You were willing to dishonor Yourself in order to get us back. Your Holy Son bore the full guilt and shame of our sin on the Cross. His empty cross, vacant tomb, and ongoing intercession conspire to free us from the paralyzing effects of shame. Continue, O Lord, to bombard our hearts with the gospel of peace. We are humbled and gladdened by the fact that the Christ of God is not ashamed to call us His brothers. We are grateful and awed that You, Father, dare to call us Your beloved sons and daughters. Your tenacious tenderness and heart-restoring kindness are a balm for us—the broken, ragged, and disgraced. We give You praise in the healing name of Jesus, amen.

The slender capacity of man's heart cannot comprehend the unfathomable depth and burning zeal of God's love toward us.

—Martin Luther

The love of God is not a mild benevolence; it is a consuming fire.

—Bede Griffiths

Divine love is incessantly restless until it turns all woundedness into health, all deformity into beauty and all embarrassment into laughter.

—Beldon Lane

CHAPTER ELEVEN

The God who hugs prodigals

"… his father saw him and felt compassion,
and ran and embraced him and kissed him."

LUKE 15:20 ESV

Some people are compulsive eaters; others are compulsive spenders; my wife is a compulsive hugger. When you meet her, she will likely hug you. If you stay within arms' reach, before long you will get hugged again. If you let your guard down, expect to get another hug. If you share something painful or joyful with her, you've got another one coming. And when you say goodbye, you can expect to be hugged once more. She can dispense more hugs in a shorter time than anyone I have ever met. Some people hug trees, others hug animals. My wife hugs people. It's her spiritual gift.

Okay, admittedly this description of my affectionate spouse is somewhat exaggerated (although only slightly). She comes from a *huggy* family, and living as we have for many years in a Latin

American country has only accentuated this ancestral tendency. She is fully convinced that arms were made for hugging.

Someone quipped, "They invented hugs to let people know you love them without saying anything." Hugging is inexpensive, does not harm the environment, requires no special equipment, and spreads happiness.

The Bible states there is *"a time to embrace, and a time to refrain from embracing."* (Eccles. 3:5). Scripture records a number of "time to embrace" incidents, but none as heart-stirring as the one Jesus depicts in His parable of Luke 15.

The Homecoming

When at last the lost son appears on the horizon the father comes to life. He catapults off the porch, dashes down the road shouting wildly, throws his arms around the boy's neck, and covers him with kisses. Before the young fellow is able to sputter a word, he is welcomed as if he had just arrived back from accomplishing some heroic mission.

Some scholars have suggested the father races out to hug his son as a protective measure. The neighbors remember well the boy's scandalous departure and would not hesitate to make their contempt known. However, before anyone can get off their porch chair, the father is already enfolding the young man in his warm embrace. The patriarch puts his forgiving love on public display, clearly forestalling any scornful actions from the villagers.

A *kezazah* ceremony is now evidently out of the question.

The townspeople look on in disbelief as Mr. Pigsty gets the welcome of his life. And no one is more flabbergasted than the prodigal himself.

When Kings Eat Humble Pie

History records a famous "reconciliation" that took place in 1077 in the northern Italian city of Canossa. German emperor Henry IV had dared to clash with Pope Gregory VII over the right to appoint bishops, and as a result the indiscreet monarch was excommunicated and threatened with deposition. Fearing the loss of his crown, Henry scrambled to make amends.

In January, in the dead of winter, he crossed the Alps and arrived at the fortress at Canossa, where the Pope was staying. Wearing a hair shirt, the king stood barefoot in the snow at the castle gate for three days waiting for the Roman Pontiff to respond. When the gates finally opened, Henry knelt before Pope Gregory and begged his forgiveness. This extreme act of royal penitence paid off and the emperor was granted absolution.

For the prodigal son to be restored to his father's good graces, an equally grueling reentry procedure was surely in order. No first-century Jew would have thought otherwise.

Most parents today in the Western world would handle this matter quite differently. We would anxiously await the return of a runaway teenager. We would welcome and forgive him, and probably avoid asking too many questions when he finally came home.

But life was different in first-century Middle Eastern communities. One writer explains,

> in conservative societies of strict moral code where the extended family is the unit of social life, age is venerated, and family possessions are the only social security, prodigal children may not violate ancient traditions, flout family and community standards, or waste family wealth with impunity. A society built on tradition doesn't welcome or forgive radical departure from inherited custom.[1]

This is the world the prodigal lives in. Major misconduct has taken place—the family name has been smeared, and an inheritance has been thrown to the wind. Such a colossal mess-up cannot be glossed over *lightly*. The returning scoundrel definitely has it coming!

Consider this example of Middle East protocol from the Old Testament: *"So Moses went out to meet his father-in-law and bowed down and kissed him"* (Ex. 18:7). Parents were given honor. And in the case of a returning wayward son, *extreme* expressions of humility would be in order.

Forgiveness could eventually be offered, but *first* there must be repentance, confession, and humility—full public penance. There must be a willingness to make amends. The seriousness of the misdeed needs to be emphasized. Disciplinary measures equal to the magnitude of the wrong committed should be applied. This was only right and appropriate.

But, as we know ... what took place was *exactly* the opposite!

The teller of the parable describes the father's response with a cascade of verbs—seeing, running, embracing, and kissing. And the man is only getting *started!*

He does not wait for confessions, explanations, or signs of deep repentance from his son. He does not give the slightest thought to salvaging his damaged honor. He is oblivious to the stares of his astounded neighbors. Time stands still for the father, as in one delirious moment of undiluted joy, he lavishes a torrent of affection on his speechless son.

What Happened to Protocol?

The onlookers are appalled. The father is acting out of turn. It is the duty of sons to kiss *paterfamilias,* not the other way around. This is a colossal blunder.

However, propriety is the *last* thing on the patriarch's mind. He is giving free rein to a heart exploding with joy. He can't refrain from kissing his son. He is, in fact, humbling himself in the eyes of the neighbors, and is surrendering the *last* remaining shreds of his dignity.

Protocol is trumped by love.

No attention is paid to the son's shoddy attire or to the unmistakable scent of swine. No mention is made of his past. He is not called upon to grovel or to give account of his shameful behavior. No apologies are called for. No promises are required.

Just a barrage of hugs and kisses.

In the Middle East kissing was and still is a customary form of greeting, but this was more than a simple salutation. The tense of the Greek verb used indicates the father kissed him repeatedly. Notice how different Bible versions render this phrase:

- *"kissed him affectionately"* (ISV)
- *"tenderly kissed him again and again"* (WUEST)
- *"covered him with kisses"* (DARBY)

The boy, caught in a thunderstorm of affection, stands grace-drenched and wonderstruck.

The Waster Gets Welcomed

In biblical times a kiss was a sign of reconciliation, a pledge that the past had been forgiven. The kissing spree means more than endearment—it demolishes *all* doubt about the father's forgiveness.

This is definitely *not* the reception the prodigal has expected. After blowing his inheritance, running all the red lights, and hanging out with the hogs, he figures the most he can hope for is a bottom-of-the-ladder job as a hired laborer. That is the *best-case* scenario. Anything beyond that is out of the question.

The boy really does not know his father!

He is going to get tackled by his dad before he can get anywhere near the house! He won't stand a chance of getting his speech out under the flurry of hugs and kisses. And his bewilderment will go off the charts as gift after gift are lavished upon him. His homecoming will be celebrated with all the stops pulled out.

This is who the father was—and his son has been blind to it.

His treachery has not turned his dad against him. It has not caused his father's love to diminish at all. If anything—it has *increased!* He has thought his "make-me-like-one-of-your-hired-servants" plan is going to be necessary to get back on good terms with his dad. How *wrong* he is!

A Love Sin Cannot Alter

There is a vital spiritual lesson for us here: *Our sin does not change God.* It does not dampen His love or alter His attitude towards us. What sin does is to alter the way we view Him. It changes *us.*

> *Through the Cross, God showed that even killing God cannot put God off from relating to and loving us. He rose again to tell us.*
>
> —John Goldingay

When we fail, we assume God "unfriends" us and stiffly turns away. We are sure that a huge effort will be required to regain His favor. Not so! Christ's attitude toward "sinners" debunks that idea. His indiscriminate compassion makes it clear that our wrongdoing is *not* powerful enough to change the heart of God. It's not that strong!

Nothing is.

Make no mistake. Sin is deadly. It destroys us, it is hateful to God (mostly because of what it does to people made in His image)—but it is utterly *incapable* of extinguishing His love. Solomon stated that many waters cannot quench love. Neither can our *sins.*

What sin does do (among other things) is to mess up our capacity to *perceive* God clearly.

And *that* is what makes it so toxic.

Love That Defies Limits

Clasped within his father's strong embrace, the prodigal's apprehensions and fears melt. Every doubt about his father's heart withers. He stands in the middle of the road dumbfounded, overtaken by a love bigger than all his failures.

What Jesus, the teller of this tale, was saying to His critics was this: "You give me flak because I dine with derelicts? You have *no* idea! My heavenly Father sprints out to embrace and kiss them, and then celebrates their return with the biggest party you have ever heard of!"

Many think that God is "loving" in a "religious" sort of way. They believe His benevolence is pious and proper. They surmise He reluctantly fulfills His theological duty to dispense good will. He wishes us well. After all—that is what gods are *supposed* to do!

What a different picture Abba's Son gives us!

He portrays the wild wonder of the Father's love—a love that is fiercely passionate and extravagant. In essence, Jesus is saying: "Dream your wildest dreams, push the limits of your most daring thoughts—my Father's love is greater than that!"

Is Christ *exaggerating?*

Not in the slightest. The Bible states that *"Christ's love is greater than anyone can ever know"* (Eph. 3:19 ERV). If there is one thing that no one could ever overestimate—it is the love of God!

Dallas Willard points out:

We must understand that God does not "love" us without liking us—through gritted teeth—as "Christian" love is sometimes thought to do. Rather, out of the eternal freshness of His perpetually self-renewed being, the heavenly Father cherishes the earth and each human being upon it. The fondness, the endearment, the unstintingly affectionate regard of God toward all His creatures is the natural outflow of what He is to the core—which we vainly try to capture with our tired but indispensable old word "love."[2]

Heart-Stopping Truth

For many, the phrase "God loves you" is a trite, worn-out cliché. It's been overworked. It states the obvious. Yawn. How unoriginal. Almost everybody understands that.

No, *not* true.

Almost everyone *fails* to understand what it means. It is heart-stopping. It is shattering. It changes everything.

This is what we once believed in a place called Eden, where we lived in the presence of our Maker who delighted in us and rejoiced over us with singing. It is what made our hearts leap and our feet dance. It made that garden a joy-filled paradise.

Hearing the Father's voice, knowing His affirmation, and reveling in His love flooded our being with light. It infused us with abounding life that overflowed in our relationship with God, one another, and the whole creation.

It is where our hearts were *meant* to live.

And our souls cry out for it.

Not a Mere Story

Jesus' parable is more than a corrective for deficient theology. It is a long-awaited rain shower for parched hearts. It is the arrival of spring after a long Siberian winter. It is a snapshot of the miracle that happens when a person turns back to God through faith in Christ.

Take a moment to process more fully the reality of this God encounter …

Put yourself in the shoes of the prodigal (forget briefly that he has no shoes). Insert yourself into this scene. You are the returning son or daughter the Father rushes out to meet. Close your eyes and let your heart take it in …

Can you see Him racing toward you? Do you see the eagerness and excitement on His face? Do you see the love in His eyes? Can you envisage Him enfolding you in His strong arms and pulling you close to His chest? Do you feel the deep intensity of His joy as He clasps you in His firm embrace? Can you sense the wonder of being overtaken by a love that is passionate and deep and true?

Pause for a moment and let the marvel of it wash over you like waves. Be still and know it's for real. Allow it to calm your fears. Let it flood your being with the deep assurance that all is forgiven and all is well. Take a deep breath, and let that *sink in.*

Homeless Hearts

Philip Yancey once remarked that when all is said and done, all we ever really wanted was to be desired by the Maker of all things. This deep craving to be "wanted and wished for and waited for"[3] is not a futile hope. It is *precisely* the way Abba feels about you.

The heart that throbs inside of us was made by God and *for* God. It was designed to live in the Father's embrace. It is *there*—and only there—that the human soul finds its center and place of rest.

"Maybe at the heart of all our traveling is the dream of someday, somehow, getting Home," wrote Frederick Buechner.[4]

I think we all know what he *means*.

We yearn for our true home—where we are welcomed and accepted and valued. Where we belong. Not just a transient dwelling but a permanent place of warmth and safety and comfort. A place filled with laughter and music and beauty, where our hearts dance with pleasure and delight.

Such a place *does* in fact exist.

There is a remedy for our homesickness. It is eloquently depicted in the prodigal's reunion with his father. Christ is pointing us to a rich spiritual reality designed for each one of us. It involves recognizing our lost-ness and returning to our *true* home—not with our feet but with our hearts. It means finding forgiveness and rest in the loving arms of the God who longs to be our Father. The One knows all and wants us back—and that is *why* He sent Jesus.

Not Mild Benevolence

There is, however, one thing we should be warned about: God's love is not only heart-warming—it is life-shaking. It is both tender *and* turbulent.

"God is not nice. God is not an uncle. God is an earthquake," writes Abraham Heschel.[5]

Was it a God of love we were hoping for? We have one. Do we ever! The Consuming Fire Himself. Here is the blazing source from which every other flame of love is ignited. Here is a love so ardent, so relentless, and so vigorous, we might find ourselves loved *more* furiously than we had wished.

This Love will forgive our most depraved actions. It will not be rebuffed by our worst behavior—however despicable. Here is love without caution, restraint, limit, logic, or expiry date. It pursues rebels to preposterous extremes.

However, if we let this Love have its way, there is one thing it will *not* do—it will not leave us the way we are.

This Love is too robust and too intense to allow twistedness and ugliness to remain. In the words of Frederick Buechner, "it is ruthless against everything in us that diminishes our joy."[6] It will love us into wholeness and goodness and virtue. It will not rest until we are well; it will not let up until we are free.

This is what love *does*.

"We read in the greatest of texts that God is Love, but we do not read anywhere that God is Sentimentalism," pointed out Chesterton.[7]

"What do people mean when they say, 'I am not afraid of God because I know He is good'?" asks Lewis. "Have they never even been to a dentist?"[8]

Love's goal is for the loved ones to become *all* they were meant to be. No price is too high. No sacrifice is too great. God not only intends to do us well, He intends to *make* us well. George MacDonald put it beautifully: "His fingers can touch nothing but to mold it into loveliness."

> *Love is something more stern and splendid than mere kindness.*
>
> C. S. LEWIS

"God just will not let us flunk out of His school of love," writes Peter Kreeft. "He insists on remedial lessons until we get it right."[9]

"God loves you" means … you're in for *quite* a ride.

Inside the Father's Embrace

As they walked together, a university student poured out his frustrations to a Christian minister. "I'm not good at praying, it's hard for me to share my faith, there are temptations I struggle with …" the young man lamented.

As the list grew longer, the man interrupted and said, "Let me ask you a question: How is your relationship with your father?"

"My father? He's a perfectionist. I can never live up to his expectations. My marks are never good enough; my performance never makes the grade. I can never please him ... That's my dad."

All his life the young fellow had longed for his father's hug of acceptance.

"You know what?" the minister said, "You think our heavenly Father is *exactly* like your earthly dad. I have some good news for you." He turned and gave the young man a ferocious hug and declared, "You already have God's embrace! Not when you get your act together, not when you become super spiritual, but right here and right *now.*"

Tears flooded the young fellow's eyes.

The man continued, "God knows there are areas of your life that need to change. There are things that need to go. But I want you to know that all those changes happen INSIDE the Father's embrace. They are *not* a condition for receiving it. They are not the basis of your acceptance. It is on the basis of *grace* that God accepts and embraces you at this very moment."

This is truth that *heals* hearts.

That makes them dance.

That dispels demons.

Is there in this universe a greater treasure than extravagant acceptance by the supreme Lord of the galaxies? To be enveloped in the affectionate embrace of the God of Infinite Love—what could possibly trump *that?*

It's the *ultimate* homecoming.

It's all our dreams come true—a million times over.

Seven hundred years ago, Julian of Norwich expressed it so well:

In His love He wraps and holds us.
He enfolds us for love,
And He will never let us go.[10]

There will be those who misjudge and mistreat you. Others will reject you and write you off. Don't waste time fretting or losing sleep over it.

The Almighty God embraces you and calls you "beloved."

Does anything else *really* matter?

PRAYER

Loving Lord, thank you for drawing us to Yourself, even when we were pushing You away. Thank you for loving us when we were matted and muddied with sin. Thank you for forgiving and accepting us, not after we clean up our acts, not when we get all our ducks in a row, not when we cease to wobble and falter, not when we memorize the Bible, but here and now—because of a blood-stained Cross. Thank you for enfolding us within the bond of an endless love. May the laughter of heaven sabotage the unbelief of our hearts. May we never cease to be amazed at the wonder of it all. May we be impelled to live in gratitude, service, and joy. Let our lives sing your praise. May we live in Your love, rejoice in Your love, and learn to love as You have loved us. In the name of Christ, the Author and Finisher of our embrace, amen.

Grace is the gravity of God grabbing us
and drawing us in to God's never ending love.
—John Manz

It wasn't enough for Him to prepare you a feast.
It wasn't enough for Him to reserve you a seat.
It wasn't enough for Him to cover the cost and
provide the transportation to the banquet.
He did something more. He let you wear
His own clothes so that you could be properly dressed.
He did that ... just for you.
—Max Lucado

For twenty centuries the Church has been proclaiming
salvation, and the grace and forgiveness of God,
to a humanity oppressed with guilt. How then is it that
even amongst the most fervent believers there
are so few free, joyous, confident souls?
—Paul Tournier

CHAPTER TWELVE

The God who robes the bedraggled

"But the father said to his servants, 'Quick! Bring the best robe and put it on him ...'"

LUKE 15:22

At first the villagers pay scant attention to the bedraggled stranger with downcast eyes. The malnourished vagrant seems nervous and apprehensive as he ventures into the village.

And he looks strangely familiar.

The stylish wardrobe he once flaunted has long since been bartered for something to eat. He has managed to put rags on his back by scrounging somebody's castoffs. And, after living with pigs, and sleeping under bridges, these are considerably worse for wear. The prodigal's shoddy appearance does not speak well for him.

People rarely give tramps a second glance.

But somebody *does.*

His father appears out of nowhere with open arms to welcome his long-lost son. Kisses rain down in ecstatic redundancy. Tears flow.

The people of the Middle East are highly expressive of their emotions. And this high-flying father is no exception.

When the patriarch finally comes up for air, he steps back, grasps his son's shoulders, and gazes affectionately at him. Then he abruptly whirls about and bellows an order to his servants, who immediately race off to fetch a special garment for the newcomer.

This is a first-century way of saying: "Roll out the red carpet." This boy is going to get a royal welcome.

And it is urgent business. Some translators have rendered the phrase thus: "Hurry! Bring out the best robe." This father wants everybody to run! No one is to drag their feet. The servants are called to drop everything they are doing and assist in welcoming the prodigal home. Everything else takes a back seat.

An Ordinary Day Disrupted

In sleepy farming communities, life routinely goes on day after day. Dawn and dusk. Seedtime and harvest. Children on the street. Neighbors on their porch. Dogs bark. Grass grows. Seldom does anything out of the ordinary happen.

Except for *today*.

Something *very much* out of the ordinary is taking place. The prodigal *persona non grata* has barely shown his face in the village when he is ambushed by his father and given an unprecedented welcome.

All eyebrows are raised. Jaws drop. The son who has messed up big time is being embraced, forgiven, and rejoiced over! This is *unthinkable!*

And, if that weren't outrageous enough, the old man then proceeds to honor the rascal with a prestigious robe!

The onlookers go from startled to stunned. It appears the father has *lost* his mind!

The patriarch is not merely calling for a clean set of clothes. He orders the servants to bring the *protos stole*—the finest robe, the "first-ranking" garment. One translation renders it "the splendid robe." This attire goes beyond elegance; it confers *honor.*

In the ancient world clothing evidenced status and position in the community. Christ once commented, *"A man wearing fine clothes? Look, those who wear fine clothes are to be found in palaces"* (Mt. 11:8 NJB). The patriarch Jacob gave his son Joseph a coat of many colors distinguishing him above his brothers (Gn. 37:3). In the biblical account of Queen Esther, when Mordecai was granted special honors, he was dressed in the king's robe, and was made to promenade through the city on the king's horse (Esth. 6:1-9). When Daniel was promoted to be the third ruler in Babylon, he was clothed with purple and a necklace of gold (Dan. 5:29). Luxurious garments highlighted the dignity and importance of a person.

Now the newly arrived tramp is being honored. A stately robe is draped over his slumped shoulders. The son's shame is hidden from view. He is cloaked with dignity.

Kezazah Cancelled

The elders of the community have likely discussed the action to be taken should the prodigal ever show his face again in the village. The decision does not require much debate: a *kezazah* is in order. According to Jewish law, such behavior should not be tolerated. The boy should be banished. A *kezazah* committee is probably lined up, ready to execute the plan if ever the occasion arises. It is pot-breaking time.

The plan never gets off the ground.

It is *sabotaged* by the father.

Before anyone else gets wind of what is happening, the old man has launched into action, dashed out to meet his son, and ordered the best robe to be put on him.

Instead of beating him, he *honors* him!

This is way too much for any decent Torah-keeping community to handle. It blows everyone's cultural gaskets!

The father is saying: "We're not breaking any pots. The *kezazah* is cancelled. My son is not getting expelled from the community. On the contrary, we are going to welcome him, accept him, and celebrate his return. And if anyone thinks of doing otherwise he is going to have to deal with me. This is my beloved son, and I am thrilled to have him back. I am giving him the best garment I have. Let it be known that today he is reinstated into my family and our community with my *full* blessing."

The robe of honor sends out a clear message. Whatever has happened in the past is forgiven and gone. It will *not* be brought up again. The son has made a complete comeback into the father's favor. Fully accepted, fully loved.

The Original Wardrobe

You will recall that in Eden's paradise, our first parents felt no need to wear clothes. It was a clothing-optional Garden. Actually it was *more* than that. Clothing never crossed their minds.

Why was *that?*

A clue may be found in an incident that took place many years later when Moses climbed Mount Sinai. After spending forty days in God's presence, the skin of Moses' face glistened so brightly he needed a veil to hide its radiance (Ex. 34:29,30,35).

Could it be that Adam and Eve, who enjoyed direct, unhindered intimacy with their Creator *every* day, *also* shone with the light of God?

Very likely.

This outer luminosity reflected an inner reality. Adam and Eve lived out of a deep inner connection with their Maker; they reveled in His goodness and love. He was the source of their security, purpose, and joy. The hearts of these original divine image-bearers throbbed with the joy of God, and their bodies shone with divine light.

However, when sin entered, the lights went out.

And now Adam and Eve felt naked. Their hearts were flooded with emotions not known before: guilt, shame, and fear. There was an inner heaviness that weighed upon their spirit and dampened their joy. How could they remedy this situation? They had no way of recovering their original garment of glory. The best they could come up with was a makeshift garb made from raw material at hand: fig leaves. A rather *clumsy* solution.

Nonetheless, the idea caught on—and went viral. All down through history we have continued to camouflage our shame through a wide assortment of fig leaves—religious activity, charitable deeds, blame, and denial. Operation cover-up.

However, *nothing* really worked. We could not shake this sense that something was wrong. We could not fabricate a covering that would truly get rid of shame.

A Garment from God

However, on that fateful day in paradise, something hopeful happened. God sought out the couple wearing fig leaves and provided a much more suitable attire. A sacrifice took place, and our first parents were soon robed with tunics made of animal skins—tailor-made by the Creator Himself.

When those animals were slain in Eden, *what* was going through God's mind? Were there tears in His eyes and a lump in His throat? (If we could use such human terms to speak of Divinity.)

Did His thoughts turn to a future day when, on a Roman cross outside the walls of Jerusalem, His own Son would be sacrificed for a fallen race? Was He thinking of the moment when Jesus would take upon Himself the collective wrongdoing of the world so that Adam's prodigal sons and daughters could be clothed with the mantle of Christ's moral perfection?

The "best robe" in God's wardrobe was made available at the Cross. It was at Calvary that the great exchange took place. Jesus wore our sin so we could wear His righteousness.

Max Lucado comments:

> *The determining factor in your relationship with God is not your past but Christ's past; not your record but Christ's record.*
>
> —Tim Keller

He offers a robe of seamless purity and dons my patchwork coat of pride, greed, and selfishness.... Though we come to the cross dressed in sin, we leave the cross dressed in ... "garments of salvation" (Isa. 61:10).[1]

Quite a change of wardrobe for prodigal people! Our soiled apparel is replaced by the white mantle of Jesus' perfection. Our dismal track record is exchanged for Christ's reputation of goodness, kindness and virtue. In fact, we are dressed in *Christ* Himself, *"You have all put on Christ as a garment"* (Gal. 3:27 NEB).

A second-century Christian writer aptly remarked, "For what else could cover our sins except His righteousness?"[2]

The Cloak of Christ

Jesus taught us, *"And if someone wants to sue you and take your tunic, let him have your cloak as well"* (Mt. 5:40). Did Christ practice what He preached? He always did. Before being crucified, He was stripped of His garments. They took His "tunic," and since that day He has been offering a cloak of righteousness to all who will trust in Him. Paul celebrated this fact when he wrote: *"Standing then acquitted as the result of faith, let us enjoy peace with God through our Lord Jesus Christ"* (Rom. 5:1 WTN).

Garments of famous people are often sold for enormous prices. A red jacket used by Elvis Presley in the 1950s was sold at an auction for $34,529. Another, belonging to the rock musician Jimi Hendrix, went for $49,200. In 2008, a garment worn by the famous Marilyn Monroe was sold for $60,000. John Lennon at one time wore a military jacket. Someone paid $158,000 for it. At another auction, a dress used by Princess Diana was sold for $315,000.

If the cloak Jesus wore were offered for sale, how much would be paid for it? The price would go into the millions! Who would not want to be the owner of a coat that belonged to the Lord Jesus Christ?

However, His coat is not on the auction block.

It's offered for *free*.

It is placed on the back of each person who returns from the far country by putting his faith in Christ. The Father's voice rings out: "Bring out the best robe and put it on him."

Nothing gives God greater delight than to place the royal raiment of heaven upon the shoulders of returning prodigals. Jesus tells us "there is joy in the presence of the angels of God" (most likely referring to joy of God) as each repentant rebel is arrayed with a garment of glory.

Attired and Accepted

French writer Henri Barbusse tells of a conversation overheard in a trench full of wounded soldiers during the First World War. Knowing he only had moments to live, one of them said to his companion, "Listen, Dominic, you've led a bad life. Everywhere you are wanted by the police. But there are no convictions against me. My name is clear, so, here, take my wallet, take my papers, my identity, my good name, my life, and hand me your papers that I may carry all your crimes away with me in death."

God did something similar but far better for believers. Our past is off the record, and Christ's past is on. Our misdemeanors are no longer taken into account, His absolute wonderfulness is. Our imperfections no longer define us, His majesty perfection does.

Is that good news or *what?*

The believer in Christ stands before God with a new garment, a new status. He never has to wonder if the Father loves him or accepts him. He never has to ask himself if the past is going to be dredged up and held against him. It's totally off the record. The robe means he has been received back with full honors and privileges.

Properly dressed ... at last.

It is no surprise Isaiah the prophet spoke of this with such exuberance:

I am overwhelmed with joy in the Lord my God!
For He has dressed me with the clothing of salvation
and draped me in a robe of righteousness.
I am like a bridegroom dressed for his wedding
or a bride with her jewels. (Isa. 61:10 NLT)

Our wardrobe is complete. Christ's righteousness is now ours. We are robed with His perfection, cloaked with the glad assurance there is "no condemnation" (Rom. 8:1) and "no separation" (Rom.

8:38,39). We are just as accepted by God as Christ is, just as loved as He is (See Jn. 17:23,26.)

Can you believe a smile comes across God's face every time He thinks about you? That He rejoices over you with joy? (See Zeph. 3:17.)

Not when you get your act together. Not when you memorize the Bible. Not when you fast forty days and forty nights.

But right *now.*

Do you dare to believe it?

If you perfectly obeyed every command in the Bible for a hundred years, you'd be no more accepted with God than when you first trusted Christ.

And you'd be no more loved than you are right *now.*

Isn't it time you started living in the sheer marvel of it?

Author Robert Capon urges us to celebrate as those who "have put on the mink of righteousness, sat down in the Rolls-Royce of salvation, and are now just laughing themselves silly over the incongruous wonderfulness of it all."[3]

A Robe to Be Worn

Religion dictates: "clothe yourselves in piety and all will be well." The gospel, in contrast, cloaks us with a perfect robe—and piety follows. Every other religion teaches: "live right and God will accept you." The gospel offers God's acceptance and favor as a free gift on the basis of Jesus' record, not our record—and *then* we can start to live right. A total reversal!

The believer does not work toward the pleasure and acceptance of God. He lives *from* it.

Grace sets us on a journey; it teaches us to walk in the reverberation of forgiveness. Grace comforts and compels. It not only brings us into God's favor, it launches us into His service. Our new robe translates into a lifestyle of constant prayer, absurd generosity, unbridled goodness, radical holiness, buoyant thankfulness, and deep involvement in the material and spiritual well-being of others. Radical grace leads to radical living; it kindles holy fires (Titus 2:11-14).

The new attire alters everything—both how we stand before God and how we live before others. Paul stated: *"for all of you who were baptized into Christ have clothed yourselves with Christ"* (Gal. 3:27). Past tense. But there's something more. The apostle *also* speaks of "putting on Christ" as something to be done in the present. He exhorts us: *"But put on the Lord Jesus Christ, and make no provision for the flesh, to gratify its desires"* (Rom. 13:14 ESV). *"Put on then, as God's chosen ones, holy and beloved, compassionate hearts, kindness, humility, meekness, and patience"* (Col. 3:12 ESV). Christ-like qualities are our new dress code.

> *God's grace turns out men and women with a strong family likeness to Jesus Christ, not milksops.*
>
> —OSWALD CHAMBERS

It is highly doubtful the prodigal hangs his pigsty garb in his closet for occasional use. He is finished with those rags. He has no intention of wearing them again. Similarly, our patchwork cloak of selfishness, greed, and pride is to be replaced by garments of grace—we now are to wear *Christ*.

The Lord Jesus Christ, by virtue of His indwelling presence, provides the believer with the status of "rightness" with God (I Cor. 1:30; Phil. 3:9), and the grace to relate to others in a Christlike way. A complete makeover!

There is a tendency to think that the ardent freeness of grace should not be diminished or clouded by ethical demands. This is contrary to the logic of the gospel of Christ. The most striking thing about our Lord, as Lewis comments, is the union of great ferocity with extreme tenderness. We should not separate mercy and morality, or disconnect justification from sanctification. Both need to be stressed side by side in creative tension. It has been pointed out that "the essence of orthodoxy is paradoxy." We cannot overstate the vast abundance of grace or the strong demands it makes upon us.

We are now called to wear the regal robe that was purchased with blood and custom-made by God. It is our high privilege. We can relax within the luxurious folds of this magnificent garment. When our conduct is out of character for a member of heaven's kingdom, we must not throw off the royal robe. We should throw off the unrighteous behavior. We are learning to live in a new way. We are learning to enjoy the gift that was fashioned for us before the foundation of the world.

Wearing His Coat Well

Marie Chapian, in her book *Of Whom the World Was Not Worthy,* relates the story of the Yugoslavian Christian church's suffering under a corrupt church hierarchy during the Second World War.[4]

Chapian tells of an evangelist named Jakob who arrived in a village, and visited the home of an elderly man by the name of Cimmerman. When Jakob tried to speak to him about the love of Christ, the old man retorted that he wanted nothing to do with this God of love. He reminded the evangelist of the sordid history of the church in his town, a history replete with plundering, torturing, and the killing of innocent people.

"Men of the cloth tortured and killed my own nephew," he burst out angrily, "and you speak to me of a God of love!"

"My heart aches with you," whispered Jakob.

Then, reflecting on the atrocities committed in the village by men wearing sacred robes, the evangelist said, "Cimmerman, can I ask you a question? Suppose I were to put on your coat and then went out and stole from someone in the village. And suppose the police sighted me running off, and recognized your coat. What would you say if they came to your house and accused you of robbery?"

The old man was silent.

"Would you not deny it?"

"Of course!" retorted Cimmerman.

"But, they would say: 'Cimmerman, we have proof. We saw your coat. You are guilty.'"

The old man said nothing.

The parallel was clear.

How can we accuse God of evils done by men who wear religious robes but whose actions betray Him? When people act contrary to their faith, *they* should be blamed, not the God they failed to represent.

Cimmerman winced. "This talk is worrisome to me."

Each week Jakob walked ten kilometers to the village. He often stopped by Cimmerman's cottage. A friendship grew. They often spoke of spiritual matters. Jakob explained the need find peace with God by repenting and trusting in Jesus Christ.

Then, on a clear winter morning, the moment finally came when Cimmerman exclaimed, "Jakob, you have convinced me. Your God is real."

The old man knelt on the soil and surrendered his life to Christ. As he rose to his feet, wiping his tears, he embraced Jakob and said, "Thank you for helping me find God."

And then, pointing heavenward, he added, "You wear His coat very well."

PRAYER

Righteous Judge of all the earth, when we stood guilty, unworthy, and condemned, it was music to our hearts to hear You declare us righteous, through Jesus Christ our Lord. You have clothed us in garments of salvation, You have enfolded us in the righteousness of Your Son. Never again will we have to wonder if we are loved and accepted. Awaken our hearts to this astounding fact. Teach us to relax in the luxuriant folds of Your magnificent robe, and lead us to live in the joy of the justified. Fill our lips with Your praise. Enable us to lay aside all the cloaks and disguises of our old life. We are tired of twilight, falsehood, and the crooked way. Lead us into paths of righteousness. Empower us to walk in Your light and love. Through the grace of Jesus our Redeemer, amen.

Grace is … is Love favoring us
when we are not favorable,
loving us when we were not lovable,
accepting us when we are not acceptable,
redeeming us when, by all the rules of the book,
we are not redeemable.

—E. STANLEY JONES

Lord I crawled across the barrenness to you
with my empty cup uncertain in asking
any small drop of refreshment.
If only I had known you better I'd have
come running with a bucket.

—NANCY SPIEGELBERG

It is so extraordinary that it must be true.

—TERTULLIAN

CHAPTER THIRTEEN

The God of preposterous grace

*"... put a ring on his finger and
sandals on his feet."*

LUKE 15:22

When the prodigal makes his reappearance in the village, he strongly suspects it is *not* going to be a good day. When he nervously starts down Main Street, he braces himself for the worst. Black sheep of the family don't expect a *warm* welcome when they come home.

And then the craziest thing happens.

He is hugged, kissed, wept over, and given a robe of honor.

This is where the story gets *flipped*.

Such a total reversal in a narrative when the least likely thing happens is called by literary people a *peripety*. Tolkien came up with the word "eucatastrophe" to describe a sudden happy turn of events "which pierces you with a joy that brings tears." Aristotle spoke of it as the most powerful part of a plot when an action veers around to its opposite. He called it *peripeteia*.

The prodigal would call it a *miracle*—on the level of the creation of the universe.

He is absolutely stunned.

He deserves flogging—but the red carpet is rolled out for him. It doesn't make *any* sense! Surely they must be confusing him with somebody else. There must be a mistake.

But no, it *is* for him.

As a matter of fact, his elated father is *only* getting started. The presents keep coming. His generosity goes into overdrive and gains momentum. This is turning into a gift-fest.

When Giving Goes Wild

As Christ paints this picture, He dips his brush deep into His rich experience of His Father's loving generosity. Jesus referred to it elsewhere like this: *"You loved Me before the foundation of the world"* (Jn. 17:24). From eternity, Jesus has reveled in His Father's overflowing goodness.

And this unimaginable blessing is *not* just for Abba's Son. (This is the amazing part!) He wants others to join the banquet. That's *why* Jesus came. And that's why He's telling this story.

So look closely. You've *never* seen a God like this.

As the prodigal's mind reels as he tries to process what is happening, the father reaches out and clasps his hand. The boy stares in disbelief as the patriarch takes a ring and slips it on to his son's finger.

Now the hand that has tended pigs is wearing the family ring!

It is not simply an ornament. It is probably a signet ring with the family crest or seal, which would identify the wearer as a person of high standing in the household. It also confers the right to give orders and to carry out transactions in the father's name. This son is being given authority over the assets of the family. In essence, he now holds his father's credit card.

This is *not* the way we deal with scoundrels.

But this father is not done yet.

His son stands decked out with an elegant robe, a gold ring—and *not* so elegant bare feet. His footgear has been swapped long ago for food. He has made the journey home barefooted. This is the attire of a servant who is forbidden by law to wear shoes. Shoelessness is a sign of servitude. His boy needs shoes.

The father commands sandals to be brought, and in short order the boy with torn feet is fitted out with shoes that evidence his privileged status as a son.

In a matter of minutes the boy goes from bedraggled to bewildered. His lot in life has skyrocketed.

The Scandal of Grace

The news of this bizarre reception goes viral.

Neighbors hurry to the scene. They stare in disbelief as the rascal is given full public honors. Extravagant privileges are heaped upon him in what looks like a lottery win. A windfall. The perplexed Torah community gasps.

This is unheard of.

It is more than that: it is *shocking*.

It would come as no surprise if someone blurted out, "Wait a minute! Have you lost your mind? Don't you know where this kid has been? He has been living with the pigs. He has been living *like* a pig! How can you treat him as if he were the greatest son in the world?"[1]

But neither scorning neighbors nor wild horses can hold this father back. There's a fire in His bosom, a passion in His heart. And he's going to give this son the most outrageous welcome imaginable. *Nothing* will deter Him.

He can't find enough gifts to shower on the boy.

Admittedly, it's unwarranted. It's ludicrous.

But this parable is an attempt to describe the indescribable—what Paul referred to as the *"unsearchable riches of Christ"* (Eph. 3:8).

Jesus is saying: "Look at this crazy extravagance. I'm trying to show you how wildly generous my Father is. There are no words to describe it."

The squanderer who knows something of prodigal spending meets a greater prodigality in the generosity of his father.

The boy is clobbered by kindness.

It's the scandalous *peripety* of grace.

A Grace Moment

Grace is the word that sums up the heart-grabbing essence of the gospel.

> *The kingdom that Jesus preached and lived was all about a glorious, uproarious, absurd generosity.*
>
> —N. T. Wright

And the illustration that stands head and shoulders above the rest is found here in Jesus' parable.

Grace is divine prodigality gone wild. It is ridiculous generosity, reckless open-handedness, audacious extravagance. It is goodness on steroids.

Grace shows flagrant disregard for moderation, fairness, or bookkeeping. It dishes out in outrageous excess to those who don't have it together and have nothing to give in return.

One writer put it like this: "Real grace is simply inexplicable, inappropriate, out of the box, out of bounds, offensive, excessive, too much, given to the wrong people and all those things."[2]

Grace completely abolishes any idea of merit. It floods the undeserving with blessing. Grace is love shown to the unlovely, favor bestowed upon the unworthy. It is indiscriminating, uncoerced, and delightfully gratuitous.

It doesn't keep score.

The Grace of Giving

Some people are givers; others are takers. My wife is definitely a giver. She *loves* to give. We live in a part of the world where there is much poverty, and when Wendy sees a need, she goes out of her way to meet it.

Things in our house disappear mysteriously. Shirts, sweaters, jackets, shoes, blankets, and a variety of other items have a tendency of vanishing into thin air. When I look for one of my belongings, I am never sure if I will find it.

Recently it was my pillow. Before that it was my shoes. It has become exceedingly difficult to keep things in our home. Any one of our possessions runs the risk of falling prey to my spouse's passion for helping needy souls.

I'm learning to hold onto things *lightly*. I'm taking a crash course in it.

Some daring individuals practice extreme sports. Wendy practices extreme generosity. Don't get me wrong: I'm all for being charitable, but my kindhearted wife stretches the concept beyond all possible recognition. She gives new meaning to the term.

It brings to mind something Christ said: *"But when you give to the needy, do not let your left hand know what your right hand is doing"* (Mt. 6:3).

I think it's my wife's life verse.

She has learned something about radical grace.

Re-Entry Strategy

Grace is something the prodigal son has *not* anticipated, and likely does not understand (the rest of us don't really get it either!). When he first crafts his confession speech in the far country, he has included the strategic phrase *"Make me as one of your hired servants."*

Hired servants ranked even lower than servants. Servants had job security. Hired servants were simply day laborers who were taken on when extra help was needed. They were paid at the end of each day and informed if their services were required or not the following day. This is the position the prodigal has in mind. He is going to put in an application for the lowest job available.

It's his *bailout* plan.

He figures he might be able to negotiate a deal. It's true, he has bungled things badly, but it is nothing a stint of good hard work shouldn't fix. He'll roll up his sleeves and make amends for his bad performance. That should bring the old man around.

But, when the moment comes ... his plan is *sabotaged* by grace. He gets mugged by a patriarch.

The Unfinished Speech

There's so much hugging and kissing going on, the boy can't manage to get in a word. It's hard to talk in the middle of a tornado.

When he recovers from this onslaught, he stammers out his speech: *"Father, I have sinned against heaven and before you. I am no longer worthy to be called your son ..."*

That's as *far* as he gets.

Before he can blurt out the part about working as a hired hand, his father butts in, shouting orders to the servants.

The boy's great spiel gets *derailed.*

His father isn't listening. He's too ecstatic about his son's arrival.

Notice the sequence of events. The wayward boy is hugged, kissed, and welcomed *before* he utters a word. The pig keeper is warmly received *before* he is able to have a bath and change into clean clothes. And his plan to salvage his reputation by signing up as a farm laborer *never* gets put into words.

In fact, as gift after gift is lavished upon him, the whole idea is scrapped.

A Royal Reception

What prompts such an extreme welcome? This is right over the top. How do we explain it?

It's not the sincerity or the depth of the boy's repentance.

It has nothing to do with his skill in navigating around the roadblocks in order to get back into his dad's good graces. *Not at all.*

It has everything to do with the overflowing *goodness* of his father's heart.

There's a great lesson here.

Coming back to God is *not* about bartering. It's not a self-improvement program. It's not a reward system. It doesn't involve ledgers or score cards. It's not about religious recipes.

It's all about *grace*—inconceivable, uncalled for, undomesticated, mind-boggling grace.

Robert Capon said it like this: "We are saved gratis by grace. We do nothing and we deserve nothing; it is all, absolutely and without qualification, one huge, hilarious gift."[3]

The prophet Isaiah depicts God's grace as an outlandish food market where goods are "sold" for free. A *ludicrous* marketing strategy! In Isaiah 55 he summons everyone to come and freely load up their shopping carts from the inexhaustible supply—and there's no cash register! It seems too good to be true. Notice how the prophet describes this preposterous divine grace...

- Its wideness—*"Come, all you who are thirsty ..."* (v. 1)
- Its freeness—*"... without money and without cost."* (v. 1)
- Its goodness—*"Listen ... and eat what is good ..."* (v. 2)
- Its lavishness—*"... you will delight itself in the richest of fare."* (v. 2)
- Its wholesomeness—*"Give ear ... that you may live."* (v. 3)
- Its sureness—*"I will make an everlasting covenant with you ..."* (v. 3).

Grace is the most outrageous bargain that could ever be made in the marketplace. Instead of "buy now and pay later," the invitation is to come and buy as much as you want—and *never* have to pay. It would be a total game loser for supermarkets, but is the ridiculously generous offer made at God's market of grace. One person admitted, "Grace could never have been a man-made idea. It had to come straight out of heaven."

Grace and Religion

The scribes and Pharisees listening to Jesus were well versed in a performance based, brownie-point-earning, merit system. These chronic scorekeepers held the copyright on correct conduct. They had mapped out every segment of life and had turned it into a complicated game of religious hopscotch. They had a rule for everything. And by all appearances, they were racking up a lot of points in this behavior competition.

The Rabbi from Galilee was not the least bit interested in their religion of rules and had the bothersome habit of *breaking* many of them. He personified a wildly irreligious idea called grace. It rocked them back on their heels and *infuriated* them.

Religion and grace are polar opposites. It comes down to the difference between a salary and a gift—between what is earned, and what is freely given. Religion requires; grace provides. Religion is advice; grace is an offer. Religion commands, "Act this way." Grace proclaims, "God acted for you."

In his book *What's so Amazing about Grace?* Philip Yancey states,

> The notion of God's love coming to us free of charge, no strings attached, seems to go against every instinct of humanity. The Buddhist eight-fold path, the Hindu doctrine of karma, the Jewish covenant, and Muslim code of law—each of these offers a way to earn approval. Only Christianity dares to make God's love unconditional.[4]

"Christianity is the 'unreligion' because it is the only one in the world that does not demand our doing but our need," remarks one Christian leader.[5]

The Irreligious Messiah

It is significant that no one opposed Jesus' message of grace as strongly as the religious leaders. We can hardly blame them! Christ did not suggest how their religion could be improved. He did not say they were doing well but needed to pull up their socks on some minor points. He came to *abolish* religion. Grace does not tweak religion—it *shuts it down.*[6]

The idea *didn't* go over well.

The religionists had Him *crucified.*

However, they didn't quite manage to get rid of Him. The One who came to replace religion came back three days later with a clear message: grace is going to have the final word—*not* religion.

"Religion," according to Robert Capon, "is the human race's vain attempt to perfect some series of transactions that will con God into doing something about its plight."[7]

It's a misguided strategy concocted by humans that aims at buying or maintaining favor with the Almighty. It is the dim-witted notion that by doing certain odd jobs God seems to have an obsession for, we can get Him to overlook the nasty items on our track record.

Religious Recipes

Religions come in a thousand varieties, but they all boil down to *one* fundamental idea: DO THIS. They all pretend to have the secret formula for fixing our spiritual dilemma, but the message is always the same—it's up to *you.*

And there are multiple options on the religious menu: helping old ladies cross the street, dancing around bonfires, lighting candles, sacrificing chickens, subscribing to the right creed, bathing in holy rivers, attending church services, sleeping on a bed of nails, gritting our moral teeth, and doing pilgrimages on our knees. And if done with sufficient sincerity and frequency, we can persuade the Ruler of the Universe to be kindhearted to us.

Is that *really* how it works?

God needs to be "persuaded" to be good to us?

Take another look at Jesus' parable. It demolishes with seismic force the bogus premise of "religion."

The prodigal doesn't need to crawl home on his knees in order to win his father over. The clincher is not his "I'm sorry" speech or his deep repentance.

It *certainly* isn't because he is thrifty, brave, or hard-working. The boy is an absolute failure. He has done everything possible to *forfeit* his father's favor.

This is all about *grace*—undiluted, unfathomable, unwarranted, undeniable, high-octane grace.

Grace for Sinners

The prodigal parable erupted out of a context of Jesus associating with sinners. This troublesome practice, however, turns out to be the *best* news we've ever heard—grace is not for the faultless folk but for the *flawed*. It is for the incompetent, the unhealthy, and the unfinished. Imperfection is the only prerequisite. Christ didn't come to call righteous people but sinners to repentance (Lk. 5:32). Those who never glitched up, who admit only to moral success are out of luck. Sinners are the *only* ones He came for.[8]

According to Scripture we all qualify—*"there is none righteous, no, not one"* (Rom. 3:10). Nobody lives up to their own standards—let alone God's. "Not only are we all in the same boat, but we are all seasick," observed G. K. Chesterton. Sin is the default setting of Adam's fallen family. Although we carry the image of God, we are like a damaged work of art and, by definition, are all sinners.

> *There are two types of sinners in the world: those who know they are scoundrels, and those who have yet to realize it.*
>
> —ANDREW STODDARD

Tragically some (like the scribes and Pharisees) prefer not to classify themselves as such and find themselves at odds with Jesus. Such people mistakenly assume they have an outstanding credit balance in their moral ledger, and they expect to make it on their own. There is a shocking reversal in our Lord's stories they need to pay attention to: the humble are exalted, and those who have it all together are brought low. The blind have their eyes opened, and those who claim to see are made blind. The losers are ushered into the banquet, and the high performers end up outside. Grace is poured out *only* on those who don't deserve it. The rest are out of luck.

"We cannot ask God to repair what we will not acknowledge and own as being broken," pointed out one writer.

Those who have discovered that their personal "righteousness" is, in fact, a huge joke, are in an *excellent* position to experience grace.

Definitely, that's me. My personal life needs more than a little touching up around the edges. God alone knows the twisted motives that drive my best actions and the tangled mix of lust, ambition, and selfishness lodged in my heart. And that's just on a good day. I have no lack of opportunities to repent.

Repentance is what turning back to God looks like. It begins with the recognition that what we had assumed was the truth, was, in fact, a lie. What we had thought was the way of life, was, in fact, the way of death. Repentance involves discarding falsehood and embracing truth, removing masks and stepping into the light. It slays demons. It is a God-inspired, hope-charged catalyst for change.

The procedure is painful, like antiseptic on a wound. It feels like death, but the results are *life-giving*.

Under New Management

Repentance is *not* an emotion. It is a feet-on-the-ground kind of word, says one writer. It declares, "I was wrong, I am unable to manage life on my own, I desperately need God." It has been pointed out that "repentance is collapsing on Christ, not promising God you'll do better." It is the joyful acceptance of the liberating Lordship of Christ. "It is above all homesickness," says German theologian Helmut Thielicke. "not just turning away from something, but turning back home."[9] It spurns sin in order to enjoy the *greater* treasure of intimacy with God.

It is *not* our repentance that prompts God to be kind. It is God's kindness that prompts us to repent.

Repentance is by no means over when we find ourselves in the Father's arms. Perhaps, that's where real repentance takes place—and *continues* to happen. The closer we get to God, the greater our awareness of how tangled up by sin we really are. Karl Barth once said, "Sin scorches us most after it comes under the scrutinizing light of God's forgiveness and not before."[10] It is precisely in the light of God's acceptance that we can get real about the monsters we harbor inside.

The Greek word for repentance literally means "a change of mind." It is a recalibration of our way of thinking and living. Lewis declares: "Repentance means unlearning all the self-conceit and self-will that we have been training ourselves into."[11] It is an excellent way of getting that ball and chain off our leg. It makes a break with what is contrary to God's heart in order to live in joyful union with Him. Repentance is relational, liberating, scary, and ongoing.

Eugene Peterson makes this helpful comment:

> Confessing our sin isn't resolving not to sin anymore; it's discovering what God has resolved to do with us as sinners. And what he has resolved to do is tune us in to the foot-tapping songs of forgiveness and set our once-broken bones to dancing.[12]

Indeed, as J. I. Packer points out, "fellowship with God becomes a real and rich reality more and more, as one lives a life of repentance."

But there's *one* thing we should understand.

Repentance is *not* the means of negotiating divine favor.

It is *not* a way of softening God's heart. It is not His heart but *ours* that needs softening.

It is *not* a pre-condition for being received back.

Nothing we do makes us forgivable. Forgiveness is something *God* does. More precisely, it is something God *did* through His Son Jesus Christ.

Born in Eternity

Forgiveness rests solidly on a foundation the Bible describes as *"the Lamb slain from the foundation of the world"* (Rev. 13:8). This refers to the death of Christ at Calvary in the year 33 A.D. Scripture, however, refers to His sacrificial death as taking place *before* the universe even existed.

Our disastrous mutiny against our Maker did not catch Him off guard. In the mind of God, comprehensive provision was made for a fallen creation *long* before the need arose. The Cross was the divine corrective for human sin that provided the basis upon which all through history God could pour out grace upon the ill-fated supporters of the revolt. Grace is free because the Giver Himself has borne the cost. We are forgiven and accepted, not because we make amends, or promise to clean up our act, but solely because God's incarnate Son died and rose again.

Jesus Christ is the *grace-bringer.*

The gospel of grace is the stunning announcement that the whole mess caused by our sin has been fully fixed by God without a scrap of human assistance. Jesus has made a way for everyone to be welcomed home, just as they are, with all their brokenness and bedraggled-ness.

Transforming Grace

Graces accepts us—and it changes us. It introduces us into a relationship with the Grace Giver, a *transforming* relationship. We are called not only to *come* to Christ, but to *live* in Christ, and to *grow* to be like Him.

Grace reconnects and *redirects* our lives (Titus 2:11-14). We need both—and *both* are good news. No longer do we have to carry guilt, and no longer do we have to serve sin. Grace is a call to full-blown freedom. It is pardon *and* power to change.[13]

Lewis explains:

> The real Son of God is at your side. He is beginning to turn you into the same kind of thing as Himself. He is beginning, so to speak, to "inject" His kind of life and thought, His Zoe, into you; beginning to turn the tin soldier into a live man. The part of you that does not like it is the part that is still tin.[14]

Similarly, E. Stanley Jones writes:

> Grace binds you with far stronger cords than the cords of duty or obligation can bind you. Grace is free, but once you take it, you are bound forever to the Giver and bound to catch the spirit of the Giver. Like produces like. Grace makes you gracious, the Giver makes you give.[15]

The gospel is an invitation to freedom and joy. It frees us from empty, self-centered living. It disposes us to be open-handed and open-hearted. It teaches us to dance, to move to the glad rhythms of grace, to run free in the open fields of God's love. It calls us to live in the Father's house, to know the Father's heart, and to reflect the Father's love.

Grace in a Bolivian Prison

Jacinto (not his real name) was one of the worst serial killers in the history of Bolivia. He is believed to have killed more than 35 people.

Jacinto was caught and sentenced to prison, but before long he escaped. The law caught up with him again, and this time he was to be sent to a maximum security penitentiary.

The inmates rose up in protest. They didn't want this dangerous criminal in their prison. Prison authorities debated what to do with the man.

Pedro, a Christ-follower in the penitentiary, spoke up and said, "I will assume responsibility for him. Send him to us. He'll be under my care."

As a result, Jacinto ended up in the correctional facility where my wife, Wendy, frequently visits.

One day she was at the prison and Pedro asked her, "Would you come and talk to Jacinto?"

The three of them sat down together in a cell, and Wendy began to share about the love of God.

Jacinto was sure God's love or forgiveness could never be for him. Wendy assured him it was. She told him of a Savior who gave His life to make forgiveness possible. She explained there are no sins that can resist the cleansing power of His atoning death.

Like a drowning man seizing a rope, Jacinto clung to every word.

Before leaving, Wendy prayed.

When she opened her eyes, she saw tears streaming down the face of this hardened criminal.

God had touched his heart. He laid hold of the rope of the saving grace of Christ.

Not long afterward, Jacinto was sent to a new correctional facility in another city where security was much tighter. For some months, Wendy was unable to contact him.

About a year later, when our travels took us to that part of Bolivia, my wife, anxious to know how he was doing, went to see this new convert.

They met and Wendy sought to encourage Jacinto in his faith. He needed little encouragement. He was full of the joy of the Lord. He was excited about the things God was teaching him. Scripture verses poured out of him. It was evident the Lord was working powerfully in his life.

Many months went by, and finally Wendy was able to visit him again. Jacinto introduced her to several other prisoners. There were thirty serious and violent offenders in his section of the prison. The warden had feared this would be a very difficult group to manage and expected serious problems.

His fears were unfounded.

The prisoners had started to hold Bible studies. Jacinto had been designated as "pastor," and twenty-nine of them had already committed their lives to Christ! The once notorious killer is now helping people to find a new life in Jesus. No longer taking lives but saving them.

And this was now one of the most peaceful sections in the entire prison!

Before his imprisonment, Jacinto had been interviewed by the press, and the hardness of this young man had shocked the nation. Society wrote him off. The worst prison in Bolivia didn't want him.

But there is a force operating in the world that changes lives, heals hearts, dispels darkness, breaks chains, instills hope, and sets our feet on a higher path.

It's called *grace*.

It's the gospel in one word, declared Karl Barth. It is unexpected, unconventional, unwarranted, uplifting, subversive, liberating, and generous.

"Grace means you're in a different universe from where you had been stuck, when you had absolutely no way to get there on your own," explains one writer.[16]

The word most used to describe it is *amazing*.

And it's real.

Just ask Jacinto.

PRAYER

Gracious God, if there is one thing that should leave us aghast it is Your stubborn grace that is not conditioned by our worthlessness, deflected by our rebellion, or diminished by our waywardness. It sought us when we were running from You. Its strong pull trumps our foolishness and willfulness, and softens our stony hearts. It continues unfailing and unending, even when we look the other way. How can we ever praise You enough for your inexhaustible grace! Thank you for not being fair with us. Thank you for being outrageously generous, immeasurably kind, and scandalously good. Drive the wonder of this gospel deeper and deeper into our hearts. Continue to batter, bend, and melt the hardness within. Keep us from daring to assume that our good fortune is of our own doing or that our ability to serve is anything other than a gift. In the Name of the One who loved us and gave Himself for us, amen.

Learn to dance, so when you get to heaven
the angels know what to do with you.
—St. Augustine of Hippo

Where did we get the idea that religion is a stiff, dull, flat business,
all pursed lips and knitted brows and gloomy looks? … How did
we ever forget to dance and laugh and play—and live?
—Mark Buchanan

He perceived that under all there was a great joy:
a fountain of mirth enough to set a kingdom
laughing, were it to gush forth.
—J. R. R. Tolkien

CHAPTER FOURTEEN

The God who throws parties for prodigals

"Bring the fattened calf and kill it.
Let's have a feast and celebrate."

LUKE 15:23

The presents just keep coming, and the prodigal stands speechless. This staggering gift-fest has *not* been on his list of possible scenarios. His mind can find no logical explanation for this extravaganza.

But his dad isn't finished.

He has showered upon the boy every conceivable privilege a man could give his son, and now he tops it off with one more: a *banquet* in his honor.

And this isn't a last-minute idea. The servants are not told to find a good side of beef but to fetch "the" fattened calf. Preparations have been made long before. A young steer has been selected from the herd and placed in a stall on a special diet. The father has been *eagerly* awaiting this moment.

A Party For The Village

This is not simply a small family event. "Bring the fattened calf" indicates a major celebration was planned. Kenneth Bailey points out that the selection of a calf, rather than a goat or sheep, means the entire community is invited. It is going to be a mega-feast.

The call to celebrate echoes the "rejoice with me" expressions in the two previous parables when the sheep and coin are found. Understandably, the villagers are hesitant to receive the boy back. The father is having none of that. He is making public his joyful acceptance of his son, and he wants the *whole* community to follow suit.

There will be *no* party poopers in this village!

Christ's parable ends with the assertion it is "necessary" to make merry and be glad (Lk. 15:32). The situation demands it. If ever there were a moment for festivity—this is it! The return of the son is the ultimate joy-bringer and *not* celebrating was inconceivable. This party is a *must*.

One theologian writes, "After he spent all his inheritance on partying, who really thinks the prodigal son needed to go to another party? Well, Jesus, apparently."[1]

And so the whole community falls to making merry, with music, feasting, and dancing. A whole afternoon of wine, roses, and hilarity—the father will have it *no other way!*

The Confucius Version

There is a story told by Confucius of a young man who steals a large portion of his father's wealth and runs away from home. He squanders the money foolishly and finally ends up in desperate poverty. Through an intermediary, the boy appeals to his father to receive him back. The father agrees, welcomes his son, and prepares a great feast to celebrate.

Thus far Confucius' story sounds all too similar, but here it takes a strange twist.

In the middle of the banquet, all eyes are fixed upon the young man. There is a sinister smile on the face of the father, which broadens as a look of horror comes over his son.

The boy grasps at his throat, realizing too late he has been poisoned.

Confucius ended his tale with a warning: "So it shall be with every son who dishonors his Father."

What a contrast between this story and the one Jesus told! The banquet in Christ's parable is not a trick to deceive and inflict punishment. It is the spillover of the father's genuine joy overrunning its banks like a torrential flooding river. It is a powerful statement of the father's deep love and total forgiveness.

Jesus is saying: "So it shall be with every wayward son or daughter who returns home to my Father."

The God Who Throws Parties

Sadly, for many, God is like the grotesque father in Confucius' story—the foreboding terror. Ever since our departure from Eden, we were convinced He was eager to execute judgment on us. We thought He was waiting for us with a club.

We never dreamed He could be waiting for us with a *party*.

Christ calls us to *repent* of our wrong thinking.

He confronts us with a picture of a delirious God who dances in sheer delight at our homecoming. He tells us of a heavenly Father who commands a blockbuster celebration on our behalf, where joy abounds and music and laughter fill the air.

Jesus is saying, "Has it ever occurred to you that God might be like *that?*"

Henri Nouwen writes:

God rejoices. Not because the problems of the world have been solved, not because all human pain and suffering have come to an end, nor because thousands of people have been converted and are now praising Him for His goodness. No, God rejoices because one of His children who was lost has been found.[2]

"Rejoicing" is a recurring theme in Luke 15. In the first of the three parables we read, *"there will be more rejoicing in heaven"* (v. 7). The second states: *"there is rejoicing in the presence of the angels of God"* (v. 10). The third does not mention joy in heaven or angels celebrating. It paints a picture of gladness we would not believe if it were not Christ who told it.

The Prophets Saw This Coming

The Old Testament passage that comes closest to this is Zephaniah 3:17.

> The Lord your God is in the midst of you, a Mighty One, a Savior [Who saves]! He will rejoice over you with joy; He will rest [in silent satisfaction] and in His love He will be silent and make no mention [of past sins, or even recall them]; He will exult over you with singing. (Zeph. 3:17 AMP)

Notice what the prophet says about God's power. He is a "mighty" Savior who overcomes all obstacles to bring us back to Himself. It doesn't matter if the final cost involved is a sin-cursed death on a cross—His passion to get us back is strong. He is "mighty" to save.

The prophet Zephaniah also refers to His love. God has finally come to be where He always longed to be—in the midst of those who are the object of His affection. It brings Him boundless delight.

The phrase *"rest in His love"* evokes the image of a mother holding her precious baby. She kisses, caresses, and gazes at the tiny bundle of joy. She loves the little one more than anything in the world. Zephaniah describes God in a similar way; His heart bursts with love for His sons and daughters.

The Hebrew prophet alludes to the joy of God using several words—delight, gladness, rejoicing, and joy.

What motivates such exuberance? *"He will exult over YOU with singing."* His loved ones are the reason for His joy. To have us in His arms brings God unbounded delight.

> **Joy is the serious business of Heaven.**
>
> —C. S. LEWIS

Such is His joy that God breaks out in song. One translation reads "loud singing." Only here in the entire biblical record do we see God singing. His lost and found children have come home, and He is jubilant.

When the Father Sings

If we take the liberty of inserting Zephaniah's image into the parable Jesus told, we get something like this ...

In the middle of the banquet the father stands up and announces, "Ladies and gentlemen, this is a very special day for me. The deep longing of my heart at last has been fulfilled—my son has come home. Since words cannot express how delighted I am—please allow me to do so with a *song*. And I dedicate this song to my son—with all the love of my heart."

Everyone in the banquet hall listens in silent wonder as the father's voice rings out in rapturous singing.

There isn't a dry eye in the place!

And no one sheds more tears than the prodigal himself.

If you are a believer in Christ, has your heart begun to perceive the wonder of the fact that God rejoices over *you* with singing? This is the heart-stopping outcome of the gospel—the God of heaven singing over *you!* Singing His love to you. Singing because He cannot be silent, He cannot contain His joy. It sounds *too* good to be true, but inspired Scripture affirms it to be so.

Well might we appropriate the words of David: *"Such knowledge is too wonderful for me, too lofty for me to attain"* (Psa. 139:6).

The Celebrating God

Celebration had prominent role in Hebrew culture. The seven annual "feasts" prescribed by Mosaic Law made for a nonstop whirlwind of festival.

Mark Buchanan explains:

> These were not quiet, sedate, well-mannered little tea parties. They were raucous, shout-at-the-top-of-your-lungs and dance-in-the-streets, weeklong shindigs. The heart of our Father God welcomes the prodigal home, shouting to His servants, "Bring the fatted calf and kill it. Let's have a feast and celebrate!" That's our God.[3]

The prodigal's return is celebrated with *"music and dancing."* A band of musicians has been called in to provide live music (the only kind of music they had back then), and it appears the music is *lively*. Pretty soon feet are tapping and people are dancing. There is feasting and frolicking. This is a party with all the stops pulled out.

How Did *That* Get into the Bible?

People of a more reserved persuasion might have difficulty with this. "Jesus, shouldn't you be a little more careful with your words? A banquet? Fine. A barbecue? Great. Music? Excellent. But— *dancing?* Is that not going a little *too* far?"

Some believe that dancing is inconsistent with godliness.

So how then did the phrase: *"music and dancing"* make it into the Holy Scriptures? Surely this was a mistake. Perhaps the translators got it wrong. Should this *really* be in the Bible?

Did Jesus really say *"music and dancing"*?

I am afraid so. It's part of the original text.

Maybe Christ knew some things about God we don't.

Hebrews Love Dancing

Dance was an integral part of Hebrew culture. Not only did people celebrate weddings and military victories with dancing, it was also a way of praising God.

Miriam led the women in dance when the Israelites rejoiced at the crossing of the Red Sea. King David danced with great fervor as an expression of devotion to God. He wrote: *"You have turned for me my mourning into dancing"* (Psa. 30:11 NKJV).

Traditionally Hebrews did not dance in couples. Men danced together, women danced together, and so did the children. It was how they expressed their gladness. It was what happened when the community came together on happy occasions.

A Time for Merriment

It comes as no surprise that the word "dancing" shows up in the homecoming celebration in Jesus' parable. It would be surprising if it *didn't*.

We can imagine a group of people holding hands and moving merrily to the music. There is laughter and joy.

And no one is as joyful as the beaming patriarch. Probably no one dances as enthusiastically as him. His gladness is contagious. He is the life of the party. It is doubtful anyone could remember a celebration *quite* like this one.

What is Jesus saying?

Is He not telling us this is what His heavenly Father is *really* like? That He is a God who celebrates, a father who sings and dances, a God who cannot help but "make merry" when a prodigal comes home?

Abba's Son is expanding our understanding of the Almighty. He is not only the Holy One who reigns on high in majestic glory—He is also the *celebrating* God. He rejoices over prodigals with singing. Jesus wants the exuberant father of His parable to be a part of our mental picture of God.

The Divine Choreography

The early Greek theologians understood that there was something extraordinarily rich and beautiful about the togetherness of the Father, Son, and Holy Spirit. They came up with a fascinating word to describe this dynamic interaction: *perichoresis.*

It literally means: a circular dance.

Theologian David Bentley Hart describes this Christian understanding of God as "a *perichoresis* of love, dynamic coinherence of the three divine persons, whose life is eternally one of shared regard, delight, fellowship, feasting, and joy."[4]

German atheist philosopher Friedrich Nietzsche once said, "I could only believe in a God who knows how to dance." According to Christian belief—that's *exactly* what we have.

At the center of the universe, there is a *dance* going on.

God is not merely a powerful celestial monarch. Through His self-revelation in His beloved Son, a breathtaking richer, fuller picture emerges.

The matrix of everything is a Trinity that celebrates, a heavenly whirlwind of goodness, joy, and beauty, a choreography of love and glory.

The heart of reality is a *celebration*.

Creation was the staggering decision of God to share the eternal dance with humans. One theologian stated that God did not want to be God without us. The Creator made people in His image, and plans to expand the celebration of love and joy got underway.

The story got off track when Adam and Eve stepped *out* of the dance. Instead of learning the choreography of the divine dance, the rhythms of other-focused love and respect, they decided to run the party their *own* way. Chaos very quickly followed as dancers stumbled, slammed into each other, stepped on toes, and crashed to the floor instead of into waiting arms.

The beauty and harmony and goodness of the original dance gave way to selfish, loveless, and prideful maneuvers. It became *ugly*.

Trying to party without God is as foolish as trying to breathe without air, or to see without light. It doesn't work well.

Seeking the Lost

God so loved the world that He sent Jesus to bring us back into the dance. The Father's resolve to have us with Him was so strong that even a cross stained with the blood of His Son was not too high a price to pay. To those who receive Him as Lord and Savior, He gives eternal life—another way to say *perichoresis*.

The "banquet" metaphor is the one Christ most often used to describe His kingdom. In the previous chapter of Luke's Gospel, Jesus tells of a man who invited his friends to a banquet. When they all turn down his offer with silly excuses, the man sends his servants to go out and summon the poor, the homeless, and the disabled to the feast.

The banquet hall ends up being crowded with these unlikely guests, and others miss out because they foolishly preferred lesser matters (Lk. 14:15-24).

If someone misses out on God's kingdom celebration, they can only thank themselves. God desires *everyone* to be there (II Pet. 3:9). Tragically many turn down the invitation for ridiculous reasons and lose out on the most joyful party in the universe.

Buchanan again:

> Joy is *an acceleration of the rhythm of celestial experience.* Joy is a direct insult to the realism, dignity, and austerity of hell. If you think—as popular lore has it—that hell is the party place where you get to slap the backs and tousle the hair of all your pals, drink a Budweiser and dance the hokeypokey with them, you've got your addresses seriously scrambled.
>
> The party's up above.
>
> Down below? Grim, sour solemnity. Long, scowling faces. Endless scolding speeches. Much wagging of the finger, knitting of the brow, quibbling over minor points. Rivalry. Hostility. Envy. The very last place you'll find a party is in hell.[5]

A Party That Never Stops

"… *And they began to be merry*" (Lk. 15:24 NKJV).

The celebration commanded by the father starts, but Jesus never mentioned anything about it *ending*. As a matter of fact, this banquet *never* does. The festival of redemption goes on forever. The kingdom of God is going to be one huge never-ending celebration. No wonder we refer to it as *glory*.

David talked about it in one of his songs: *"At Your right hand are pleasures forevermore"* (Psa. 16:11 NKJV).

That sounds like a fabulous party!

Timothy Keller writes:

> Our future is not an ethereal, impersonal form of consciousness. We will not float through air, but rather will eat, embrace, sing, laugh, and dance in the kingdom of God, in degrees of power, glory, and joy that we can't at present imagine. Jesus will make the world our perfect home again. We will no longer be living "east of Eden," always wandering and never arriving. We will come, and the father will meet us and embrace us, and we will be brought into the feast.[6]

The story is told of John Hyde, a missionary to India known as Praying Hyde. This godly saint was approached by a woman who asked: "Mr. Hyde, are Christians allowed to dance?"

Hyde's answer took her by surprise.

He retorted, "Lady, I don't know how someone could be a Christian and *not* dance!"

Perhaps you need to grab one of those silly hats and join the party.

Heaven is not just the existence of joy, it is the increase of joy forever.

—SAM STORMS

PRAYER

Lord of the Feast, this story heightens our longing for the day when You will gather Your redeemed into the Banquet of the Kingdom, the joyful dance for which all things were made. Thank you, Lord Jesus, for turning our sadness into joy, our brokenness into dancing, our heaviness into hope. Unlock our hearts to rejoice in Your salvation. We look forward to the day when all inhibitions and limitations will be gone forever, and we will sing, and laugh, and dance with unbridled joy in the everlasting dance of the glory of God. We bless You that in this universe gladness will have the final word, and goodness will triumph. Holy Spirit, deepen our wonder, fill us with hope, and lead us in the way of the severely astonished in the breathless realization that the Father rejoices over us with singing. May the joy of the Lord be our strength in a world where we struggle and serve and stumble and live in the hope of coming glory. Through Christ Jesus, the Alpha and Omega of this outrageous bliss, amen.

You can more easily catch a hurricane
in a shrimp net than understand
the wild, relentless, love of God.
—Brennan Manning

The gospel is always bigger, more disruptive,
more liberating, more tenacious, and more healing
than we bargained for.
—Scotty W. Smith

Christianity, whatever else it is, is an explosion.
Unless it is sensational there is simply no sense in it.
Unless the gospel sounds like a gun going off
it has not been uttered at all.
—G. K. Chesterton

CHAPTER FIFTEEN

The God of scandalous mercy

"Meanwhile, the older son was in the field.
When he came near the house,
he heard music and dancing."

LUKE 15:25

J ust when a "they lived happily ever after" ending is expected, Jesus' parable veers off in a new direction. Shifting His gaze to the Pharisees and religious scholars in His audience, He continues His tale.

These men are about to get *broadsided*.

Not Everyone Rejoices

The father's party is in full swing, and that's when the elder brother shows up. He arrives home dusting his hands after a hard day's work and is startled to find a huge celebration is underway.

He asks one of the servants what is going on. *"'Your brother has come,' he replied, 'and your father has killed the fattened calf because he has him back safe and sound'"* (Lk. 15:27).

Upon hearing such stupendous news one would expect a shout of jubilation from the older son. Surely he will toss his shovel aside and dash into the party to give a hearty welcome to his long-lost brother.

Here the story takes another crazy twist.

> *The older brother became angry and refused to go in. So his father went out and pleaded with him. But he answered his father, "Look! All these years I've been slaving for you and never disobeyed your orders. Yet you never gave me even a young goat so I could celebrate with my friends. But when this son of yours who has squandered your property with prostitutes comes home, you kill the fattened calf for him!"* (Lk. 15:28-30)

The young man is furious and refuses to join the party. If anyone deserves a banquet it's *him*—not his brother who screwed up. And off he stalks.

Bellyaching at the Banquet

When the father comes out and appeals to his son, the boy explodes and launches into a tirade.

He is upset—and for good reason.

He cannot fathom how this loser of a brother could deserve a five-star celebration. How can you make a train wreck of your life and then expect a homecoming bash? It's not right. Forgiveness should not be dished out with such hilarious openhandedness. It's irresponsible.

The party pooper has a valid point.

He seems to be the only character in this story with a *good* notion of fairness and sound judgment.

Bunglers don't deserve banquets! Misconduct should not be rewarded in this fashion. The crazy celebration makes no sense. It is unjust, misguided, and unthinkable.

The feast is a *farce*.

Things have clearly gotten out of hand. It appears the old man has lost all sense of propriety. This is not a parable. It is a *travesty*. It makes a mockery of decency and shows contempt for God's law.

It is madness!

A Preposterous Party

The storyteller from Nazareth had an irksome habit of inserting an extreme element into His parables. In one of His stories, a debtor gets forgiven a sum of money that rivals the nation's foreign debt. In another, He has a farmer scattering seed crazily in every possible direction and on the most unpromising soil. In still another, He has farm workers getting paid more than ten times what they had coming to them. This "scandalous mathematics of grace" crops up constantly in Jesus' narratives.

But the prodigal story *takes the cake*.

Here we have a boy who has taken all the wrong turns. He is a father's worst nightmare. He disgraces the family, blows his inheritance, messes up badly, hits the skids, mucks around with pigs, and when the loser comes home—he gets honored like a hero! It's like striking out all season and then getting celebrated as the best hitter in the league.

Something is absurdly *wrong* with this picture.

The Gospel Is a Shocker

If we are going to come to terms with the God Jesus revealed, we will need to face squarely the *scandalous* nature of His mercy. There is an outrageousness to it.

The elder son sees this clearly—and it angers him.

It is not because his brother has been welcomed and forgiven that the stay-at-home son blows a gasket. That he could accept—maybe.

What he *cannot* accept is the *extravagance* of the welcome. The father has given his brother a robe, a ring, shoes, and a banquet! They *even* kill the fatted calf! (That is first-century lingo to say it is a blockbuster of a celebration.) And now the knucklehead is in there dancing up a storm at the party.

It goes beyond *all* reason and good measure.

One scholar expresses the elder brother's sentiments: "of course, let the penitent come home, … but to bread and water, not fatted calf; to sackcloth, not a new robe; to ashes, not jewelry; to kneeling, not dancing; to tears, not merriment."[1]

Definitely *overkill*.

Offensive Mercy

The New Testament repeatedly refers to the "scandal" of the Good News (Rom. 9:33; Gal. 5:11; I Pet. 2:8). The gospel not only redeemed, it also *rattled* people. It was offensive.

Hymn-writer Frederick Faber wrote:

There's a wideness in God's mercy,
Like the wideness of the sea.

Faber continues:

But we make His love too narrow
By false limits of our own;

And we magnify His strictness
With a zeal He will not own.

"Magnifying His strictness" was precisely the specialty of the Pharisees and scribes. They had it down to a fine art. They were experts in scrupulosity, skilled in fussiness.

They were the *only* ones who were getting it right!

These pious fault-finders were spreading the word that Jesus was getting it all wrong: *"But the Pharisees and the teachers of the law muttered, 'This man welcomes sinners and eats with them'"* (Lk. 15:2).

It was a put-down, spoken in contempt. Jesus' choice of table companions was reprehensible to the religious leaders, and they were defaming Him.

"Then Jesus told them this parable ..." (Lk. 15:3).

The prodigal story targeted a specific audience—it was the religious mudslingers. They were about to take a hit. This was Jesus' response to their smear campaign.

Throughout the Gospels an ongoing skirmish takes place between Christ and these religious bureaucrats. It is a clash between a *true* understanding of God (as shown in Christ) and a mistaken understanding of God (as seen in the Pharisees and scribes). This clash is the backdrop to Luke 15.

> *A God of grace will endlessly frustrate those who've built their lives upon an economy of merit.*
>
> —A.J. Swoboda

Conflicting Ideas about God

According to His critics, Jesus "did God" all wrong. The truth is that Abba's Son is the *only* one who ever "did God" right. Jesus was vexed and grieved at these religious snobs who totally misunderstood the nature of God. He once stated flatly, *"You do not know me or my Father"* (Jn. 8:19). The Rabbi from Galilee challenged their upside-down notions about His Father.

And here He goes for the *jugular.*

Notice how Jesus does it.

He artfully inserts the Pharisees and the scribes into His story. They are about to be faced with a spitting image of *themselves* in the obnoxious older son who does not want to celebrate with his "sinful" brother.

This is where Jesus rubs their noses in it.

The elder brother is a bona fide card-carrying Pharisee. Notice his words: *"I never transgressed your commandments at any time"* (Lk. 15:29 NKJV). He has kept the rules and done it all right. He has earned all the air miles. He has stopped at all the traffic lights. He hasn't strayed out of bounds like his brother—and he strongly feels he should be *rewarded* for that.

This fellow thinks it's all about bookkeeping and he is proud of his performance. According to all sensible accounting, *he's* the one who deserves the party!

This is *classic* Pharisaical theology.

Fuming about the Feast

When the prodigal son is reinstated with a welcome-home bash, the villagers in Jesus' story are probably aghast. This is *not* on their list of options.

The Pharisees thought, "The kid deserves to be taken out to the woodshed." The father says in effect, "You're right, but instead we're going to give him a banquet." The religious experts esteem that a time of probation would be appropriate. The prodigal's dad responds by throwing, without further ado, a blockbuster of a reception.

It is *disturbing*. The pious zealots are flabbergasted by this outrageous mercy. They don't like it one bit.

In his excellent book on the parables, Helmut Thielicke tells the story of setting his little son in front of a large mirror. The tiny fellow was too young to recognize the image on the glass wall, but enjoyed seeing the face that smiled back at him. Suddenly the boy's expression changed as he recognized the similarity of the movements, and he seemed to be saying, "That's me!"

Jesus was setting the Pharisees up for a "that's me" moment. In true elder brother style, they had been annoyed and angry about the way Jesus casually and freely shared meals with lawbreakers and losers. And now He tells of an irate brother fuming outside the father's banquet. It is a strangely familiar picture. Were these uptight Jews catching a glimpse of themselves in the mirror of Jesus' parable?

The Meaning of Meals

In first-century Palestine, table fellowship established social boundaries. The elite ate with the elite; peasants ate with peasants. People invited their social, religious, and economic equals to dine with them—*not* their inferiors. It was a way of defining who was in and who was out of their circle. Even the seating arrangements highlighted the relative social status of each guest.

However, for devout Jews, meals involved much more. They had taken on deep religious meaning.

The Pharisees were not of the priestly caste; they were laymen who earnestly sought to live out the holiness required by the Law of Moses. God had said, *"Be holy as I am holy"* (Lev. 11:44-45), and they took that *very* seriously. In their religious fervor they sought to practice, in non-temple settings, the ritual purity exacted of the priesthood. Temple etiquette became normative for *everyone*.

The Pharisees regarded the meal-table in their homes as an equivalent for God's altar in the Temple. Eating together was not simply about nourishment; it was a sacred activity laden with theological meaning. It meant fellowship with God.

An elaborate road map was followed to maintain the sanctity of the family altar. Table fellowship with a holy God required paying close attention to ritual washing and matters of "clean and unclean." It called for strict adherence to the dietary laws of kosher (meaning "fit"). Maintaining ritual purity had huge importance.

A vital concern for Jews was: *with whom can I eat?*

Food defined fellowship. All "unclean" outsiders were blacklisted. Contaminating contact with sinners was carefully avoided. There was a huge KEEP OUT sign on the fence of the inner circle of the righteous. Meals mattered.

Having lunch was about holiness.

Miffed about Meals

It is not surprising that Jesus' eating habits caused these Jews to hit the roof. They were shocked to see Him dine with delinquents and undesirables.

Basically Jesus' response was to shock them even more: "You accuse me of eating with sinners. You are absolutely right. That is precisely what I do. But, as a matter of fact, I not only sit down and eat with sinners, I rush down the road, shower them with kisses and drag them in that I might eat with them. It is much worse than you imagined!"[2]

For the Rabbi from Galilee to show up at dinner parties in the homes of despised and "unclean" tax collectors, like Matthew or Zacchaeus, was a *dangerous* move. He was accepting the worst of the untouchables as table companions. Not just the Pharisees, but *everyone* was shocked (Lk. 19:7). It really rocked the religious boat.

Some feared He was going to *capsize* the boat.

One writer went so far as suggesting that "Jesus got crucified because of the way He ate."[3] His wholesale acceptance of outsiders was threatening to the exclusive religious establishment. And it led to His death.

Doing Theology at the Table

Why did Jesus engage in such exasperating behavior? Could He not have toned it down a bit? What was He up to?

He was *altering* the theological landscape—forever.

He was revealing God as He truly is. He was giving us a new definition of Deity.

God is like Jesus.

His unmistakable message was: "You are misunderstanding God. You are misrepresenting God. He is not at all as you perceive Him to be. He is more shockingly beautiful than anything you can imagine. Let me show you what He's *really* like."

"Jesus brought a revolution in the understanding of God," writes Brennan Manning. "It is impossible to exaggerate the extravagance of the Father's compassion and love."[4]

In the ministry of Christ, the Old Testament command to *"be holy as God is holy"* gets expressed this way: *"Be merciful, just as your Father is merciful"* (Lk. 6:38). The Pharisees had reduced holiness to "pickiness." Jesus demonstrated the delightful, captivating loveliness of authentic holiness—a holiness that does not wear a prudish scowl but is compassionate, self-sacrificing, other-focused, and overwhelmingly beautiful. A holiness that hates sin, but loves the sinner to the point of giving one's life for him.

By eating with the lost and the broken, Jesus portrayed the wild intensity of the Father's love. His scandalous table-fellowship with sinners was a dramatic expression of the indiscriminate *wideness* of God's compassion. The multitudes excluded by the religious system of Jerusalem were welcomed by Jesus. The door of God's kingdom was thrown open to everyone.

Dallas Willard elaborates:

> The flunk-outs and drop-outs and burned-outs. The broke and the broken. The drug heads and the divorced. The HIV-positive and herpes-ridden. The brain-damaged, the incurably ill. The barren and the pregnant too-many-times or at the wrong time. The overemployed, the underemployed, the unemployed. The swindled, the shoved aside, the replaced. The parents with children living on the street, the children with parents not dying in the "rest" home. The lonely, the incompetent, the stupid. The emotionally starved or emotionally dead … Jesus offers to all such people as these the present blessedness of the present kingdom—regardless of circumstances.[5]

Jesus befriended "publicans and sinners"—and was vilified for it. He genuinely cared for them, knowing full well the price He would pay for doing so. One writer said, "For Jesus, salvation is having a seat at the table of grace and the transformation that happens there."[6] His love flowed out to sinners *before* they got their act together and even if they never did. He was much more eager to forgive than to condemn.

He scattered mercy in wild excess—as if He had an unending supply.

Because *He did.*

"*God's mercy,*" the psalmist declared, "*reaches to the heavens*" (Psa. 57:10). The Scriptures, for good reason, affirm over forty times: "*His mercy endures forever.*"

Puritan theologian Thomas Goodwin points out: "You shall not read in all the Scripture that God is rich in wrath, or rich in justice, or rich in power. He is only rich in mercy."[7]

It was the reckless liberality with mercy that scandalized the Pharisees. It was what offended the elder brother. It was too excessive, too generous, and too *free.*

It was *out of control.*

Over-The-Top Mercy

This divine extravagance is reflected in a term the apostle Paul used to describe grace. We get our English word "hyperbole," meaning an obvious exaggeration, directly from this Greek word *hyperbole.* The term literally means a throwing beyond, perhaps not unlike our phrase "to hit one out of the ballpark," when a batter slugs a baseball so hard it lands outside the stadium. "Hyperbole" is going beyond the ordinary, surpassing the usual limits, going into uncharted territory, over the top.

> *When grace seems excessive and love is absurd—we finally are beginning to fathom the gospel.*
>
> —JONATHAN MARTIN

In Ephesians 2:4 Paul uses the word *riches* to refer to God's mercy. However, there's a lavishness here that demands more extravagant language. The apostle takes another shot at it in verse 7, and speaks of *"the immeasurable [hyperbole] riches of His grace in kindness toward us in Christ Jesus"* (Eph. 2:7 ESV). There's a reckless abundance, a wild exuberance to the grace of God, that goes beyond anything we have ever heard of.

Notice upon *whom* this grace is bestowed: those who are *"dead in the trespasses,"* *"sons of disobedience,"* and *"children of wrath"* (Eph. 2:1-3). This is what our life was like without Christ. To such down-and-outers, God imparts new life and confers the honor of a privileged seat in heavenly places (Eph. 2:4-6). This is an extreme unruly outpouring of grace for prodigals.

But God is *only* getting started. Verse 7 goes on to say that *"in the ages to come"* there will be a "hyperbole" deluge of grace. There is so much of it that it's going to take eternal ages to get it all out. This is unheard-of excessiveness. God has an amazing grace-fest lined up. He is going to knock it clear out of the cosmic ballpark.

Such is the *riotous* abundance of His mercy.

Shocking Vastness

One of the great Bible expositors of the twentieth century, Martyn Lloyd-Jones, made this bold statement:

> If your preaching of the gospel of God's free grace in Jesus Christ does not provoke the charge from some of antinomianism, [a disregard for the law] you're not preaching the gospel of the free grace of God in Jesus Christ.[8]

"The gospel is always bigger, more disruptive, more liberating, more tenacious, and more healing than we bargained for," writes one author.[9]

What ever made us conclude that divine mercy would be restricted, limited, and *unscandalous?* Did we think that the one who taught us to give in *"good measure, pressed down, shaken together, running over"* (Lk. 6:38) would not do so Himself?

Did we expect that the grace of the Lord of the star-fields would *not* mystify the mind of earth dwellers?

Did we think that the mercy of the God of infinite greatness would *not* be of a shocking magnitude?

Did we suppose it would be a ripple and not a *tsunami?*

Robert Capon asserts, "Grace is wildly irreligious stuff ... any serious doctrine of grace is going to scare the rockers right off our little theological hobbyhorses."[10]

Frederick Buechner remarks:

> People are prepared for everything except for the fact that beyond the darkness of their blindness there is a great light. They are prepared to go on breaking their backs plowing the same old field until the cows come home without seeing, until they stub their toes on it, that there is a treasure buried in that field rich enough to buy Texas. They are prepared for a God who strikes hard bargains but not for a God who gives as much for an hour's work as for a day's. They are prepared for a mustard-seed kingdom of God no bigger than the eye of a newt but not for the great banyan it becomes with birds in its branches singing Mozart. They are prepared for the potluck supper at First Presbyterian but not for the marriage supper of the lamb.[11]

The "Mercy" of Allah

Some years ago, while traveling on a train, I struck up a conversation with a Muslim. I said to him, "I understand that Islam teaches that two angels follow each person around every day of their life. One records the good deeds, and the other keeps track of the bad deeds. At the final judgment the two angels read the books, and if the good deeds outweigh the bad deeds, that person will be allowed into heaven. Is that correct?"

My fellow traveler said, "Yes, that is correct, but I must add one detail—if the good deeds outweigh the bad deeds, Allah will be *merciful,* and allow the person into heaven."

With that clarification, I replied, "Let me tell you about the God I believe in." I told him the story of the Prodigal Son—a rascal whose bad deeds *far* outweigh the good ones. The boy wouldn't stand a chance at Allah's judgment. However, when he returns to his father he is given the most fabulous welcome imaginable. He receives preposterous mercy.

I said to the Muslim, "That's what my God is like."

He mumbled something about a similar story in Islam. It was clear, however, that the wild abundant grace of the gospel of Christ made the "mercy" of Allah look rather measly—hardly deserving of the term. The message of Islam was good advice, perhaps, but certainly *not* Good News.

The gospel is such a jaw-dropper that one is easily tempted to think that it couldn't possibly be as good as it is. Fifth-century Cyril of Alexandria admitted: "Indeed the mystery of Christ runs the risk of being disbelieved precisely because it is so incredibly wonderful."

Timothy Keller comments: One way to put the gospel in a nutshell is this. You are more wicked than you ever dared believe and yet, you are more loved and accepted in Jesus Christ than you ever dared hope.[12]

Capon put it this way:

> And if there is a God who can take the dead and, without a single condition of credit-worthiness or a single pointless promise of reform, raise them up whole and forgiven, free for nothing—well, that would not only be wild and wonderful; it would be the single piece of Good News in a world drowning in an ocean of blame.[13]

Scandalous mercy, indeed.

PRAYER

O God, we are easily confused about who You are. We are prone to believe in the score-keeping god of the Pharisees. The god who monitors conformity and clobbers sinners. Our hearts struggle to realize that the running, forgiving, banqueting father is You. We are so steeped in Pharisaical theology that we find ourselves outside the banquet, frowning, judging, and looking with disdain upon failing people who are the objects of Your love. How foolish to think we somehow earned or did something to deserve Your favor. Lord, we renounce our self-righteousness and pride. Sweep away the lies. May Your grace be our only boast. May our hearts become so mercy-soaked that we will not only welcome prodigals, but drench them with affection and draw them into Your loving arms. In the Name of the One who is the Friend of sinners, amen.

*I understand God's patience with
the wicked but I wonder how He can
be so patient with the pious.*

—GEORGE MACDONALD

*You can run from God either by
breaking His rules, or by keeping them.
The former says God doesn't own me.
The latter says God owes me.*

—TIMOTHY KELLER

*How long will it take before
we discover we cannot dazzle God
with our accomplishments?*

—BRENNAN MANNING

CHAPTER SIXTEEN

The God who calls us to join the party

"'My son,' the father said, 'you are always with me, and everything I have is yours. But we had to celebrate and be glad, because this brother of yours was dead and is alive again; he was lost and is found.'"

LUKE 15:31,32

A ruckus erupts outside the banquet hall. An angry fellow is raising his voice and making a scene—and it is the host's elder son! He can see no good reason for the celebration and absolutely refuses to come in.

The guests exchange uncomfortable glances.

Custom requires the presence of the older son. "At such a banquet the older son has a semi-official responsibility," explains Kenneth Bailey. "He is expected to move among the guests, offering compliments, making sure everyone has enough to eat, ordering the servants around and, in general, becoming a sort of mayordomo of the feast."[1]

Any objections should be postponed until later. They can be discussed in private when everyone has gone home. Meanwhile the celebration *must* go on—and the son's participation is crucial. He should be honoring his father.

Not *this* boy.

He isn't backing down. He is furious about the party and is giving his father an earful. The smart aleck has no qualms about humiliating his dad by quarreling with visitors present.

The loud outburst does not go unnoticed. Eyebrows go up. It is an awkward moment.

Pleading with a Party Pooper

It was unthinkable in first-century Jewish culture for a son to refuse to attend a major celebration put on by his father. And *highly* disrespectful.

The father has found it necessary to slip out of the banquet to attend to this "family crisis." He stands in the courtyard, reasons with the agitated son, and urges him to join the party. The tense of the verb indicates he *repeatedly* begs him to enter.

This is a demeaning act for the host of the great feast. His honor is taking a major setback—and it's happening in front of the *whole* community.

Furthermore, the young man does not address his father with the appropriate deference. Instead of saying, "Father," he brazenly exclaims, "Look here!" In a patriarchal society such behavior is way out of line.

We would expect the lord of the estate to explode at such insolence. A slap in the face would have been in order, perhaps a good thrashing. By all rights the patriarch should be sternly putting this impertinent upstart in his place.

Not this dad.

"My son," the father replies, "you are always with me, and everything I have is yours."

The father responds with gentle words. It's totally unexpected. The brash fellow has insulted and humiliated his father. The boy's appalling manners warrant a harsh response, but his dad bypasses the offense and patiently implores the son to join the party.

His humility surprises us. He seems totally unconcerned with defending his dignity. He has every right to command obedience, but instead he appeals to the hothead, and affectionately calls him "my son."

Unparalleled Patience

Jesus is giving us a fascinating sidelight on His Father.

Instead of demanding respect, He portrays God as *imploring*, not retaliating but appealing. Remarkable. The one who spoke the universe into existence patiently pleads with disrespectful creatures. He beseeches brats. Instead of putting an end to their insolence and arrogance, He *reasons* with them.

We don't expect the Lord of the universe to respond to defiance in this fashion.

This is a *very* unusual God.

In the Old Testament book of Esther, Queen Vashti was summoned by King Ahasuerus to attend a royal banquet. She dared to decline—not a good idea! The king *"became furious and burned with anger"* (Esth. 1:11). An invitation from a king is *never* a suggestion but a command. The queen was deposed.

Eastern monarchs were not known to be "long-suffering."

Not so the King of heaven.

God's unwearying patience with rebels is astounding. Such individuals have chosen a path leading to "everlasting destruction." The Father's obstinate purpose is to turn them to the way of "everlasting life," and to this end He entreats, rebukes, whispers, shouts, appeals, and waits. Even the disgrace and agony of crucifixion was not too *high* a price to pay.

Who has ever heard of a God like *this*?

"Loving humility is a terrible force," observed Fyodor Dostoyevsky, "it is the strongest of all things, and there is nothing else like it."[2]

Two Ways to Get Lost

There is more than *one* lost son in this parable. One left home; the other stayed. Both were alienated from their father—each in his own way. It was not the badness of the elder son that was the problem; it was his *"goodness."* It was not his sins that drove a wedge between him and his dad, but his self-righteousness.

The elder son is proud of his outstanding performance and thinks his father *owes* him something. The boy feels he has the right to determine how robes, rings, shoes, and fatted calves should be managed. And his father *isn't* going about it the right way!

Frederick Buechner comments on the elder brother:

> He is what Mark Twain called a good man in the worst sense
> of the word. He is a caricature of all that is joyless and petty
> and self-serving about all of us. The joke of it is that of course
> his father loves him even so, and has always loved him and
> will always love him, only the elder brother never noticed it
> because it was never love he was bucking for but only his due.[3]

Many suffer from an "elder son complex" and believe their morality gives them certain leverage with God. They think they have a right to be blessed and prospered and favored. They deserve entrance into heaven. They have worked hard, followed the rules, and God "owes" it to them.

As if the Owner of the universe could *ever* be "in debt" to anyone!

The only thing He "owes" any of us is the payment our countless sins deserve. *"The wages of sin is death"* (Rom. 3:23). That's what we *all* have coming. Thankfully God in His mercy has been holding back the full amount owed to us.

Eternal life is not something God *owes* anybody. It is a gift, not an entitlement. It is *only* through the mercy and grace of God. We don't earn it; we don't deserve it. We receive it by surrendering to Jesus Christ as Lord and Savior. It was fully paid for at the Cross. Period. No hired-hand nonsense. It's an unqualified gift.

The striving, the earning, and the deserving are irrelevant. Jesus makes it clear He doesn't care a fig about our balance sheet. It is not the high achievers but the unworthy who are welcomed with banners flying into the hilarious banquet of the God known as Abba (See Luke 15:7). In the kingdom of heaven *grace* reigns.

A Ridiculous Notion Called Grace

The high-performance son thinks his father is a bookkeeper. *"All these years I have served you, and you never gave me ..."* By hard labor he has racked up a lot of points on the credit side of the ledger, and he feels he has been shortchanged. He wants the father to review his record.

This fellow holds to a theology of retribution that says: "I give to you and you give to me." It's standard marketplace methodology. It expects a return on investments, a

> *The sad truth is that most Christians spend their entire lives trying to score points with Someone who is not keeping score.*
>
> —WAYNE JACOBSEN

paycheck for hard work. It's simple. It's fair. And *everyone* should play by the rules.

Even God.

And that's where we run into trouble. The Lord of heaven and earth does not play by our rules. He is not a prisoner of our market mentality. He does not subscribe to our tidy retribution theology of demerits and rewards.

The Father of our Lord Jesus Christ does *not* live in a world of retribution—He lives in a world of gratuitousness. He makes the sun to shine and the rain to fall on the just and unjust. He forgives rebels, scoundrels, and hypocrites. He throws blockbuster parties for prodigals who smell like pigs.

Righteousness is the foundation of His kingdom, but His favorite activity is a crazy idea called "grace." It's something we don't control, it defies measurement, and it's available to everyone.[4]

When Elder Brothers Balk

Kenneth Bailey points out: "The father's speech is ... primarily a cry from the heart for an understanding of grace."[5]

Grace is precisely what the older brother couldn't and *didn't* want to understand. With tongue in cheek, Robert Capon articulates the prayer of his grace-resistant heart:

> Lord, please restore to us the comfort of merit and demerit. Show us that there is at least something we can do. Tell us that at the end of the day there will at least be one redeeming card of our very own. Lord, if it is not too much to ask, send us to bed with a few shreds of self-respect upon which we can congratulate ourselves. But whatever you do, do not preach grace. Give us something to do, anything; but spare us the indignity of this indiscriminate acceptance.[6]

The gospel is not a try-harder program of ledgers and score-cards. God does not operate on the basis of "fairness." If He did we'd all be in the soup. He operates on the basis of grace—wild, unsettling, unreasonable, out-of-the-ballpark, risky, unfair grace. It levels the playing field for all the younger and older brothers of Adam's family. It opens wide the banquet hall doors to both deadbeats and religious diehards.

But the latter often balk at the sheer *freeness* of it all. Few things are harder to take than grace squandered on someone else—especially if they are not as holy as *we* are.

Capon described the older brother's reaction this way:

> He's angry about the party. He complains that his father is lowering standards and ignoring virtue. The music, dancing, and feasting are, in effect, condoning wrong behavior. And to that, Jesus has the father say only one thing: "Cut that out! We're not playing good boys and bad boys any more. Your brother was dead and he's alive again. The name of the game from now on is resurrection, not bookkeeping."[7]

The Eternal Party

Look closely at the picture Jesus is painting.

The party is in full swing. The father stands at the door appealing to a belligerent boy. His heart is breaking at the hardness of his son's heart. The father desperately wants him in the festivity, but his words fall on deaf ears. It's a heart-rending struggle, and a touching scene.

Don't *skip* past this incident.

It's more than a banquet on a Jewish farm. It has cosmic dimensions. It's a picture of the meta-narrative we are a part of, involving a celebration some refuse to attend. It reflects the divine drama being played out on planet Earth,

Let's step back to consider the big picture for a moment.

The famous atheist philosopher Bertrand Russell suggested that if we could penetrate to the center of the universe we would find a mathematical equation.

Not *exactly* a heart-warming proposition.

The Bible paints a radically different picture of ultimate reality. What is found at the heart of everything is a *celebration*—the eternal dance of the Trinity. The God who is Father, Son, and Holy Spirit has been forever caught up in a symphony of joy, goodness, and love that is beautiful beyond description. At the center of the universe is a God-fest of glory.

The Original Celebration

The matrix of all existence is not a formula, a machine, or a monastery—it is a fellowship, a *perichoresis*, an interaction of love.

It is so delightful, so exuberant, so marvelous, that the Three-in-One God could not keep it to Himself. He came up with an astonishing plan. He decided to create humans in His image and *incorporate* them into the Triune choreography of glory.

The plan got derailed by *sin.*

Sin hides the true nature of God (His infinite love and goodness) from our consciousness. A fundamental breakdown took place in our understanding of God. We turned from Him to search in other places for life, wholeness, and fulfillment, not suspecting that the answer to our longing for joy might be *God.* After all, what does "religion" have to do with *life?*

We thought the party was somewhere *else.* We were under the impression that God was strongly opposed to partying, and we tried to keep Him at a distance. We didn't want a cosmic killjoy around.

We were disastrously *wrong.*

Without knowing it, like blockheads we walked away from the only REAL party in the universe. We believed the lie, and we ended up lost and dead in our sins. We were duped.

Abba's Son came to us in our darkness. His incarnation brought God to us, His words declared Him, His deeds demonstrated Him, and His Cross revealed His heart.

God is more wonderful than we *ever* imagined.

Jesus declared that the kingdom of God was like a wedding reception, and invited people to the celebration (Mt. 22:1-4). He repeatedly described the kingdom in terms of a supper, a banquet, or a feast—it was His favorite metaphor.

This King loves to celebrate.

And He has not abandoned His original plan to include us in the eternal festivity.

By laying down His life, Jesus reconciles us to God, and by giving us His Spirit, He unites us with God. Thus Christ brings us back into the enjoyment of the Great Dance of abounding joy shared by the Father, Son, and Spirit. It's the party we were looking for.

It's the party we were *created* for.

The Entreating Father

The word Jesus employed in His parable to describe the father's pleading at the banquet door is used primarily to describe the activity of the Holy Spirit, the *Paraclete*. One scholar explains: "It is a coming alongside word. A wooing, inviting, welcoming, encouraging word that draws us into the singing and feasting and congratulating community of the lost and found."[8]

Jesus' parable concludes with one son inside the banquet and another outside. Now it is the "respectable" sibling who needs to repent. The patriarch wants them both in the happy celebration, but the older son is *not* about to give in. The father graciously urges the grumbler to reconsider.

Similarly our heavenly Father urges *every* outsider to join the party.

Listen to Capon:

> Grace is the celebration of life, relentlessly hounding all the non-celebrants in the world. It is a floating, cosmic bash shouting its way through the streets of the universe, flinging the sweetness of its cassations [serenade music] to every window, pounding at every door in a hilarity beyond all liking and happening, until the prodigals come out at last and dance, and the elder brothers finally take their fingers out of their ears.[9]

The Banquet of the Kingdom

> *When the God you worship turns water into wine to perpetuate a party that had begun to wind down, you don't belong to an austere religion.*
>
> —BRIAN ZAHND

The kingdom feast is entirely "on the house." *"Let the one who is thirsty come; and let the one who wishes take the free gift of the water of life"* (Rev. 22:17). This is the extravagant *freeness* of the gospel. It is not an upward struggle to attain. It is a heaven-sent gift (Rom. 6:23) that is *"without money and without cost"* (Isa. 55:1).

The gospel is a call to a joy-filled banquet. Christ's first and constantly repeated word in the Sermon on the Mount is "blessed" (Mt. 5:3). Helmut Thielicke points out that whenever the New Testament speaks of repentance, there is always great joy in the background.[10] Essayist F. W. Boreham wrote: "We make religion a drudgery, a grind, a slavery, when it should be a revelry, a festival, an everlasting song."[11]

The Kingdom and Hardships

There is something, however, we must understand. In a fallen world, believers not only celebrate—they often suffer. They tread a path of privilege and peril. Hardship and even martyrdom have been endured by Christ followers for two thousand years. Our Lord warned us it would be so.

It's part of living in a world that rejects our King. It's part of following a Christ who shouldered a cross and called us to self-sacrificing love. This entails laying down our lives for the gospel (Mk. 8:35), and for our brethren (I Jn. 3:16). It is as we lay down our lives that we find them again (Mt. 16:25). Our lifestyle is now defined by a cross.

We must not think that faith secures avoidance of adversities such as the ones mentioned by Paul in Romans 8—*"trouble or hardship or persecution or famine or nakedness or danger or sword"* (v. 35). The promise is *not* that we will be exempt from such hardships. The promise is that *none* of them can separate us from the love of Christ (vv. 38,39).

Though shaken by trials and fears, we belong to *"a kingdom that cannot be shaken"* (Heb. 12:28). Though we stumble and fall, we are safe in the hands of a love that will not let us go. And in that *firm* hope we rejoice.

Hugging Block Throwers

A preschool teacher called her students to put away their toys. Turning to one boy she asked, "Johnny, will you help me put your blocks away?"

The little fellow looked up and responded, "No."

Without skipping a beat the teacher replied, "Well, today I'll help you and perhaps tomorrow you will help me."

After storing the blocks, the teacher began to read a story to the children. Johnny picked up a block and threw it at her, striking her in the head.

The teacher turned and drew Johnny into her arms, saying, "Johnny, I suspect you are angry with me, and I'm angry with you, but we have to learn to talk with our mouths and not with our hands; and anyway, I need to hold you until I feel better about myself."

After a few minutes, he stopped kicking and fussing. She set him down and turned to the group. Johnny went back to play with the blocks. Shortly after, he returned, climbed onto her lap, interrupted the story she was reading, and said, "I like you."

We are very much like Johnny. Although we act like unruly block throwers, God doesn't write us off. He patiently and tenderly holds us in His arms, intent on breaking through to our willful hearts. Even when His words are stern—they are words of love. We are assaulted by grace—and it is hard to resist. Who can stay away from someone who sees everything wrong with you and loves you *all* the more for it?

A young man surrendered his life to Christ but struggled to break with his immoral past. When he finally turned from his old ways, he was asked *what* had happened. His response was: "I just could not continue to sin in the arms of mercy."

It is God's goodness that leads us to repentance (Rom. 2:4).

The Amazing Invitation

Few verses in the Bible are more remarkable than Revelation 3:20: *"Here I am! I stand at the door and knock. If anyone hears my voice and opens the door, I will come in and eat with him, and he with Me."*

"Here I am! I stand at the door and knock." This is *not* heaven's door, and *we* are not the ones knocking. This is the door of *our* hearts, and the *Lord of the universe* is doing the knocking! He is

not at the right hand of God in heaven. He is calling at the door of human hearts. Not demanding entrance but *knocking*. Awaiting a response from within.

"If anyone ..." It matters not who you are or where you've been. He knocks on every door.

"... hears my voice and opens the door ..." The door is opened from within, not battered down from without. He respects our choice.

"I will come in and eat with him ..." Can you imagine *that?* He wants to sit down and be your guest. Once He had table fellowship with tax collectors and sinners. Now He sits down to eat with *you*.

"... and he with Me." In the end *He* becomes the host, and we are the guests. He comes to dine with us with a view to bring us into in *His* banquet—the eternal banquet of the kingdom.

Capon put it like this: "He finds the door of every last one of us and lands the party on our porch. All we have to do is say yes to him and open the door."[12]

The Great Celebration

The gospel confers the unspeakable privilege of sitting where many kings and princes have not sat. It calls us to table fellowship with the Lord of glory. *"Indeed our fellowship is with the Father and with His Son Jesus Christ"* (I Jn. 1:3 ESV). It is a privilege God's sons and daughters can enjoy every day.

"He brought me to the banqueting-house, and His banner over me was love" (Song of Sol. 2:4).

To be a part this celebration is the greatest windfall of all. *"Blessed is the man who will eat at the feast in the kingdom of God"* (Lk. 14:15). Each guest finds himself overtaken by lavish forgiveness, ridiculous favor, and unrestrained love.

We noticed previously that Jesus said, "they *began* to be merry," but He did not say they *ever* finished. This party never ends. It goes on forever. Chesterton described it as "one eternal and uproarious banquet."

"If the Lord is our host at the great feast, then the sky is the limit," wrote Frederick Buechner.[13]

One theologian put it like this: "This is the eternal feast of heaven and earth. This is the dance of the redeemed. This is the laughter of the universe."[14]

How awesome is *that?*

Bookkeeping has been banned. No ledgers or scorecards allowed. This banquet is not for high scorers but for the *redeemed*— the lost and found. Some of us were pig keepers, others pigheaded. Some of us, like a sheep, were lost in the far country. Others, like a coin, were lost at home. The Father brought us back. We have no entitlements to claim, no merits to boast of. We celebrate the unspeakable mercy of God through our Redeemer Jesus Christ. It is a veritable grace-fest.

It is the ultimate Homecoming.

We are *commanded* to rejoice.

And it's time to get on with the party.

PRAYER

*O God, You never cease to amaze us. Your mercy, patience
and humility exceed our wildest thoughts. You are incessantly
saying to each one of us in our grumbling and complaining,
"My son/daughter, you're always with me and everything I
have is yours." You are constantly running toward us in the
gospel—inviting, imploring, entreating us to get on the dance
floor of Your grace, to enjoy the music of reconciliation, to sing
the songs of redemption. You summon us into Your banquet
and Your banner over us is love. You also call us to share Your
heart for broken lost people. Forgive us for having a faith that
does not translate into loving others, into caring for the weak
and the wandering. Change us by your grace. "Mess" with us in
any way necessary, that we might love quicker, deeper, and more
sacrificially in the joyful wonder of Your beauty, mercy, and
goodness. We pray in the name of the Christ of Calvary, amen.*

*To be a Christian means you become
a part of the most significant story
the world has ever heard.*
—STANLEY HAUERWAS

*Christianity is the story of how the
rightful King has landed and is calling us
to His great campaign of sabotage.*
—C. S. LEWIS

*You don't just read the stories
of the Bible, you live in them.*
—LEONARD SWEET

CHAPTER SEVENTEEN

The God who calls us into His story

W hat a magnificent story Jesus gave us in Luke 15! It is a tale of a father and son, of God and humanity, misery and mercy, death and life, heartbreak and joy. It encapsulates the saga of our planet and the miracle of the gospel.

And what an astounding God Jesus reveals to us!

We have contemplated with wonder the portrait of a Father, displayed on the canvas of a parable, painted by His Son. We have pondered a picture too beautiful for words.

It is more than a parable. It is the unveiling of Deity. It is heaven-sent truth. It is a revelation, an earthquake, a feast, a waterfall, a love story, a symphony, a tsunami, a homecoming, a thirst quencher, a game changer, an explosion of hope, and a healing balm for the wounds of our broken and flawed lives.

We have heard the music of another world seeping through the cracks of this one.

We knew the high and holy Lord reigns in unapproachable glory and majesty. What we didn't know is that He runs in wild abandon to clasp lost sons and daughters in His effusive embrace.

We knew He scattered galaxies in space, but we didn't know He throws blowout parties for pig-keepers and rebels. We knew about His holiness but not His hilarity. We have discovered Him to be both awesome and winsome. Terrifying and tender.

An Unfinished Story

There's only one thing lacking in Jesus' parable—a conclusion. The story ends abruptly with one issue left dangling. We don't know if the older brother gets off his high horse and joins the festivities or not. We don't know if the two brothers are reconciled. We are left to surmise.

On purpose.

Jesus wants *us* to finish the narrative. The whole point of His parable is that we not only hear it but step *into* it. He was not hoping to hear us say, "Great parable, Rabbi." He was challenging us to be a part of the story.

"Stories are verbal acts of hospitality," observed Eugene Peterson. The prodigal parable is precisely that.

Like the wardrobe that gave children entrance into C. S. Lewis' land of Narnia, Christ's words have the potential of drawing us into a wonderful new reality. They invite us into the Father's house, to taste and feel and experience life in His embrace, to live in God's Story.

J. R. R. Tolkien's words come to mind: "Too long have you sat in shadows and trusted to twisted tales and crooked promptings."[1]

Following the Right Script

According to Walter Brueggemann, everyone lives according to a social or cultural script that shapes their beliefs and behaviors. Since being scripted is unavoidable, the pressing need is to follow the *right* script: the biblical "counter-drama."[2] Scripture records the true mega-narrative that subverts the fictitious cultural scripts of this world and calls us back into the Real Story.

Living in God's Story requires that we allow Christ to recalibrate our thoughts about God. "All our prevailing images and understandings of God must crumble in the earthquake of Jesus' self-disclosure," affirms Brennan Manning.[3] If we do not listen to Jesus of Nazareth, that will not mean we have no beliefs about God. It will mean we will have *wrong* ones. Christ needs to be our definition of Deity.

Jesus confronts us with a God who is *not* what we expected—a God of shocking beauty, majestic humility, and holy compassion.

Abba's beloved Son gives us a ravishing glimpse of a God whose goodness is larger, deeper, wider, and more beautiful than we can imagine. He brings into view a love that is wild and dangerous and big and free.

Not at all like the God most of us had in our heads.

And *that* is precisely what lies at the root of this world's troubles. And how they began.

A False Picture of God

In earlier chapters we reflected on the fact that confidence in God's goodness is a *crucial* issue for human beings. The undermining of that confidence rocked the world of our first parents. They were subsequently unable to rely and lean on their Creator as their source of life. Like deep-sea divers cut off from their air supply, they desperately needed to find a new life source—and they began looking in all the *wrong* places.

A disfigured view of God is the *matrix* of all sin. It launches us into all kinds of wrongful, idolatrous behavior in a futile attempt to meet our innermost need for love, worth, affirmation, and security. We turn to counterfeit gods. We anxiously try to get *life* from achievements, possessions, or sensual pleasures.

And it *doesn't* work.

We were created to have the love of God poured into us and flow through us. "To say that I am made in the image of God is to say that love is the reason for my existence: for God is love," stated Thomas Merton.[4] However, when our mental picture of God is distorted, this abundant life shuts down. Disconnected from love, we turn elsewhere to satisfy our inner thirst.

We become addicted to *idols*.

And idols don't give life, they *suck* life from us.

The Truth about God

Jesus came to us in our darkness. Through His life and death He put on display the beauty, goodness, and love of God. He shattered the lies about the Lord of glory that kept us messing up in the far country or slaving to get into His good graces. He told us who God really is. Abba's Son is the living, concrete, unerring, captivating revelation of the Father. He is the *truth* about God.

We never dreamed God was so wonderful.

"You will never find a more relieved person in all the world than me when I discovered that God was just like Jesus Christ," a well-known author exclaimed.

The gospel calls us to resolve in our minds that *God is as beautiful and loving as Jesus.* Jürgen Moltmann writes: "When the crucified Jesus is called 'the image of the invisible God,' the meaning is that THIS is God, and God is like THIS."[5] He is a God of unfathomable love who gave His life for sinners on a God-forsaken cross. *This is what God is like.*

The most important thing we can now say about God is this: *God is like Jesus.*

"Anything that one imagines of God apart from Christ is only useless thinking and vain idolatry," cautioned Martin Luther.

E. Stanley Jones elaborates:

> The gospel begins with Jesus, the Incarnate. If you don't begin with Jesus, you don't begin—you don't begin with anything except roads with dead ends. We know little or nothing about God, and what we know is wrong, unless we begin with Jesus. If you do not see God in the face of Jesus, you see something other than God—and different.[6]

The un-Christlike God is no fun to live with. He always wears a frown, always demands more. You never make the grade. When you have the wrong God, you have someone who doesn't care about your *heart.* He cares about your performance, and you can *never* do enough.

In Jesus, God shows us God. That I believe, is the whole secret of the Christian faith.

—BEN MYERS

It's exhausting, and you either work yourself into the ground, or you bail out.

Getting "Life" from God

Our relationship with God needs to be built solidly on the fact that His character is fully reflected in Jesus the Messiah who gave His life for us. This is where true spirituality happens. This provides firm ground for assurance, and enables us to live life in a liberated way that is born out of gratitude and joy, rather than fear and guilt.

The truth about God liberates us to find *life* in God. Jesus came to reveal the Father and reconnect us with Him as our life source. The gospel is concerned with the core issue of our relatedness to God, with whether we are alive to God or dead to Him. The father in Jesus' parable twice describes his lost son as "dead" (Lk. 15:24,32). The gospel does not aim at making bad people good, but at making dead people alive.

"*But because of his great love for us, God, who is rich in mercy, made us alive with Christ even when we were dead in transgressions ...*" (Eph. 2:4,5).

The issue is not betterment but *resurrection*. It is not a matter of tidying up the edges; it is coming to life at the center.

The Bible says: "*Whoever has the Son has life; whoever does not have the Son of God does not have life*" (I Jn. 5:12).

This is not just about going to heaven. It is about life with God here and now. It is often termed "eternal life." Jesus explains: "*Now this is eternal life: that they know you, the only true God, and Jesus Christ, whom you have sent*" (Jn. 17:3). Eternal life is relational. It is not something we *possess* on our own; it involves connectedness with God. It is the restoration of the spiritual intimacy for which we were created.

Eternal life implies receiving life from God, as a branch on a grapevine derives its vitality from the plant (see John 15:1-12).

It means living life energized by His love.

This can only take place to the extent that Jesus becomes the lens through which we see God. As our false images of deity collapse before the incarnate portrayal of the Father, our hearts are freed to turn and trust and leap for joy. As we see the glory of God shining in the face of Jesus Christ (II Cor. 4:6), we are inspired with child-like confidence to run into the open arms of the Father.

Living in God's Story

This revelation of God's love allows us to breathe a new air of freedom, to abandon our anxious self-assertion, to sense we have truly come home, and to drink of the fountain that imparts life to our souls.

We can abandon trying to get life from what one biblical prophet called "broken cisterns" (Jer. 2:13). We no longer need to scrounge for fulfillment by being better, smarter, more attractive, more successful, or more spiritual than others. We have found the *source* of life. We have been embraced by eternal love. We can live out of God's fullness rather than our emptiness.

One author explains:

> Having a Father like this moves one to action. Such enormous love overwhelms. Like the man who found a treasure in the field, the Father's children are swept off their feet with great joy in the presence of such incomprehensible forgiveness. This dramatic act on the part of the Father energizes a chain reaction. The children get caught up with this love and pass it on. They are merciful as He is merciful. As He loved, they love. Because the disciple has been forgiven, He can forgive. This gratitude for God's vast acceptance is the motive for action in the Upside-Down Kingdom [of God].[7]

By faith in Christ we obtain grace and we give grace. We receive enough love from God to be able to love others even when they don't love us back. We can bless those who curse us, do good to those who hate us, go the second mile, and forgive seventy times seven. We are enabled to do so by drinking from a fountain that will never run dry (Jn. 7:37,38). We are living in a love that will never let us go (Rom. 8:38,39).

When we surrender to Him, we surrender to Love, we surrender to Life. When we submit to Him, we find true freedom.

Compassion and affection for others emerge. We spread goodness. We practice righteousness. We love holiness. The death-defying, joy-giving beauty and sweetness of the gospel leads us to take up our cross and follow Christ.

And in the process we find *life*.

We are not truly alive until we live in love.

N. T. Wright stated:

> Once we have been grasped afresh by the love of God in Jesus liberating us from our own idolatries so that our work for the kingdom may be free from distortions of our own making, then we must lift our eyes to the world around and see the new work that awaits us.[8]

Missionary theologian Lesslie Newbigin put it this way:

> The logic of mission is this: the true meaning of the human story has been disclosed. Because it is the truth, it must be shared universally. It cannot be private opinion. When we share it with all peoples, we give them the opportunity to know the truth about themselves, to know who they are because they can know the true story of which their lives are a part.[9]

The three parables of Luke 15 are Christ's answer to the question: Why are you eating with sinners? The stories make one truth very clear: *lost people matter to God.* His heart beats with compassion for each one.

And now those who were once lost and now found are called be a part of God's search-and-rescue operation.

One Bible teacher says: "The Pharisees listening to Jesus learned what we often forget: faithful followers of Christ aren't on earth to assign blame; we're here to free the trapped, bandage the wounded, help the hurting, and celebrate homecomings."[10]

A Profound Mundane Incident

In the first chapter of John's Gospel Jesus is introduced as the Messiah, and two of John the Baptist's disciples turned to follow Him. Jesus suddenly spun around and asked, "What is it you want?" They were caught off guard and didn't know what to say. Finally one of them blurted out, "Where are you staying?"

Not *exactly* a deep theological question.

Jesus replied, "Why don't you come and see?" And the two spent the rest of the day with Him.

This incident seems totally mundane. Nothing like the remarkable miracles we get in the rest of John's Gospel. Did the author throw this paragraph in as mere filler? Why mention this humdrum episode?

Then it *dawned* on me.

This is no humdrum conversation. It sums up the message of the entire book of John. The apostle John loves to use different levels of meaning in his writings—and he does so here.

John has a lot to say about where Jesus "was staying." Although Nazareth was where He lived most of his life, Jesus had a more important dwelling place—*"The only begotten Son, who is in the bosom of the Father ..."* (Jn. 1:18).

On the inside, Jesus lived in His Father's embrace. That was his *heart* address. He dwelt in the daily enjoyment of his Father's love.

Jesus responded to the inquiry by saying, "Come and see."

A New Place to Live

Where does He take these disciples? That's what the rest of the Gospel of John is all about. Through His words and miracles Jesus leads them into a deeper knowledge of the Father. He wants them to *know* Him, which in biblical terms refers to an intimate, personal, interactive relationship. He wants to take them to *live* where He lived—inside the Father's embrace.

He wants *all* of us to live there.

In John 15:9, Jesus declared, *"As the Father has loved me, so have I loved you. Now remain in my love."* In essence He is saying, "I live in the constant awareness and enjoyment of my Father's love, and I have shared that love with you. You've seen it, tasted it, and enjoyed it. This is where I live—and it is where I want *you* to live."

We are called to live in a *place of love.*

When Jesus tells them to "remain" in his love, he employs the same Greek verb the disciples used when they asked, where are you "staying?" It means "to take up residence" as opposed to "occasionally visit." His followers are to live their lives where the Son of God has always lived His—inside the Father's love. *That* is to be their permanent home.

> **To know that the Lord of the universe loves you is the strongest foundation that any human being can have.**
>
> —Tim Keller

Our response to Christ's commands does not cause His love for us to diminish or increase, but it affects our practical *enjoyment* of it. To live in His love means learning to live as Christ lived and to love as Christ loved. Our delight in Christ's love deepens as we overflow to others with the same radical, no-strings-attached, Calvary-like love that God gives to us. In order to live in the Father's love, we must share it.

In John 15:11 Jesus adds, *"I have said this to you so that my joy may be in you, and your joy be complete."*

What does Jesus' "joy" consist of? It comes from knowing, enjoying, and sharing His Father's love. Abba's Son now says, "This joy is not just for me. It's for you. My joy is going to be *your* joy. Live in the full enjoyment of My Father's love."

This is the privilege, *not* of those who achieve outstanding performance, but of those who, in all their unworthiness, have cast themselves on the mercy of Christ. It is for those who have responded to the gospel with faith and repentance and have landed securely in the Father's embrace.

That's where we are now called to live.

The Main Concern

The overriding goal in the Christian walk is learning to *rest in* and to *reflect* the love of God. This is what we were created and redeemed for—*to participate in God's love and life and joy.* The Bible calls it "abiding in Christ."

This is not something I claim to have mastered. I am growing and moving forward and sometimes wavering and stumbling—but my heart has found its home, and I'm learning to live there.

Our fundamental job description comes down to this: *We are to live each day in the awareness that we are constantly engulfed in God's loving presence.*

This is no easy task.

George MacDonald once said that every day we have to fight the God-denying look of things. We live in a fallen world where evil and lies run riot. Evangelist Dwight Moody affirmed there is nothing in the Bible the Enemy would so much like to blot out as the truth of the Love of God.[11] We will be assailed by doubts, fears, trials, and tears, and we must learn to stand our ground and fight the good fight of faith.

Author John Eldredge alerts us to this struggle: "The story of your life is the story of the long and brutal assault on your heart by the one [Satan] who knows what could be, and fears it."[12]

We will need to learn to pray, to nourish our hearts with the Word of God, to renew our minds, to listen to the Spirit's whispers of love, and to walk with others of like faith.

A Home and a Journey

One writer explained:

> Life with God involves, not only a home, but a journey. A
> home provides security and comfort, a journey involves
> adventure and uncertainty; it entails going somewhere,
> learning, growing, and changing. It is a journey into the heart
> of God.[13]

In the course of a dinner party conversation, Albert Einstein was asked by a young lady, "What is your profession?"

"I devote myself to the study of physics," replied the white-haired scientist.

The girl looked at him in astonishment. "You mean to say you study physics at your age?" she exclaimed. "I finished mine a year ago."

"Faith is never something 'finished' which one could smugly boast of possessing," stated Helmut Thielicke. "No, faith is always traveling a definite way, a particular road."[14]

The apostle Paul described it like this: *"I press on to take hold of that for which Christ Jesus took hold of me"* (Phil. 3:12).

To be sublimely loved and outrageously blessed launches us on a quest. We have tasted and seen that God is good—and we want to experience more of this sacred romance. We long to explore it, live in it, savor it, grasp it, delight in it, share it, and celebrate it. "Thirsty hearts are those whose longings have been awakened by the touch of God within them," remarks Tozer.[15]

Author Madeleine L'Engle declares:

> What I believe is so magnificent, so glorious, that it is beyond
> finite comprehension. To believe that the universe was created
> by a purposeful, benign Creator is one thing. To believe that
> this Creator took on human vesture, accepted death and

mortality, was tempted, betrayed, broken, and all for love of us, defies reason. It is so wild that it terrifies some Christians who try to dogmatize their fear by lashing out at other Christians, because tidy Christianity with all answers given is easier than one which reaches out to the wild wonder of God's love, a love we don't even have to earn.[16]

Living in the Father's Love

When Jesus launched His public ministry at His baptism, His Father had one word for Him. It was not a word about strategy, guidelines, or ministry focus. It was a word about son-ship: *"You are my beloved Son, in whom I am well pleased"* (Mk. 1:11). And with those words resounding in His ears, Jesus launched into three years of service that changed the world. He lived enjoying and sharing the Father's love.

We can accumulate spiritual insights, study theology, and acquire ministry skills, but if we have not heard *this* word from heaven, we are not ready to serve. We need to hear what the Father says to each of His children, the word our hearts were made to hear: *"You are my beloved son, you are my beloved daughter, in whom I am well pleased."*

If that word hasn't reached our hearts, our service will become an arduous attempt to *earn* His love. If we are not confident of His acceptance, we will try to work for it.

And it will be burdensome and exhausting.

Living for God is not about earning His favor; it is about *enjoying* and *spreading* God's favor.

Keller reminds us:

> God does not love us because we are serviceable; He loves us simply because He loves us. This is the only kind of love we

can ever be secure in, of course, since it is the only kind of love we cannot possibly lose.[17]

Finishing the Parable

Ultimately each of us is faced with writing our own ending to Jesus' unfinished parable. As either younger or elder brothers (or sisters), we are confronted with the need to respond to the God Christ told us about. What is the conclusion that we give to this famous story?

The younger brother returns home. What about the elder brother? Does he finally come around?

One can only hope so. Wouldn't it be great if Jesus' story ended with the following scenario?

"My son," declares the father, "the banquet is going ahead—with you or without you." All at once the elder son falls silent. Gazing at the firm gentleness of his father's face, he is suddenly overcome with a flash of self-awareness, and something inside crumbles. What an obnoxious snob he has become! What ugly attitudes he has displayed!

Casting aside his foolish pride, he throws himself into his father's arms, imploring his forgiveness.

The doors of the festive hall open and the father emerges, his arm wrapped around his elder son, both faces beaming. All eyes turn in their direction, and surprised murmurs of approval sweep across the room.

Spotting his younger sibling, the elder brother pushes through the crowd, clasps him in his strong arms, and whispers, "Welcome home, my brother." The two embrace for a long time, sobbing for joy. Tears flow.

There are few dry eyes in the place.

One of their friends hurries over to insist the brothers join their dance. The two are quickly pulled into a circle of young men who are leaping and laughing and swirling in typical Jewish fashion.

The happy occasion has just got *happier.*

The father sits and looks on, his eyes glistening, his heart bursting for joy.

He has longed for this moment for a *very* long time.

The Open Invitation

Christianity tells us we are part of a story that has an Author. It tells us He is good—indisputably, overwhelmingly, irresistibly good—and He is the source of everything that is beautiful and worthwhile and true. He created us to play a role in His story and placed in our hearts a deep longing to know Him. Christianity warns us there is a villain and dangers and distortions and perversions of the truth. It declares that tragedy, evil, and chaos have been defeated in Jesus Christ. It calls us to believe that the gospel is not only the greatest truth—but the most *wonderful* one of all. It invites us to become the beloved sons and daughters of the Writer of the story.

Could there be anything more astounding than *that?*

It would make this book worth writing if God used it to prompt one more person to join the eternal banquet. I hope you have caught a glimpse of the beauty of God and sensed the gladness of the feast of the redemption. I trust you have heard the sound of music and excitement and laughter that floats through the night air from a great celebration. This festivity is what Christ followers mean by salvation—the supreme causing for rejoicing in this universe. To miss out on it is the *greatest* tragedy of all.

To trust the Lord Jesus Christ is to choose life. It is to embrace joy. It is to abandon our trivial stories and enter the banquet of the magnificent, eternal, ridiculous, overwhelming love of God. The only other alternative is to starve—*forever.* There is only *one* place where hopes are realized, hearts are fulfilled, and joy is unending. It is in the Father's house. It is where, as Tolkien said, "everything sad is going to come untrue." It is where redeeming grace is celebrated by the laughing, leaping, praising company of the lost and found.

There is a seat with your name on it. What are you *waiting* for?

John Chrysostom, in the fourth century, said it well:

The table is laid: come all of you without misgivings.
The fatted calf is served, let all take their fill.
All of you share in the banquet of faith:
All of you draw on the wealth of his mercy.[18]

PRAYER

Lord God of unrestrained goodness, thank you for authoring the most incredible love story of all. Thank you for sending light into our darkness. We have seen Your beauty in Your Beloved Son, and we have heard the music of Your grace. Never did we imagine You were so wonderful. We are left speechless, breathless, and grateful. Savior of the world, we gladly surrender to Your love. Save us from our sin, our waywardness, and our self-deception. Teach us to live within the Father's strong embrace and to walk in Your ways. Free our hearts of all that is a traitor to Your redemptive purposes until we love as You have loved us, and we stand for others in their need as You have stood for us in ours. Teach us to live gratefully and grace-fully within the clasp of a love that will not let us go, through the Lord Jesus Christ, our only hope and glory, amen.

ENDNOTES

THE PARABLE—LUKE 15:1-32

1. This rendering of Luke 15 is from THE MESSAGE, by Eugene H. Peterson (Colorado Springs: NavPress, 1993).

INTRODUCTION

1. Timothy Keller, *The Prodigal God* (New York: Dutton, 2008), 101.
2. From New Century Bible, cited on website: http://www.studyjesus.com/Life_of_Christ/64_Prodigal_Son.htm (accessed Jan. 26, 2016).
3. Kenneth E. Bailey, *Poet and Peasant and Through Peasant Eyes* (Grand Rapids, MI: Eerdmans, 1983), 41.
4. N. T. Wright's meditations for Lent on Matthew 13, goo.gl/YE7Zc (accessed Jan. 26, 2016).
5. G. Campbell Morgan, *The Parables and Metaphors of our Lord* (London: Marshall, Morgan & Scott, 1943), 187.
6. Kenneth E. Bailey, *Poet and Peasant and Through Peasant Eyes* (Grand Rapids, MI: Eerdmans, 1983), 158.
7. George Murray, *Jesus and His Parables* (Edinburgh: T & T Clark, 1914), 163.
8. George Buttrick, *The Parables of Jesus* (Grand Rapids, MI: Baker Publishing, 1973), 189.
9. J. C. Lavater (1741–1801), Minister of the gospel at Zurich.
10. A. W. Tozer, *The Knowledge of the Holy* (New York: Harper & Row, 1961), 9.

CHAPTER ONE
THE GOD WHO LOOKS LIKE JESUS

1. Quote from Anthony de Mello, http://www.brainyquote.com/quotes/quotes/a/anthonydem169894.html (accessed Jan. 16, 2016).
2. John Henry Jowett, *The Friend on the Road and Other Studies in the Gospels* (New York: George H. Doran Company, 1922), 116–8.

3. Philip Yancey, *What's So Amazing About Grace? Participant's Guide* (Grand Rapids, MI: Zondervan, 2000), 22.

4. Donald Miller. Twitter post. 22 Mar 2013. https://twitter.com/donaldmiller/status/315147134456459264.

5. Eugene H. Peterson, *The Contemplative Pastor: Returning to the Art of Spiritual Direction* (Grand Rapids, MI: Eerdmans, 1989), 32.

6. Michael Spencer, *Mere Churchianity* (Colorado Springs, CO: Waterbrook Press, 2010), 218.

7. Eugene H. Peterson, *Traveling Light: Reflections on the Free Life* (Downers Grove, IL: InterVarsity Press, 1982), 35.

8. Gregory A. Boyd, *Benefit of the Doubt: Breaking the Idol of Certainty* (Grand Rapids, MI: Baker Publishing Group, 2013), 62.

9. William Blake, *The Marriage of Heaven and Hell* (first published 1790).

10. A. W. Tozer, *The Root of the Righteous* (Harrisburg, PA: Christian Publications, 1955), 13.

11. Baxter Kruger, *Across All Worlds* (Vancouver, BC: Regent College Publishing, 2007), 17.

12. A. W. Tozer, *Ibid.*, 13.

13. Thomas A. Whiting, *Sermons on the Prodigal Son* (Nashville, TN: Abingdon Press, 1959), 35.

14. F. W. Boreham, "18 December: Boreham on Ludwig van Beethoven," http://www.thisdaywithfwboreham.blogspot.com/2006/12/18-december-boreham-on-ludwig-van.html (accessed 10 Jan 2015).

15. From Mike Reeves' sermon "The Trinity and Mission." http://www.theologynetwork.org/christian-beliefs/doctrine-of-god/starting-out/the-trinity-and-mission.htm (accessed 10 Jan 2015).

16. Judah Smith, *Jesus Is: Find a New Way to be Human* (Nashville, TN: Thomas Nelson, 2013), 26.

17. Victor Hugo, http://www.consolatio.com/2005/02/written_beneath.html (accessed 10 Jan 2015).

18. Fyodor Dostoevsky, "Letter To Mme. N. D. Fonvisin" (1854), as published in *Letters of Fyodor Michailovitch Dostoevsky to his Family and Friends* (1914), translated by Ethel Golburn Mayne, Letter XXI, p. 71.

19. Luther gives us this advice: "There is nothing more dangerous than to speculate about the incomprehensible power, wisdom, and majesty of God … Begin with Christ. He came down to earth, lived among men, suffered, was crucified, and then He died, standing clearly before us, so that our hearts and eyes may fasten upon Him. Thus we shall be kept from climbing into heaven in a curious and futile search after the nature of God. If you ask how God may be found, who justifies sinners, know that there is no other God besides this man Christ Jesus. Embrace Him, and forget

about [trying to figure out] the nature of God." Martin Luther, *Commentary on Galatians* (written in 1539).

20. S. D. Gordon, *Quiet Talks about Jesus* (New York: Eaton & Mains, 1906), 171.

21. A. J. Swoboda. Twitter post. 12 Sep 2014. https://twitter.com/mrajswoboda/status/510538860162732032.

CHAPTER TWO
THE GOD WHO IS FATHER

1. In a world where sovereignty and authority have a bad name, it is helpful to note that God's sovereignty is nothing like that of Pharoah, Caesar, or Stalin. It is not about raw power. It is, as John Newton said, "another name for the unlimited exercise of wisdom and goodness." God's sovereignty centers, not in His control, but in His love. It is the self-sacrificing sovereignty of the God who wore a crown on a cross at Calvary, who lays down His life to redeem rebels, who turns evil to good in the gospel. His sovereignty is cruciform.

2. Timothy George, *Is the Father of Jesus the God of Muhammad?* http://www.christianitytoday.com/ct/2002/february4/is-god-of-muhammad-father-of-jesus.html (accessed 17 Mar 2017).

3. Michael Reeves, *Delighting in the Trinity* (Downers Grove, IL: InterVarsity Press, 2012), 9.

4. James I. Packer, *Knowing God* (Downers Grove, IL: InterVarsity Press, 1973), 182.

5. George MacDonald, *Unspoken Sermons*.

6. Tim Keller. Twitter post. 12 Aug 2015. https://twitter.com/timkellernyc/status/569890726349307904.

7. Belden Lane, *The Solace of Fierce Landscapes: Exploring Desert and Mountain Spirituality* (New York: Oxford University Press, 1998), 53.

8. The Psalm that declares, *"The LORD reigns, let the nations tremble"* is found right alongside another that says, *"Shout for joy to the LORD, all the earth"* (Psa. 99:1; 100:1). This God evokes both holy trembling and happy shouting. In His presence we are constrained not only to bow down but also to dance, to be awestruck, and joy-filled. Neither reverence or rejoicing should be absent. A fascinating and powerful combination.

9. Eugene H. Peterson, *Living the Resurrection* (Colorado Springs, CO: Tyndale House, 2006), 16.

10. Brennan Manning, *The Signature of Jesus* (Colorado Springs, CO: Multnomah Books, 1996), 155.

11. Michael P. V. Barrett writes: "Our sonship rests on a love that never began as well as a love that will never end. In eternity, before the beginning of

time and obviously before the beginning of us, God chose to make us His children. The gospel was not God's afterthought or even His forethought; it was His eternal thought." *Complete in Him: A Guide to Understanding and Enjoying the Gospel* (Bingley, UK: Emerald House Group, 2000), 170.

12. George MacDonald, *Ibid.*

CHAPTER THREE
THE GOD OF EXTREME GOODNESS

1. Dwight Pryor, "The Prodigal Son—The Story of a Loving Father," *Return to God Magazine*, Vol. I, No. 2, p. 12.

2. John Piper, *Future Grace, Revised Edition: The Purifying Power of the Promises of God* (Colorado Springs, CO: Multnomah Books, 2012), 74.

3. Richard Sibbes, *The Complete Works of Richard Sibbes,* Vol. 6 (Edinburgh, 1863), 113.

4. C. S. Lewis, *Screwtape Letters* (New York: HarperCollins, 2001), 39.

5. Walter Brueggemann, "The Liturgy of Abundance, The Myth of Scarcity," http://www.religion-online.org/showarticle.asp?title=533.

6. Nicholas Wolterstorff, *Lament for a Son* (Grand Rapids, MI: Eerdmans, 1987), 80.

7. Jürgen Moltmann. Twitter post. 26 Dec 2015. https://twitter.com/karlbarthfordum/status/680912906456666112.

8. Wolterstorff, *Ibid.*

9. John R. W. Stott, *The Cross of Christ* (Downers Grove, IL: Inter-Varsity, 1986), 335.

10. Timothy Keller, "My Faith: The danger of asking God 'Why me?'" http://religion.blogs.cnn.com/2012/08/04/my-faith-the-danger-of-asking-god-why-me/ (accessed 16 Jan 2016).

11. Peter Kreeft, "God's Answer to Suffering," http://www.peterkreeft.com/topics/suffering.htm (Accessed Jan 11, 2014).

12. Lesslie Newbigin, *Truth and Authority in Modernity* (Valley Forge, PA: Trinity Press, 1996), 15.

CHAPTER FOUR
THE GOD WHO GRANTS DANGEROUS FREEDOM

1. The author is indebted to Jay Kesler for his insights on this story.

2. Henri J. M. Nouwen, *The Return of the Prodigal Son: A Story of Homecoming* (New York: Doubleday, 1994), 44.

3. Eugene Peterson, *Christ Plays in Ten Thousand Places* (Grand Rapids, MI: Eerdmans, 2005), 78.

4. Frederick Buechner, *The Magnificent Defeat* (New York: HarperCollins, 1985), 88.

5. Douglas John Hall, *God and Human Suffering, An Exercise in the Theology of the Cross* (Minneapolis, MN: Augsburg, 1996), 156.

6. Cited by William Curtis Holtzen in: "Fide: A Relational Theology of the Faith of God" [D.Th. diss., University of South Africa, 2007] http://uir.unisa.ac.za/bitstream/handle/10500/2550/thesis.pdf.txt?sequence=2.

7. C. S. Lewis, *Mere Christianity,* 145.

8. Philip Yancey, *Disappointment with God: Three Questions No One Asks Aloud* (Grand Rapids, MI: Zondervan, 1988), 75.

9. Bo Jinn, *Utopia, The Secular Delusion* (Kindle version: 2013), 463.

10. Sarah Ban Breathnach, *Simple Abundance* (New York: Grand Central Publishing, 1995), 51.

11. From an essay by Dorothy L. Sayers in *Christian Letters to a Post-Christian World* also available under the title *The Whimsical Christian: 18 Essays.*

12. Brent Curtis & John Eldridge, *The Sacred Romance* (Nashville, TN: Thomas Nelson, 1997), 78.

13. C. S. Lewis comments in *The Problem of Pain* (New York: HarperCollins, 1996 [1940]), 86: "The possibility of pain is inherent in the very existence of a world where souls can meet. When souls become wicked they will certainly use this possibility to hurt one another; and this, perhaps, accounts for four-fifths of the sufferings of men."

14. Philip Yancey, *Reaching for the Invisible God* (Grand Rapids, MI: Zondervan, 2000), 56.

15. Theologian David Bentley Hart comments: "There is, of course, some comfort to be derived from the thought that everything that occurs at the level of secondary causality—in nature or history—is governed not only by a transcendent providence but by a universal teleology that makes every instance of pain and loss an indispensable moment in a grand scheme whose ultimate synthesis will justify all things. But one should consider the price at which the comfort is purchased: it requires us to believe in and love a God whose good ends will be realized not only in spite of—but entirely by way of—every cruelty, every fortuitous misery, every catastrophe, every betrayal, every sin the world has ever known; it requires us to believe in the eternal spiritual necessity of a child dying an agonizing death from diphtheria, of a young mother ravaged by cancer, of tens of thousands of Asians swallowed in an instant by the sea, of millions murdered in death camps and gulags and forced famines (and so on). It is a strange thing indeed to seek peace in a universe rendered morally intelligible at the cost of a God rendered morally loathsome." David Bentley Hart, *The Doors of*

the Sea: Where Was God in the Tsunami? (Grand Rapids, MI: Eerdmans, 2005), 98.

16. Frederick Buechner, *Wishful Thinking: A Theological ABC* (New York: HarperCollins, 1993), 149.

17. Nicholas Loudovikos, "Hell and Heaven, Nature and Person. Chr. Yannaras, D. Stăniloae and Maximus the Confessor," *International Journal of Orthodox Theology* 5:1 (2014). Available at http://orthodox-theology.com/media/PDF/IJOT1.2014/Loudovikos.pdf, 32. (accessed Aug. 22, 2016).

18. J. I. Packer, *Knowing God* (Downers Grove, IL: InterVarsity: 1973), 139.

19. C. S. Lewis, *Mere Christianity,* 139.

20. Robert Farrar Capon, *Kingdom, Grace, Judgment* (Grand Rapids, MI: Eerdmans, 2002), 132.

21. Henri J. M. Nouwen, *Bread for the Journey* (New York: HarperCollins, 1997), Dec. 16.

22. N. T. Wright, "God, 9/11, The Tsunami, and the New Problem of Evil," Transcript of N. T. Wright's May 18–19, 2005, lecture at the Church Leaders' Forum, Seattle Pacific University, http://spu.edu/depts/uc/response/summer2k5/features/evil.asp (accessed Jan. 16, 2016).

23. S. Craig Glickman, *Knowing Christ* (Chicago, IL: Moody Press, 1980), 89.

24. Annie Dillard, *Teaching a Stone to Talk: Expeditions and Encounters* (New York: Harper & Row, 1982).

25. C. S. Lewis, *Mere Christianity,* 38, 39.

CHAPTER FIVE

THE GOD WHO MADE PLEASURE POSSIBLE

1. Dallas Willard, *The Divine Conspiracy* (San Francisco: HarperCollins, 1998), 62.

2. C. F. Wishart, *The Book of Day* (New York: Oxford Press, 1935).

3. Philip Yancey, *Soul Survivor* (New York: Random House, 2001), 55.

4. Karl Barth. Twitter post. 28 Nov 2013. https://twitter.com/k_barth/status/724192672525615109.

5. G. K. Chesterton, *Irish Impressions* (New York: W. Collins Sons & Co., 1919).

6. G. K. Chesterton, cited by William Oddie, in *Chesterton and the Romance of Orthodoxy: The Making of GKC, 1874–1908* (Oxford: Oxford University Press, 2008), 150.

7. Jürgen Moltmann, *A Broad Place: An Autobiography* (London: SCM Press, 2007), 350.

8. From a sermon delivered by C.H. Spurgeon, http://www.ccel.org/ccel/spurgeon/sermons40.li.html (accessed 16 Jan 2016).

9. Hugh Evan Hopkins, *Charles Simeon of Cambridge* (Eugene, OR: Wipf & Stock, 2011), 203.

10. Philip Yancey, *Soul Survivor,* 55.

11. Ravi Zacharias, cited in "Christian Apologist Ravi Zacharias Answers: What Is the Greatest Lie Facing Today's Culture?" http://www.christianpost.com/news/christian-apologist-ravi-zacharias-answers-what-is-the-greatest-lie-facing-todays-culture-106997/ (Accessed Jan. 27, 2016).

12. C. S. Lewis, *The Great Divorce* (New York: HarperCollins, 2001), 92.

13. C. S. Lewis, *Mere Christianity,* 40.

14. C. S. Lewis, *The Weight of Glory, and Other Addresses* (Grand Rapids, MI: Eerdmans: 1977), 14.

15. Timothy Keller, *Walking with God through Pain and Suffering* (New York: Penguin Group, 2013), 117–8.

CHAPTER SIX
THE GOD WE CANNOT LIVE WITHOUT

1. William Shakespeare, *Hamlet,* Act IV, scene 5, line 78.

2. J. I. Packer, *God's Words* (Grand Rapids, MI: Baker, 1981), 71.

3. Karl Barth, *Deliverance to the Captives* (New York: Harper & Brothers SCM Press, 1961), 146.

4. In the Bible, the harmful effects of sin are depicted more as consequence than as direct divine retribution (Psa. 7:14-16; 9:15; Jer. 2:19; 4:18). This is not a tidy tit-for-tat arrangement, but the fact that sin, as a general rule, brings regret, indignity, pain, and ruin. Someone put it this way: "Sin turns you on and then turns on you." Divine judgment is generally the normal outcome of our actions; it is God withdrawing and giving us over to our evil choices (Rom. 1:18-32). This is how God judged His Son for our sin at the Cross; He withdrew and hid His face (Mk. 15:34). During this present age of grace what God appears to do most of the time is to *hold back* the full lethal effects of our sins. When He occasionally ceases to restrain evil, He is said to be "judging." One of the complaints most often voiced in Scripture is that God seems too reluctant to intervene in judgment: *"Lord, how long will the wicked, how long will the wicked triumph?"* (Psa. 94:3 NKJV). "If you struggle with the idea of a loving God judging people," asks Amy Orr-Ewing, "have you really faced the darkness of the world?"

5. E. Stanley Jones, *The Christ of the Mount* (Toronto: McClelland & Stewart, 1931), 152.

6. Ravi Zacharias, "The Scandal of the Cross," http://rzim.org/a-slice-of-infinity/the-scandal-of-the-cross-4 (accessed 25 Nov 2015).

7. Simone Weil, *Waiting for God* (New York, Harper & Row, 1973), 128.

8. C. S. Lewis, *God in the Dock: Essays on Theology and Ethics* (Grand Rapids, MI: Eerdmans, 1970), 155.

9. C. S. Lewis, *Mere Christianity,* 73.

10. C. S. Lewis, quoted by Walter Hooper in *C. S. Lewis: A Companion & Guide* (New York: HarperCollins, 1996), 389.

11. Edward Abbey, http://www.brainyquote.com/quotes/quotes/e/edwardabbe384419.html (Accessed 17 Feb 2016).

12. Tertullian, *Against Marcion* 1:25-26.

13. George MacDonald, *The Tutor's First Love* (Minneapolis, MN: Bethany House, 1984).

14. Miroslav Volf, *Free of Charge* (Grand Rapids, MI: Zondervan, 2009), 139.

15. David Wells, "Prayer: Rebellion against the Status Quo," http://www.worldevangelicals.org/resources/source.htm?id=427 (accessed 24 Nov 2015).

16. R. J. Campbell, *The Call of Christ* (London: Skeffington & Son, 1932).

17. Peter Kreeft, *The God Who Loves You: "Love Divine, All Loves Excelling"* (San Francisco: Ignatius Press, 2004), 166.

18. Thomas Aquinas, *Summa Theologica,* II–II, q. 35, art. 4, ad. 2.

19. Simone Weil, *Gravity and Grace* (Lincoln, NE: University of Nebraska Press, 1997), 69.

20. Philip James Bailey, https://en.wikiquote.org/wiki/Sorrow (accessed 30 July 2016).

21. François Fénelon, *Selections from Fénelon,* ed. Mary Wilder Tileston (Boston: Roberts Bros, 1879), 188.

CHAPTER SEVEN
THE GOD WHO IS OUR TRUE HOME

1. Dante Alighieri, *The Divine Comedy.*

2. This phrased was coined by Charles Taylor in his classic work *A Secular Age* (Harvard University Press, 2007).

3. C. S. Lewis, *The Weight of Glory,* 5.

4. Ronald Rolheiser, *The Holy Longing* (New York: Doubleday, 1999), 3.

5. One of John Milton's drafts for *Paradise Lost* bore the title: "Adam unparadiz'd."

6. C. S. Lewis, *The Weight of Glory,* 12.

7. David Foster Wallace, "This Is Water," Commencement speech, Kenyon College https://www.youtube.com/watch?v=8CrOL-ydFMI&feature=youtu.be&a (accessed 16 Jan 2016).

8. C. Baxter Kruger, *The Great Dance* (Vancouver, BC: Regent College Publishing: 2005), 89.

9. John Blase, "Just a Hunch," http://thebeautifuldue.wordpress.com, March 20, 2014 (accessed 27 Dec 2015).

10. F. F. Bruce, *The Gospel of John,* (Grand Rapids, MI: Eerdmans, 1983), 105.

11. C. S. Lewis, *The Problem of Pain,* 40, 41.

12. From "nostalgia," http://www.etymonline.com (accessed 16 Jan 2016).

13. C. S. Lewis, *Letters of C. S. Lewis* (San Diego, CA: Harcourt Brace, 1993), 231.

14. Mark Buchanan, *Things Unseen: Living in Light of Forever* (Colorado Springs, CO: Multnomah Publishers, 2002).

15. Peter Kreeft, *The God Who Loves You,* 31.

16. Frederick Buechner, *The Magnificent Defeat* (New York: HarperCollins, 1985), 65.

17. Katherine Sonderegger, *Systematic Theology: The Doctrine of God,* Vol. 1 (Minneapolis, MN: Fortress Press, 2015), 456.

18. Malcolm Muggeridge, *Conversion: The Spiritual Journey of a Twentieth Century Pilgrim* (Eugene, OR: Wipf & Stock, 2005), 13.

CHAPTER EIGHT
THE GOD WITH TEAR-FILLED EYES

1. Kenneth Bailey comments that the prodigal brought nothing home but a handful of filthy rags, bringing to mind the words of Isa. 64:6 *"All of us have become like one who is unclean, and all our righteous acts are like filthy rags"* (Kenneth E. Bailey, *The Cross & the Prodigal: Luke 15 Through the Eyes of Middle Eastern Peasants* (Downers Grove, IL: InterVarsity Press, 2005), 72.

2. Alexander McLaren, *Expositions of Holy Scripture,* St. Luke, Vol. II (New York: Hodder & Stoughton), 63.

3. Marcus Dods, *The Parables of Our Lord* (New York: Thomas Whittaker, 1951), 348.

4. Abraham Joshua Heschel, *The Prophets* (New York: HarperCollins, 2001), 241.

5. Cited by Thomas Wilkins, "Why me?" http://a-workinprogress.net/2008/10/13/why-me/ (accessed 16 Jan 2016).

6. Jürgen Moltmann. Twitter post. 23 Feb 2014. https://twitter.com/moltmannjuergen/status/800273995576774656.

7. Philip Yancey, *Reaching for the Invisible God,* 139.

8. Theologian Jim Gordon comments: "Campbell Morgan's commentary on Hosea is still one of the few that explores the full range of emotions in God that makes Hosea 11 amongst the most theologically subversive chapters for those who want a God predictably sovereign or indulgently loving—Holy Love is agony, but agony that persists in mercy." (http://livingwittily.typepad.com).

9. Philip Yancey, *Disappointment with God*, 71.

10. Mike Mason, *The Mystery of Marriage* (Portland, OR: Multnomah Press, 1985), 142.

11. Frederick Buechner, *Wishful Thinking: A Theological ABC* (New York: HarperCollins, 1993), 65.

12. Athanasius, *On the Incarnation of the Word*: http://www.ccel.org/ccel/athanasius/incarnation.

13. Horace Bushnell, *Vicarious Sacrifice Grounded in Principles or Universal Obligation* (New York: Charles Scribner, 1866), 42, 43.

14. C. S. Lewis, *Letters of C. S. Lewis* (San Diego, CA: Harcourt Brace, 1993), 231.

15. If the law of God is summed up in love (Rom. 13:10), and if the greatest commandment centers in love (Mk. 12:28-31), then it should not surprise us that the dominant truth about God is *love*. The self-giving life of the Son of God and His death on a cross reveal the true nature of God (Mk. 10:45; Jn. 14:9; I Jn. 4:9,10). Never does Scripture affirm that God is wisdom, holiness or power, although He is wise and holy and powerful, but twice it declares that *God is love* (I Jn. 4:8,16). Love is the very essence of the nature and life of God and not merely one of his many attributes. God is love because God is a Trinity. Love is His relational bond; it is what eternally goes on between Father, Son and Holy Spirit (Jn. 1:18; 17:24). God does not have "a dark side." The wrath of God is not in opposition to His love, it is an expression of it. His wrath is His firm opposition to all that militates against love and harms His creation. Love is the defining characteristic of God's nature.

16. C. S. Lewis, *Mere Christianity*, 138.

17. The great eighteenth-century theologian Jonathan Edwards, in his famous work *The End for Which God Created the World*, argues that the Triune God spoke creation into being with a view to inviting humans to share in the abounding life of God. Edwards describes Father, Son, and Holy Spirit enjoying a passionate, other-centered, self-giving love, and mutual delight that was so full and intense, that it could not be contained. The fullness overflowed in creation. It was God's purpose to not live without us. The Triune God set His abounding love upon us and determined we would be given a place inside the divine circle of life and joy and glory. An astounding truth, indeed.

18. Peter Kreeft, *The Philosophy of Jesus* (South Bend, IN: St. Augustine's Press, 2007), 22.

19. Jacob Reagan Goff. Twitter post. 14 Jun 2015. https://twitter.com/jacobgoff/status/610171273314832384.

20. Annie Dillard, *Teaching a Stone to Talk*, 141.

21. C. S. Lewis, *Mere Christianity*, 105.

22. Brennan Manning, *Lion and Lamb* (Grand Rapids, MI: Baker, 1986), 22.

CHAPTER NINE
THE GOD WHO COMES RUNNING

1. Leonard Sweet, *Out of the Question … Into the Mystery* (Colorado Springs, CO: Waterbrook Press, 2004), 146.
2. Bible commentator Alexander MacLaren suggests, "His stomach, and it only, urged him to go home." Alexander McLaren, *Expositions of Holy Scripture, St. Luke* (New York: Hodder & Stoughton), 62.
3. Consider this example of Middle East protocol from the Old Testament: *"So Moses went out to meet his father-in-law and bowed down and kissed him"* (Ex. 18:7). If such was the custom of greeting parents after a time of absence, what extreme measures would not be expected of a returning wayward son?
4. G. K. Chesterton, *Heretics/Orthodoxy* (Nashville, TN: Thomas Nelson, 2009), 249.
5. Ravi Zacharias, *Cries of The Heart* (Nashville, TN: Thomas Nelson, 2002), 24.
6. C. S. Lewis, *The Collected Letters of C. S. Lewis,* Volume III: Narnia, Cambridge, and Joy 1950–1963 (London: HarperCollins, 2007).
7. Mike Yaconelli, source unknown.
8. Charles Spurgeon. Twitter post. 7 Aug 2011. https://twitter.com/spurgeon_/status/100307759869853697.
9. J. S. Whale, *Christian Doctrine* (Cambridge: Cambridge University Press, 1961), 64.
10. Graham Greene, *Brighton Rock* (London: Random House, 2010), 268.
11. John Piper, *The Pleasures of God* (Colorado Springs, CO: Multnomah, 2012).
12. Quoted in: Gerard Stephen Sloyan, *Crucifixion of Jesus: History, Myth, Faith* (Minneapolis: Augsburg Fortress Press, 1995), 123–124.
13. Alastair Roberts, "The 'Atheistic' Character of Christianity and the Question," http://alastairadversaria.wordpress.com/2011/12/29/atheism-and-christ/.
14. Frederick Buechner, *The Clown in the Belfry* (San Francisco: HarperCollins, 1992), 171.

CHAPTER TEN
THE GOD WHO TAKES OUR SHAME

1. I am greatly indebted to Mark Moore for his helpful insights on this topic in his sermon: "The Shame of God."

http://providencecommunity.com/resources/sermons/the-shame-of-god/ (accessed 16 Jan 2016).

2. From Rudyard Kipling's famous poem, "The Ballad of East and West."

3. G. K. Chesterton, "The Morality of the Hat," *The Speaker*, March 2, 1901, Available at http://chestertonwritings.blogspot.com/2012/01/morality-of-hat.html (accessed Aug. 30, 2015).

4. Kenneth E. Bailey, *Poet and Peasant and Through Peasant Eyes* (Grand Rapids, MI: Eerdmans, 1983), 181.

5. Cited by L. P. Weatherhead, *In Quest of a Kingdom* (London: Hodder and Stoughton, 1943), 90.

6. Kenneth E. Bailey, *The Cross & The Prodigal: Luke 15 Through the Eyes of Middle Eastern Peasants* (Downers Grove, IL: InterVarsity Press, 2005), 41.

7. See Genesis 3:15.

8. N. T. Wright, *Jesus and the Victory of God* (Minneapolis: Fortress Press, 1996), 543.

9. Stephen Seamands, *Give them Christ: Preaching His Incarnation, Crucifixion, Resurrection, Ascension and Return* (Downers Grove, IL: InterVarsity Press, 2012), 57.

10. Deut. 21:23; Gal. 3:13.

11. J. S. Whale, *Christian Doctrine* (Cambridge: Cambridge University Press, 1961), 98.

12. Author: Philip P. Bliss (1875).

13. Frederick Buechner, *Secrets in the Dark: A Life in Sermons* (New York: Harper Collins, 2006), 24.

14. From C.H. Spurgeon's sermon: "God's first words to the first sinner," https://www.biblegateway.com/devotionals/spurgeon-365-2/1804/10/05 (Accessed Jan. 24, 2016).

15. Frederick Buechner, *The Magnificent Defeat* (New York: HarperCollins, 1985), 89.

16. Karl Barth, *Dogmatics in Outline* (New York: Harper & Row, 1959), 104.

17. Lesslie Newbigin. Twitter post. 15 March 2016. https://twitter.com/lesslienewbigin/status/713549809462943746.

18. James S. Stewart, *A Faith to Proclaim* (Vancouver, BC: Regent College Publishing, 2002), 59.

19. From a sermon by Friedrich Schleiermacher, "The Prayers of Stephen."

CHAPTER ELEVEN
THE GOD WHO HUGS PRODIGALS

1. Mark Moore, "The Shame of God," *ibid.*

2. Dallas Willard, *The Divine Conspiracy* (San Francisco: HarperCollins, 1998), 64.

3. Jürgen Moltmann. Twitter post. 15 Oct 2012. https://twitter.com/moltmannjuergen/status/803832705448374273.
4. Frederick Buechner, *Wishful Thinking: A Theological ABC* (New York, HarperCollins: 1993), 393.
5. Quote is attributed to Abraham Heschel. Source unknown.
6. Frederick Buechner, *Wishful Thinking*, 60.
7. G. K. Chesterton. Twitter post. 7 Mar 2016. https://twitter.com/GKCDaily/status/832317209523388416.
8. C. S. Lewis, *A Grief Observed* (HarperCollins ebooks), 43. http://www.harpercollinsebooks.com.
9. Peter Kreeft, *The God Who Loves You* (San Francisco: Ignatius Press, 2004).
10. Julian of Norwich, *The Revelations of Divine Love.*

CHAPTER TWELVE
THE GOD WHO ROBES THE BEDRAGGLED

1. Max Lucado, *He Chose the Nails* (Nashville, TN: Thomas Nelson, 2000), 75.
2. Epistle to Diognetus, http://www.ccel.org/ccel/schaff/anf01.iii.i.html (Accessed Jan. 26, 2016).
3. Robert Farrar Capon, *Kingdom, Grace, Judgment,* 123.
4. Marie Chapian, *Of Whom the World Was Not Worthy* (Minneapolis, MI: Bethany House, 1978), 122, 123.

CHAPTER THIRTEEN
THE GOD OF PREPOSTEROUS GRACE

1. With regard to the robe, the ring, and the sandals, Alfred Plummer comments: "None of the three things ordered are necessities. The father is not merely supplying the wants of his son, who has returned in miserable and scanty clothing. He is doing him honour." Alfred Plummer, *A Critical and Exegetical Commentary on the Gospel According to St. Luke* (Edinburgh: T. & T. Clark, 1901), 376.
2. Michael Spencer, "Grace Is As Dangerous As Ever," http://www.internetmonk.com/archive/grace-is-as-dangerous-as-ever (accessed Oct. 25, 2015).
3. Robert Farrar Capon, *Kingdom, Grace, Judgment* (Grand Rapids, MI: Eerdmans, 2002), 230.
4. Philip Yancey, *What's so Amazing about Grace?* (Grand Rapids, MI: Zondervan, 1997), 45.
5. Justin Buzzard, *The Big Story: How the Bible Makes Sense out of Life* (Chicago: Moody, 2013).

6. "Religion," as I use the term in this book, is any system of belief and/or behavior that is embraced as a means of obtaining or maintaining divine favor. It is man's misguided attempt to reconnect with God by cooking up salvation on his own. It's the fig leaf formula invented by Adam in Eden. As such, it is part of the idolatrous fallen world, and a denial of the gospel of Jesus Christ. The gospel is not a system of religious merit; it is an undeserved provision of divine grace. It does not depend on human effort but on God's redeeming work on our behalf through the Lord Jesus Christ. "All religions are man's attempt to climb to God; Jesus is God's descent to man," wrote E. Stanley Jones. The free gift of the gospel evokes obedience born of gratitude, not of striving to earn God's approval. Jesus did not come to offer an improved religion but an *alternative* to religion: the gospel. "Religion makes us proud of what we have done," stated Timothy Keller. "The Gospel makes us proud of what Jesus has done."

7. Robert Farrar Capon, *The Romance of the Word: One Man's Love Affair with Theology* (Grand Rapids, MI: Eerdmans, 1995), 31.

8. C. S. Lewis comments: "Christianity tells people to repent and promises them forgiveness. It therefore has nothing (as far as I know) to say to people who do not know they have done anything to repent of and who do not feel that they need any forgiveness. It is after you have realized that there is a real Moral Law, and a Power behind the law, and that you have broken that law and put yourself wrong with that Power—it is after all this, and not a moment sooner, that Christianity begins to talk. When you know you are sick, you will listen, to the doctor." (*Mere Christianity*, pp. 24, 25).

9. Helmut Thielicke, *The Waiting Father* (San Francisco: Harper and Row, 1959), 26.

10. Karl Barth. Available at http://quoteaddicts.com/1158753 (accessed Jan. 24, 2016).

11. C. S. Lewis, *Mere Christianity*, 46.

12. Eugene Peterson, *Conversations: The Message with Its Translator* (Colorado Springs, CO: NavPress, 2002), 830.

13. E. Stanley Jones writes: "The Gospel of Jesus is not the Gospel of a Demand but the Gospel of an Offer. Christ offers life to men: 'He that drinketh of the waters that *I shall give unto him* shall never thirst,' for 'they shall become in him a well.' Here is not an agonizing to live, but an acceptance of life—abundant and full ... Of course, at the center of that offer is a demand—for repentance, for self-surrender, for following—but once the offer is accepted, the demand dances its way into a delight and is gone." E. Stanley Jones, *Christ at the Round Table* (Toronto, ON: McClelland & Stewart, 1928), 138–140.

14. C. S. Lewis, *Mere Christianity*, 150.

15. Source unknown.

16. Anne Lamott, *Plan B: Further Thoughts on Faith* (New York: Penguin Group, 2005), 54–55.

CHAPTER FOURTEEN
THE GOD WHO THROWS PARTIES FOR PRODIGALS

1. Douglas Wilson. Twitter post. 2 Mar 2014. https://twitter.com/douglaswils/status/440334997602701312.
2. Henri J. M. Nouwen, *The Return of the Prodigal Son: A Story of Homecoming* (New York: Doubleday, 1992), 114.
3. Mark Buchanan, *Your God is Too Safe* (Colorado Springs, CO: Multnomah, 2001), 242.
4. David Bentley Hart, *The Beauty of the Infinite: The Aesthetics of Christian Truth* (Grand Rapids, MI: Eerdmans, 2004), 155.
5. Mark Buchanan, *Your God is Too Safe,* 241.
6. Timothy Keller, *The Prodigal God,* 104.

CHAPTER FIFTEEN
THE GOD OF SCANDALOUS MERCY

1. Fred B. Craddock, Editor, *Preaching Through the Christian Year* (Harrisburg, PA: Trinity Press International, 1994), 158.
2. Kenneth E. Bailey, *Jacob & the Prodigal: How Jesus Retold Israel's Story* (Downers Grove, IL: InterVarsity, 2003), 62.
3. Robert K. Jarris, *Luke: Artist and Theologian* (New York: Paulist, 1985), 70.
4. Brennan Manning, *A Glimpse of Jesus* (New York: HarperCollins, 2003), 45.
5. Dallas Willard, *The Divine Conspiracy* (San Francisco: HarperCollins, 1998), 123, 124.
6. Derek Vreeland. Twitter post. 17 Mar 2013. https://twitter.com/DerekVreeland/status/313336188066992128.
7. Thomas Goodwin, *The Works of Thomas Goodwin. Vol. 2.* 1890. Reprint. (London: Forgotten Books, 2013), 184–5.
8. From "The Faith of God Without Effect?" a sermon by Martyn Lloyd Jones, originally delivered Jan. 18, 1857 at Westminster Chapel, London, England. MlJTrust.org http://www.mljtrust.org/sermons/the-faith-of-god-without-effect/ (Accessed 18 March 2016).
9. Scotty Smith. Twitter post. 3 Jun 2015. https://twitter.com/ScottyWardSmith/status/606210017847611392.
10. Robert Farrar Capon, *The Romance of the Word,* 11.
11. Frederick Buechner, *Telling the Truth: The Gospel as Tragedy, Comedy, and Fairy Tale* (New York: HarperCollins, 1977), 78.

12. Timothy Keller, *The Meaning of Marriage: Facing the Complexities of Commitment with the Wisdom of God* (New York: Dutton, 2008).

13. Robert Farrar Capon, *The Romance of the Word*, 8.

CHAPTER SIXTEEN

THE GOD WHO CALLS US TO JOIN THE PARTY

1. Kenneth E. Bailey, *Poet and Peasant and Through Peasant Eyes* (Grand Rapids, MI: Eerdmans, 1983), 194.

2. Fyodor Dostoyevsky, *The Brothers Karamazov*.

3. Frederick Buechner, *Telling The Truth: The Gospel as Tragedy, Comedy & Fairy Tale*, cited on: http://day1.org/7181-weekly_sermon_illustration_parables_as_comedy (accessed March 1, 2016).

4. Thomas Merton writes: "[N]o man, whether good or bad, can lay claim in strict justice to the love of God, because love is not like that at all. It has to be given as a free gift, or not at all. The sinner who is ready to accept love as a gift from God is far closer to God than the "just" man who insists on being loved for his own merits. For the former will soon stop sinning (since he will be loved by God), and the latter has probably already begun to sin." Thomas Merton, *The New Man* (London: Burns & Oates, 2003), 67.

5. Bailey, *Ibid.*, 202.

6. Robert Farrar Capon, *Between Noon & Three: Romance, Law & the Outrage of Grace* (Grand Rapids, MI: Eerdmans, 1997), 7.

7. Robert Farrar Capon, "Between Noon and Three," *Christianity Today*, Vol. 30, no. 7.

8. Eugene Peterson, *Tell It Slant* (Grand Rapids, MI: Eerdmans, 2008), 96.

9. Robert Farrar Capon, *Between Noon & Three*, 72.

10. Helmut Thielicke, *The Waiting Father*, 26.

11. F. W. Boreham. Twitter post. 3 Aug 2011. https://twitter.com/FWBoreham/status/98767706546909184.

12. Robert Farrar Capon. Twitter post. 14 April 2016. https://twitter.com/Robert_F_Capon/status/720664110052954112.

13. Frederick Buechner, *Secrets in the Dark: A Life in Sermons* (Grand Rapids, MI: Zondervan, 2007), 130.

14. Jürgen Moltmann, Twitter post. 9 Dec 2015. https://twitter.com/Karlbarthfordum/status/674555929656819712.

CHAPTER SEVENTEEN
THE GOD WHO INVITES US INTO HIS STORY

1. J. R. R. Tolkien. Twitter post. 14 Jun 2014. https://twitter.com/JRRTolkien/status/660165983877902336.

2. Walter Brueggemann, *Texts Under Negotiation: The Bible and Postmodern Imagination* (Minneapolis, MN: Fortress Press, 1993), 57–91.

3. Brennan Manning, *Ruthless Trust, The Ragamuffin's Path to God* (San Francisco: HarperSanFrancisco, 2000), 88.

4. Thomas Merton, *New Seeds of Contemplation* (New York: New Direction Publishing, 1972), 60.

5. Jürgen Moltmann, *The Crucified God: The Cross of Christ as the Foundation and Criticism of Christian Theology* (Minneapolis, MN: Fortress Press, 1974), 205.

6. E. Stanley Jones, *The Word Became Flesh* (Nashville, TN: Abingdon Press: 2006), 192.

7. Donald B. Kraybill, *The Upside-Down Kingdom* (Scottsdale, PA: Herald Press, 1978), 200.

8. N. T. Wright, *Bringing the Church to the World* (Minneapolis, MI: Bethany House, 1992), 209–15.

9. Lesslie Newbigin, *The Gospel in a Pluralist Society* (Grand Rapids, MI: Eerdmans, 1989), 125.

10. Kyle Idleman, *AHA: The God Moment That Changes Everything* (Colorado Springs, CO: David C. Cook, 2014), 201, 202.

11. D. L. Moody, *The Way to GOD And How to Find It,* Ch. 1, http://www.whatsaiththescripture.com/Voice/Moody.The.Way.to.GOD.html (accessed Jan. 21, 2016).

12. John Eldredge, *Waking the Dead: The Glory of a Heart Fully Alive,* (Nashville, TN: Thomas Nelson, 2006), 34.

13. Source unknown.

14. Helmut Thielicke, *Man in God's World* (London: James Clark & Co. 1967), 140.

15. A. W. Tozer, *The Pursuit of God* (Harrisburg, PA: Christian Publications, 1958), 33.

16. Madeleine L'Engle, *Penguins + Golden Calves: Icons and Idols* (Wheaton, IL: Harold Shaw Publishers, 1996).

17. Timothy Keller, *Galatians for You: For Reading, for Feeding, for Leading* (Epsom, Surrey, UK: Good Book Company, 2013).

18. John Chrysostom, *Paschal Homily,* tr. Theodore Berkeley (New City, 1993), pp. 53–54. cited in *The Westminster Collection of Christian Meditations,* edited by Hannah Ward, Jennifer Wild, p. 420.